The Backdoor to Medicine

The Back Door to Medicine

Medicine

An Embedded Anthropologist Tells All

Robert Anderson, M.D.

iUniverse, Inc.

New York   Bloomington

The Back Door to Medicine
An Embedded Anthropologist Tells All

iUniverse books may be ordered through booksellers or by contacting:

iUniverse
1663 Liberty Drive
Bloomington, IN 47403
www.iuniverse.com
1-800-Authors (1-800-288-4677)

ISBN: 978-1-4401-7289-2 (pbk)
ISBN: 978-1-4401-7290-8 (ebk)

Printed in the United States of America

iUniverse rev. date: 9/28/2009

Celebrating 50 Years of Intellectual Adventures
As an Anthropology Professor at Mills College

1960-2010

This 1976-1986 Adventure is Dedicated
To Physicians in My Family
Who Never Experienced
The Ordeals and Rewards of
Successfully Struggling Through
The Back Door to Medicine

Scott Anderson, M.D., Ph.D., my son
Clinical Professor of Medicine (Rheumatology)
University of California at Davis

Kristin Mitchell Sun, M.D., my daughter
Clinical Assistant Professor of Medicine (Pediatric Anesthesiology)
Stanford University

Yao Sun, M.D., Ph.D., my son-in-law
Associate Professor of Medicine (Neonatology)
University of California at San Francisco

Emily Asaro Morell, B.A., my granddaughter
Medical Student and Truman Scholar

Harvard University School of Medicine

Also by Robert Anderson

The Vanishing Village: A Danish Maritime Community (with B. G. Anderson), 1964

Bus Stop for Paris: The Transformation of a French Village (with B. G. Anderson), 1965

Traditional Europe: A Study in Anthropology and History, 1971

Modern Europe: An Anthropological Perspective, 1973

Denmark: Success of a Developing Nation, 1975

The Conservative Care of Low Back Pain, (Editor and author, with Arthur H. White), 1991

Magic, Science, and Health: The Aims and Achievements of Medical Anthropology, 1996

Alternative and Conventional Medicine in Iceland: The Diagnosis and Treatment of Low Back Pain (monograph), 2000

The Ghosts of Iceland, 2005

The Labyrinth of Cultural Complexity: Fremont High Teachers, The Small School Policy, and Oakland Inner-City Realities, 2008

Headbutting in Academe: An Autoethnography, 2010

Contents

Dedication   v

Preface   ix

Chapter 1:   Role Models and Childhood Dreams   1

Chapter 2:   Admission to a College of Chiropractic   13

Chapter 3:   Student Life as Chiropractic Culture   27

Chapter 4:   Learning to Be a Chiropractic Doctor   41

Chapter 5:   The Culture of Clinic Interns   57

Chapter 6:   Interlude - Establishing My Own Clinic   69

Chapter 7:   Medical School in a Chiropractic College   75

Chapter 8:   Public Policy and Scope of Practice   87

Chapter 9:   Chiropractic as Medical Practice   105

Chapter 10: Across the Border to Medical School   113

Chapter 11: Students in a Medical No Man's Land   127

Chapter 12: Corruption and Conflict   145

Chapter 13: Clinical Rotations in Mexico   167

Chapter 14: Day One in an American Hospital   187

Chapter 15: The American Year   203

Chapter 16: Was it Worth While?   227

Appendix 1: Publications as Life-West Research Director   245

Appendix 2: Publications as a Chiropractor Anthropologist   253

References   259

Preface

The title and subtitle of this book beg for clarification. I chose the title as a way to indicate that I have written about how you can become a doctor without graduating from a fully accredited medical school in the United States. More precisely, I have written about how you can become a doctor by graduating from a chiropractic college or by graduating from a foreign medical school. Either way, you will need to come to terms with challenges in terms of personal agency and self-identity (Vallacher & Wegner, 1989).

In Part One I describe how that goal can be achieved based on my own experience in a chiropractic college from which I graduated as a Doctor of Chiropractic (D.C.). As concerns personal agency, as a D.C. you will exult in being able to offer relief without harmful side effects to patients suffering pain and immobility. You will work as a specialist in the diagnosis and treatment of back, neck and peripheral joint problems. Personal agency will be limited, because you will not be qualified to prescribe medication or perform surgery as required to cope with the full range of health problems. In itself, that limitation should be unimportant. Back pain is ubiquitous and diminishes quality of life. You will serve the needs of numberless grateful patients in a busy practice. And remember this, a medical doctor is less effective for the very spinal conditions that you manage successfully. A big drawback has to do with social and professional status, your self-identity. Medical doctors are generally accorded higher prestige. That can be hard to accept by an otherwise proud doctor. I will offer a suggestion on how that shortcoming might be lessened in the last chapter of the book.

In Part Two I describe how your goal can be achieved by graduating as I did from a foreign medical school as a Doctor of Medicine (M.D.). In terms of personal agency, as an M.D. you will rank at the top. It is the same for self-identity, but only after you earn certification as a medical doctor by the Educational Commission for Foreign Medical Graduates (ECFMG) in the United States. During the years when you are struggling as a medical student to earn that certification your self-identity is at risk. You entered your profession through a back door.

Now I need to explain the subtitle. In my world of academe, for highest respect in terms of personal agency and self-identity the only "real" doctor is a Doctor of Philosophy (Ph.D.), although most of us prefer to downplay titles in favor of appreciating scientific and scholarly achievements as such, along with good teaching. The culture of academe differs from the culture of health care in that way, and that brings me to an important observation about the research that led to this book. It was never my intent to change careers in order to become a chiropractic or medical doctor. As a cultural anthropologist, my intellectual adventure began as an effort to practice ethnography relevant to the then new subfield of medical anthropology. In that effort I virtually stumbled into getting trained in chiropractic, medicine and surgery. In describing my ten-year adventure here I offer a case study of what it is like to live the life of an ethnographer, to work as an embedded anthropologist.

By the way, I changed subfield specialization beginning a decade ago when I embedded myself in a failing inner-city high school in East Oakland and wrote my most recent book, *Headbutting in Academe: An Autoethnography*. Anthropology is endlessly challenging and rewarding. Think about it.

Chapter One

Role Models and Childhood Dreams

Working Class Realities

"He may not make it this time," the doctor muttered to my mom in funereal tones. He gazed down at my dad to catch his eye and add in a firm voice, "I'll do what I can to pull you through, Vic, but you've destroyed your liver. If this bust doesn't kill you, the next one definitely will."

Stan and I, about 11 and 12 at the time, watched and listened silently at the foot of the bed. Except that this time it looked as though he might die, it was a familiar scene repeated once or twice a year for as long as we could remember, but with an onset that Stella dated to shortly after 1929 as the Great Depression increasingly squeezed East Oakland in its hellish grasp.

Victor was a binge drinker but not a drunkard. He was a good family man who attended Melrose Baptist Church every Sunday morning with his wife and two boys and even occasionally on Wednesday evenings for prayer meetings. Anxious and emasculated as the head of household in a desperate era, he managed to stay sober for months at a time, sitting helplessly day after day in his small barbershop at the front of our house where a large sign advertised haircuts reduced to only 35¢ as an inducement for men who, like Victor himself, needed every nickel they could get just to put a bit of food on the table for their families. A drink would help ease his sense of despair. Sooner or later, but most likely on a day when he wasn't able to add even thirty-five cents to his till, he would calm himself from a bottle of wine or, if it was the only alcohol he could get his hands on, even from his flask of Bay Rum hair tonic.

Once having downed a first drink he would totally lose control and stay drunk for a week or ten days – he would "go on a bust" - until, having spent every quarter he brought in and every dollar Stella contributed from seasonal work at the cannery, having squandered every hard earned coin put aside to pay bills and buy groceries, he would collapse in an exhausted stupor. Usually Stella would gently nurse him back to health by herself, but when he was really sick and she became especially worried, Dr. Newton would be called in to examine him, and, predictably, to prescribe paregoric, a horrible smelling concoction of liquefied opium that would help Vic sleep off his demons and resurrect as the kindhearted father and husband we loved and respected.

As a boy, rather than become a barber like my dad, I thought I would like to be a physician/surgeon like Dr. Newton, a man others turned to as a source of strength when they were weak. When Victor suffered from hemorrhoids and couldn't afford a hospital stay, Dr. Newton, a general practice physician, performed the bloody surgery as an office procedure in his examination room. When I was thirteen and became anxious about some of the strange-feeling bodily changes of puberty, my mother had me examined in Dr. Newton's office where I was completely healed by his reassurance that I was perfectly normal and healthy. He had a good solid reputation in the neighborhood. Always addressed as "Doctor," he lived a secure life, wore a suit with vest and tie, spoke proper English, and was highly respected. Having no knowledge at all of what the practice of medicine entailed or how one was trained for it, I did know that I would like to earn the high status inherent in being a doctor, like Dr. Newton.

The point of reminiscing about my boyhood is to illustrate how an early ambition can motivate a career choice unrealistically as a desire to achieve a personal identity – in my case, to achieve respect as a doctor - that might well be a wrong decision because of the realities of temperament, innate abilities, and other culturally organized aspects of self. It was misleading for me insofar as Dr. Newton was an early role model. It was equally misleading as concerned Dr. Harry O. Anderson, another powerful role model in my youth.

My grandmother, Victor's Danish mother, spoke English with a strong accent and, her Danish husband long out of the picture, lived meagerly by taking in laundry to support four growing boys as a single mom. Her three oldest sons dropped out of school in the fifth grade in order to contribute to the family income at a time when child labor was legal, or at least tolerated. As adults, Fred ended up with a secure job cleaning Pullman sleeping cars for the Southern Pacific Railroad System. Jim became a carpenter and Vic worked first as a house painter and later as a barber.

The baby in the family was Harry, who managed to get an education, partly because his older brothers and mother made enough to live on, and mainly because his goal was to save lost souls, and the family was devoutly religious. After graduating from Fremont High in Oakland and working his way through the University of California in neighboring Berkeley he was ordained as a Baptist minister (Anderson, 2008: chapter 2). His childhood dream to become a medical missionary had to be abandoned when he flunked biology in his senior year at Berkeley, and he was not suited to pastor a church. Instead of traveling to a foreign country to preach and practice medicine he ended up traveling here and there in the Western United States as a charismatic evangelist. At revival meetings he sold copies of his self-published a book, *How Far Can You See? And Other Sermons* (1928), at $1.50 a copy. His interpersonal skills were excellent.

In mid-career he was awarded an honorary Doctor of Divinity (D.D.) degree by the Northern Baptist Theological Seminary in Chicago, where he was hired for a short time to handle public relations. In actuality, the degree was awarded in an attempt to enhance his status for soliciting donations, but he flopped on that and soon returned to evangelism, advertising himself thereafter as Dr. Harry O. Anderson. He was a compelling role model for me.

I still have a vivid memory from when I was no more than five years old and stood on a small stool to play that I was delivering a sermon, just like Uncle Harry. As a young man following in my uncle's footsteps I graduated from Fremont High School and managed to gain admission to the University of California (Anderson. 2008: chapters 3-4). I even pre-registered at the Berkeley Baptist Divinity School, which qualified me for an exemption from the draft during World War II, because even a nation at war was thought to need future ministers and chaplains. I told the Dean I wanted to be a medical missionary, but, not only did I have no idea about what the lifestyle of a physician entailed, I also eventually came to realize that I couldn't possibly qualify for ordination. The more I learned at the university, the more I was forced to abandon my belief in the infallibility of the Bible as God's literal truth, including that the world was created in six days about 6000 years ago (according to the Baptist interpretation).

By the time I was twenty I had totally withdrawn from Melrose Baptist Church and everything biblical that it stood for. That left me with the ambition to become a doctor, even though I knew nothing about the practice of medicine and surgery as a way of life.

Lost in an Educational Jungle

So how would a working-class boy qualify himself to become a medical doctor? The culture of East Oakland, especially in the flatlands near the railroad tracks, factories, and warehouses, including the cannery near us where Stella worked, was that of minimally educated families whose livelihoods derived from hard physical labor. We were all low-class in terms of socioeconomic status, but not low in terms of family values and the work ethic. I find it meaningful to think of the families in our part of town as a laboring class.

The residents of East Oakland were mainly white, with a scattering of Chinese and Japanese and only one "Negro" family. But Oakland whites were not culturally uniform. Our part of town was heavily populated with immigrants from Europe. Many had their origins in Scandinavia and Germany. They were readily assimilated. Victor's parents came from Denmark where his oldest brother Frederick was born. Stella was 21 years old when she arrived, also from Denmark, followed a year later by her brother and divorced mother. However, not all white families were equally respected. American born migrants who escaped the mid-western Dust Bowl, especially from Oklahoma, were considered very low class because of their extreme poverty, rural mannerisms, and disparaged dialect. Other families had their origins in Catholic Southern Europe, especially Portugal, Spain, and Italy, along with a smaller number from Mexico. Racism found expression in those days as prejudice against "Okies," Asians and Catholics, but it was often low key or out of awareness as I recall and acted upon more by adults than by children. Examples of subtle and frankly ignorant racism can be found in my Uncle Harry's sermons.

He unthinkingly denigrated Asians in one sermon on the virtues of Christian charity: "How often my good mother prepared the best soup ever to carry over to that sick mother in the neighbor's house," he said. "If an epidemic hits China, they all flee and leave the victims to their fate" (1928: 40). And of Italy and Italians: "Roman Catholicism prevails and my heart goes out to the poor benighted people" (1928: 219).

As youngsters, Stan and I were influenced by those attitudes, but we played easily with boys from any of those families, fearing a couple who were bullies and respecting others who were good athletes. The most admired baseball player was a Japanese boy a year older than I. His parents, characterized by strong accents and reticent mannerisms, were proprietors of the grocery store two blocks up East 14th Street from our house-cum-barber shop. They lost everything they had when they were transported to a relocation camp at the beginning of World War II. It happened just before I started high school, and I remember feeling it was unjust, but soon forgot about it. It is worth noting in hindsight that a smaller grocery store at the other end of our block provided a livelihood for an Italian family, equally a wartime "enemy" ethnicity, but being white and culturally less different apparently saved them from relocation and internment.

The point is, although I wanted to be a doctor, I did not live in a community in which boys, and certainly not girls, grew up to go to medical school. Those who worked at Highland Hospital did so as orderlies, nurses aids, kitchen workers, cleaning staff, guards, or ambulance drivers.

Moreover, to meet the high academic standards that medical school admission increasingly required after World War I, you had to succeed well as a student. Victor dropped out of elementary school in order to work in the nearby cotton mill. Stella finished middle school in Copenhagen after which she took courses in machine embroidery and hat making. They had no idea at all about how to parent Stan and me in our school work. Grades of C and even D were no cause for comment. They never asked about homework, never attended PTA (parent) meetings or scheduled conferences with our teachers. We didn't play hooky or get sent to the principal's office. Being well-behaved was an adequate measure of our success in their eyes, especially in a neighborhood where the oldest brother of one of our friends for a time was listed on the FBI's "ten most wanted" list.

In senior high school (grades 10 to 12 at that time) I finally realized it was important to pay attention and do homework if I wanted to become a medical missionary. My grades improved. I was even tracked into college preparatory courses where I got a piece of advice that changed my life.

Mrs. Bridges taught a senior English class for college-bound students. Occasionally she would tell us what college was like, and one day she advised us, "No matter what else you study, be sure to take an anthropology course." She told us a bit about a course she had taken, even though her major was English literature, and advised us to do the same, no matter what we majored in, because it was such an eye-opener about peoples of the world. A few months later I found myself sitting in Wheeler Auditorium between two other Fremont graduates who had also signed up for Anthropology 1A, Cultural Anthropology, taught by Professor Robert Lowie.

At Berkeley in those days we were not assigned individually to academic advisors in the first year or two. Premed was not a formal major. I suppose it existed somewhere in the catalogue as a list of recommended courses, I'm not sure. When I stood in a long line to register as an entering freshman I made decisions by consulting with other students. I declared my major as physics, correctly assuming that medical schools would approve. As a newly declared physics major I took physics 1A and did quite well, but I liked anthropology much better and decided to put off Physics 1B. By the end of my sophomore year I had taken one course each in physics, biology, and physiology, plus several in math, but I never got around to chemistry, even though I had a good background in it from a high school course. Each semester I registered without advising other than to stop at a desk in a large auditorium where a professor took a peremptory look at my proposed schedule, signed approval, and turned to the next student in line.

Each semester I took an anthropology course, because Mrs. Bridges was right. It was a captivating subject. In hindsight I was clearly foolish not to seek formal advising on the premedical curriculum, but at the time I never thought to do it, didn't know how to go about it, and was not counseled to do it. It certainly did not occur to my parents to suggest it; I almost never saw my uncle, and it did not occur to me to look up Dr. Newton. The university was an enormous institution in which no one noticed a naïve undergraduate who needed career guidance and encouragement.

Reality Testing

At the end of my sophomore year, though still virgins, my girlfriend and I got caught in the middle of a weekend night almost having sex. Her father was an austere Catholic from the Old Country who enforced a strict moral code. He insisted that we marry. I escaped by joining the Navy, which is how I became a veteran of World War II.

On enlisting I stated that I had completed two years as a premed student, so after Boot Camp in San Diego I was transferred to Long Beach to be trained as a hospital corpsman. The Naval Hospital there offered a splendid opportunity to test my interest in medicine. We were taught basic nursing skills, from making beds, giving bed baths, and cleaning bedpans to first aid, handling medications and injecting patients with hypodermic syringes.

After qualifying as a corpsman I was assigned to the Eye, Ear, Nose, and Throat (EENT) Department. It was a splendid experience for a young person interested in becoming a doctor. My responsibilities in the outpatient clinic were to prepare patients for procedures and to assist physicians who carried them out. It was much like being a third year medical student in the first year of clinical training. For month after month I made myself useful and observed how doctors worked. One doctor showed me how to use an otoscope to look at an ear drum and identify lesions and inflammations. The ophthalmologist taught me how to use an ophthalmoscope and showed me retinal tears, vitreous floaters, and lens opacities. I learned to identify a deviated septum in the nose and what the vocal cords look like when viewed through a broncoscope.

Best of all, I was taught how to scrub for surgery and assist by identifying instruments, placing them firmly in the surgeon's hands, and holding retractors to maintain the visual field while the doctor explained what he was doing and taught me to identify basic anatomy. I gained experience in using a microscope to examine diseased tissue and bacteria. And, of course, I spent long days doing scut work as a reminder that I was only an enlisted man.

Naturally I didn't socialize with physicians in their off-duty hours, but I did spend day after day with them when they were on duty. In multiple ways I acquired a basis for evaluating the medical profession as a way of life rather than merely as cultural capital. I liked what I experienced, and continued to think that it would be fulfilling to go on in medicine. By the end of my enlistment, however, I realized that I would much rather study to be an anthropologist like Professor Lowie than to become a physician like Dr. Newton. When I returned to Berkeley as a junior I took a course in human anatomy as a last gesture toward medicine, but I took it because it was recommended as background for biological anthropology. With Professor Theodore McCown as my major advisor I graduated "with honors" in 1949, the proud possessor of a bachelor's degree in anthropology.

On to Earn Two Doctoral Degrees

Stella, a mother and wife who bore adversity bravely and cheerfully, loved to quote a Biblical promise for troubled times that the Great Depression turned into a daily mantra: ". . . all things work together for good. . ." The verse as a whole has an escape clause that Stella seemed completely to have forgotten. I never heard her add ". . . to them that love God, to them who are the called according to his purpose" (Romans 8:28). Perhaps that's why things often did not work out at all well for a lot of good Christians, including my dad. Not called, I suppose.

Fortunately for me, getting caught in a sinful act of heavy petting worked well to make possible two years of hands-on participant-observation in hospital medical practice. In addition, being caught in apparent flagrante delicto also worked out for me to pursue my first two years of anthropological graduate work in Denmark at the University of Copenhagen. After finishing my two-year enlistment I was eligible as a veteran of World War II to have tuition and living expenses paid for by the G. I. Bill of Rights. Without that benefit I could never have afforded such an enriching educational experience. (Stan joined me for a year to study international law, also on the G. I. Bill.) So much for the wages of sin.

After Denmark I returned to Berkeley where I graduated in 1956 with a Ph.D. in anthropology, also paid for by the G. I. Bill. The subsequent four years seemed to pass very rapidly: a year of fieldwork in Denmark, two years in France doing research and studying urban sociology at the Sorbonne (where I graduated as a *Docteur en Sociologie*), and one year as a neophyte assistant professor at the University of Washington. Then in 1960 I returned to Oakland to earn my living as a tenure-track Assistant Professor of Anthropology and Sociology at Mills College, where I have remained to this day, except that I did move up through the ranks to full professor.

Mills College is only ten minutes by car from East 14th Street where Stan and I lived as boys and where I decided that I wanted to grow up to be a doctor. It is equally close to Fremont High School where I first experienced success as a student. To this day, I love being an anthropologist. I love teaching anthropology and pursuing my research and writing interests at Mills College. So how can it be that I am writing about fulfilling my childhood dream of becoming a medical doctor? Because, you see, with the passage of time I really did unexpectedly stumble through *The Back Door to Medicine*.

PART I:
CHIROPRACTIC

1925

"If osteopathy is essentially a method of entering medicine by the back door . . . chiropractic by contrast is an attempt to arrive through the cellar."

> Morris Fishbein, M.D., *The Medical Follies.*
> Editor, 1924-1950, *Journal of the American Medical Association*

1992

"Chiropractors are no longer isolated in their private practice or excluded from government and privately funded health care institutions and facilities. . . . Increasing numbers of chiropractors have hospital privileges and all now have access to medical specialist consultations."

> Scott Haldeman, D.C., Ph.D., M.D.,
> Editor, *Principles and Practice of Chiropractic*
> Clinical Professor, Department of Neurology,
> University of California at Irvine

Disclosure

I describe the chiropractic college I attended as it was thirty years ago during its first four years of solving start-up problems. My observations should not be taken to represent the college as it has become in the twenty-first century.

Chapter Two

Admission to a College of Chiropractic

It Began with Becoming a Medical Anthropologist

Conventional wisdom teaches that to make the most of a lifetime it is important to seek out new challenges and opportunities as much as you can. As a general rule, it can be enriching if you are lucky enough to change jobs or work assignments from time to time in a growth process that calls for you to acquire new skills that build on and enhance previous training and experience. It has been my good fortune to do that several times as an anthropologist at Mills College, and it is relevant to how I ended up knocking at the back door of medicine.

Based on having earned a first doctorate at the University of California in anthropology and a second doctorate in sociology at the University of Paris (Sorbonne), I was appointed to the Mills College faculty in 1960 as an Assistant Professor of Anthropology and Sociology, tasked to institutionalize those subjects as a new academic department. I found it difficult but enriching to split my teaching responsibilities equally between the two disciplines. From the start it has always been my practice, to the extent possible, to do original research and publish in every subject I teach as a way to continually improve my competence as a scientist and an educator. So, even though I was much more an anthropologist than a sociologist, I published an article in the *American Journal of Sociology* as well as one in *The American Anthropologist*. That modeled what was to follow as I continued my teaching career.

Three years after I arrived, Ted Thomas joined the faculty to increase our sociology offerings and release me to teach only anthropology. As the years passed I worked and taught in several subfields, but for many years my heaviest commitment was to medical anthropology.

Since the 19th century when anthropology first emerged as an academic field, some practitioners have included health and healing in their interests. *Medicine, Magic, and Religion* by W. H. R. Rivers, a physician anthropologist, was published in 1923. However, it was not until 1967-1968, that a substantial number of American anthropologists, although fewer than a hundred, were sufficiently specialized to establish the Organization of Medical Anthropology (since 1970, the Society for Medical Anthropology). Research funding was becoming increasingly available. By 1978 enough courses were being taught nation-wide to support publication of a first textbook, aptly titled *Medical Anthropology*, written by George Foster and Barbara Anderson, both of whom I knew intimately.

The field was dynamic and grew rapidly in prominence and influence, so it is not surprising that I decided it needed to be added to our curriculum at Mills. In the fall of 1977 I taught a medical anthropology course for the first time. In 1996 I published my own textbook, *Magic, Science, and Health: The Aims and Achievements of Medical Anthropology*. Alas, it was never much used except, unsurprisingly, at Mills. So, as part of designing and implementing a new course and a new direction in my career, I needed to identify an appropriate field for research.

That fall I talked with people at the California College of Podiatric Medicine in San Francisco. A month later I drove to Sacramento to spend time with a naturopathic physician. As months passed I was able to visit the Kansas City College of Osteopathic Medicine on one occasion and the College of Osteopathic Medicine of the Pacific in Southern California on another.

Later, I completed a "three day intensive" course with William Pseudonym, D.C., N.D. (Doctor of Naturopathy). That long weekend almost qualified me to practice as an iridologist. Practitioners of iridology identify diseases by examining the color and configuration of the iris of the eye. On that basis they treat by prescribing dietary supplements and lifestyle modifications.

To illustrate, one case study presented in his lectures described a woman found by her medical doctor to have normal thyroid function. Dr. Pseudonym, to the contrary, demonstrated on a photograph, that where the thyroid was mirrored on the left iris it was enlarged and therefore overactive while on the right side it was small and underactive. Since the double dysfunction balanced out, the medical doctor was misled into a false diagnosis. In iridology theory the two sides of the body function more or less independently of one another, so she was treated with protein for the left lobe of the thyroid gland and with starches for the right lobe.

How could such obvious nonsense be taken seriously by anybody? Yet, iridology does attract patients - though perhaps not many - and it has been taken up by some health-care providers. How could that be? It is clear that the answer is complex and multifaceted. In part, however, the success of iridology may well derive from therapeutic prescriptions which require the patient to eat a balanced diet, avoid harmful intakes of junk food, cigarette smoke, and alcohol, to sleep eight hours every night, and to engage in exercise. In short, Dr. Pseudonym advocated life-style changes demonstrated in medical research at that time to contribute to reduced morbidity and mortality (Breslow, 1978). Add to that the placebo benefits of a laying on of hands and the "power of positive thinking," and the iridologist probably contributed to improved health. In all events, it convinced some licensed practitioners of chiropractic, naturopathy, and even optometry to add it to their healing repertoires, even if it did seem strange nonsense on a scientific basis (Simon, et al, 1979).

So I was almost certified to practice medicine as an iridologist. Why almost? Because to receive the certificate I was told I would have to sign and date a "memorandum" affirming to Dr. Pseudonym that "I fully understand that you do *not* treat nor do you make any recommendations for the treatment of cancer in any form or in any manner whatsoever and I wish to assure you that I am in no way asking for such information." I could not attest to such a manifest untruth, so I walked away without a certificate to hang on my office wall.

Although ethnographically interesting, iridology was scientifically unconvincing and too much of an odd offshoot to warrant further investigation. One three-day intensive was enough. I would look in other directions for research possibilities. I decided it would be a good idea to focus on Traditional Chinese Medicine (TCM).

My enthusiasm and scattered background for work in China reached back to 1948 when I took an undergraduate course on the Sociology of China from Wolfram Eberhard at Berkeley. Later, it included the summer of 1967 on a Fulbright Grant in Taiwan with China expert Morton Fried, a professor of anthropology at Columbia University in New York. Mort arranged a briefing for half a dozen other anthropologists and me with a practitioner of TCM.

At a time when Americans like us were very uninformed about acupuncture, the doctor asked one of us to volunteer for a demonstration treatment. Everyone pulled back, like kids fearing a vaccination, so, in my own eyes at least, I became the macho male. While Mort translated, I rapidly scanned a diagram on the wall showing where meridians connected with different parts of the body. I didn't want to involve a meridian that would require inserting a needle at the corner of my eye or in some other sensitive spot, and I lucked out. I complained vaguely of an upset stomach, which only required one needle in my foot.

I took off my shoe and sock and watched calmly. (After all, I had administered penicillin injections when I was a Navy medic, so I did not feel threatened.) After inserting the needle the doctor asked if I felt better. Since I did not actually have a stomach problem I answered honestly that I felt no different. Ouch. That was a mistake. He responded by unexpectedly plunging the needle deeper into my flesh and pumping it up and down. Startled by the sudden onset of sharp pain, I immediately assured him that I now felt fine. That ended the demonstration. Later my companions let me know that needle anxiety was not the reason for failing to volunteer. It was because they feared infection from an inadequately sterilized needle. Perhaps hepatitis. HIV/ Aids came along much later but Hepatitis B was scary enough. They were so much smarter than I!

Building on that admittedly meager background, I decided to enroll in a school of traditional Chinese medicine in the Bay Area as an orientation to research possibilities. As a trial run I sat in on the acupuncture class with a room full of other would-be American acupuncturists, but I couldn't stand it. It was so boring. As it happened, I arrived when, hour after hour, all the instructor did was to move his finger along one meridian at a time, one of twelve shown on a big chart at the front of the class, halting about every centimeter at an acupuncture point to pronounce its Chinese name, write the ideogram for us to copy from the blackboard, and then s-l-o-w-l-y with endless detail, explain the pathology each point could impact depending on the angle and depth of needling.

After two weeks the head of admissions informed me that I would have to pay tuition just like the others if I intended to become a serious student. I became a drop-out instead and responded submissively to my wife's advice.

Edna had counseled against Chinese medicine from the start, and she was right. She reminded me after our visit to Beijing and Canton on a January interterm break that to do first-rate work as an anthropologist would take years just to learn to speak and read Chinese minimally, and if I elected to work in China I would have to spend months in the field away from her and our children. So we agreed that it would make better sense to develop research expertise in a field indigenous to the United States and located in Oakland where we lived and worked. But what should it be?

In the end, three possibilities seemed to hold the most promise: Native American medicine, osteopathy, and chiropractic. I was attracted to chiropractic because at the time it had been almost completely overlooked by other anthropologists and yet was prominent on the alternative medicine scene. By contrast, many anthropologists had done fieldwork relating to Indian healing practices and osteopathic medicine, for its part, had a low profile in Oakland.

Preliminary Orientation in the Library

So chiropractic it would be, but there was a problem. I had never met a practitioner and knew absolutely nothing about the discipline. So, the obvious first step was to read whatever I could get my hands on.

I learned that chiropractic was "discovered" by Daniel David Palmer, an itinerant healer who had tried several ways to make his living as an alternative practitioner before settling down in Davenport, Iowa, to offer his services as a magnetic healer (Gielow, 1981).

An epiphany occurred in his office in 1895 or, according to Joseph Keating, maybe it was 1896 (Keating, et al, 1998: 1), when Palmer got into a conversation with Harvey Lillard, the janitor in his building. Lillard explained that he had lost his hearing 17 years earlier when he was straining to lift a heavy object while crouched in an awkward position. He remembered pushing as hard as he could until he felt something snap in his back and immediately lost his hearing. He became so deaf that he couldn't hear the ticking of a watch or the racket of a horse-drawn wagon clanking iron-rimmed wooden wheels over cobble-stone streets.

Palmer, it seems, knew something of osteopathic spinal manipulation as practiced and taught by Andrew Still, an apostate medical doctor in Kirksville, Missouri, only a day's journey from Davenport (Gibbons, 1980). "In fact," as Timothy Gorski notes, "it appears that . . . he borrowed a number of his ideas from his contemporary Andrew Taylor Still" (1994). Perhaps having those concepts in mind, Palmer asked to examine Lillard's back and, as he later recalled, took note of "a vertebra racked from its normal position." After convincing his reluctant patient to trust him, he "racked it into position by using the spinous process as a lever." Within minutes Lillard once again could hear ticking watches and carts bouncing along roads (cited in Gielow, 1981: 78). Inspired by that experience, Palmer eventually abandoned magnets as he taught himself to diagnose and treat by adjusting vertebral subluxations. He thrived, and within a year or two had established a school. Chiropractic was born.

Throughout his lifetime, Palmer was caricatured by the medical profession as an ignorant huckster. Morris Fishbein, M.D., excoriated him in his popular books, including *Fads and Quackery in Healing* (1932). More than sixty years later Timothy Gorski, M.D., Assistant Clinical Professor at the University of North Texas Health Science Center, wrote "It's time – well past time, actually – to address what is certainly the most successful and widespread form of medical quackery in America: the pseudoscience of chiropractic. . . . , said to have been discovered by grocer and 'magnetic healer' Daniel David Palmer in 1895" (1994).

In contrast to persistent hostile criticism in medical circles, anthropologist Thomas McCorkle offered a far more balanced evaluation (1961). Intrigued by the popularity of chiropractic in the Midwest, and particularly in Iowa where Palmer lived and worked, he wondered, why chiropractic succeeded so well in competition with conventional medicine. Two features of rural Iowa culture seemed to offer a reasonable explanation.

McCorkle noted, first, that the Christian-European heritage of those farming people supported an ethic of work. "Work is a prime value, . . . everyone is supposed to work physically and to use all his waking time in getting things done." To that he added that farmers engaged in heavy field work with a high risk of injury. "They accidentally strike themselves with hand tools; suffer bruises, dislocations, and strains in striving with animals or machines; and often are exposed to extremely cold and wet conditions while performing winter work. Stiff necks, lame backs and strained ligaments are frequent" (1961: 21).

When a farmer found that pain and incapacity were great enough to keep him from work, he wanted help that would let him get back to his plowing or harvesting with the least possible delay. The medical doctor could only offer bed rest, liniment, and analgesics. However, bed rest was not an option when it was urgent that crops be planted or harvested. James Fisk, a physician, took note of that problem in the New Zealand farming area where he was established in general practice. His patients were sheep and dairy farmers, much like the hardworking farmers of the Midwest. He noted that, as a medical doctor, he was considered "no good with backs." Yet, when one of those farmers hurt his back he could, as Fisk wrote, "ill afford the luxury of being off work" (1977: 3). In New Zealand as in the United States, farmers went to chiropractors because they got quick results that allowed them to return to work faster than if they went to the medical doctors (Greenland, et al, 1980).

The second reason cited by McCorkle was also grounded in the Christian-European heritage of those hard working people. They preferred "natural" remedies to medicine and surgery. Hands-on healing was familiar from Sunday school lessons, sermons, and the "laying on of hands" in prayer meetings. The practice of chiropractic was readily accepted as consistent with their experience as Protestant Christians.

I would add a third reason to those of McCorkle. A balanced

perspective requires that we go beyond an examination of reasons why chiropractic had appeal to consider good reasons why a medical alternative might be rejected. Medicine in the time of D. D. Palmer was often harmful and ineffective. It was particularly so in late 19th century rural America when chiropractic appeared on the scene (Gibbons 1981).

Most country doctors at that time earned their credentials by apprenticing to older doctors or by spending some months in a medical school. That's how Andrew Still became a medical doctor. Even those who graduated from medical schools were surprisingly ignorant. The President of the Kansas City Academy of Medicine confessed, "We are obliged to admit, that the standing of our profession with the community is not what it should, or even what it might be" (Bonner, 1959: 70-79.)   In 1870, even the head of Harvard Medical School was forced to admit that "written examinations could not be given because most of the students could not write well enough" (Gebhard, 1976: 21).

Nineteenth century country doctors perpetuated outmoded concepts of medical practice. A generation before the time of Palmer, Oliver Wendell Holmes, M.D., encapsulated an indictment of medical practice with his observation that if most the medicines in use were thrown into the sea it would be better for people and all the worse for fish (1981: 39). That indictment remained valid in the Midwest until the end of the century.

Historian Richard Harrison Shryock noted for rural American medicine that "it took time for new light to penetrate the nooks and crannies of everyday practice" (1966: 224). Until well into the 1890's the practice of medicine was largely archaic and useless. For example, despite a first successful vaccination by Pasteur in 1885, Kansas doctors continued to treat rabies with porous "stones" taken from the stomachs of cows. Known as madstones, they supposedly cured by "drawing out" the infection. "A doctor in Paola and a druggist in Fort Scott were reported to own especially potent stones, which supposedly attacked the disease by adhering to open wounds inflicted by a mad dog" (Bonner, 1959: 59).

Many of the treatments offered by 19th century doctors were worse than useless; they were harmful survivors of failed medical theorizing.

A particularly dangerous approach to medicine was first advocated by Benjamin Rush, M.D. (1746-1813) during a severe epidemic of yellow fever. Dismayed by the failure of his treatments to cure dying patients, Rush concluded that to conquer a powerful infection it was essential to invoke extreme measures. Physicians should not allow themselves to be fooled "by the seeming weakness in a patient since yellow fever was caused by an over-excitement of the body. Even if the pulse were so thin you could hardly find it, you should nonetheless prescribe the most violent purges." Rush was convinced that depletion of the patient was essential for a cure. "Away then with cowardice: he would purge and bleed to an extent never dared in Philadelphia before!" (Flexner, 1962: 99-101). He had invented "heroic medicine."

Surgeon James Marion Sims (1813-1883) described heroic medicine as he encountered it in 1840. "It was heroic, it was murderous. Physicians killed their patients; it was preferable to put one's confidence into nature and not into the dangerous skill of physicians" (cited in Gebhard, 1976: 91).

By the end of the century, heroic medicine was out of vogue in urban medical centers as doctors shifted to mild methods, trusting to the self-limited quality of most diseases and finding wisdom in letting nature do the healing. As early as 1840, in a speech delivered to medical graduates of the University of Pennsylvania, Samuel Jackson stated that "the least important part of the science . . . is the dosing of patients with medicine." He argued instead that nature provided the real cure (cited in Shryock, 1966: 223).

Although heroic medicine was no longer espoused by leading American physicians at the end of the 19th century, it persisted among rural practitioners throughout the Midwest. Until well into the days of Palmer, bleeding was widely practiced as was the prescribing of mercurials, tartar emetic, and calomel, along with cauterizing and blistering to promote the healing of wounds. Doctors tended to over-prescribe opium and morphine for pain control and they poisoned patients with arsenic and strychnine tonics.

As the Harvard University biochemist L. J. Henderson famously observed, "Somewhere between 1910 and 1912 in this country, a random patient, with a random disease, consulting a doctor chosen at random, had, for the first time in the history of mankind, a better than

50/50 chance of profiting from the encounter" (cited in Ingelfinger, 1978: 945).

When the founder of chiropractic is looked at in the perspective of the Midwest at the end of the 19th century, he looks far more a saint than a sinner. His simple approach to human health appealed to patients who harbored a tradition of faith in natural methods and was consistent with the return to natural methods espoused by medical leaders in urban centers. He was able to get hardworking farming people out of pain and back to work faster than could medical doctors. Perhaps equally important in his time, he also saved patients from the harm that medical doctors often perpetrated through the use of exceedingly harsh procedures and medications. Palmer was a plain, rough frontiersman, but in balanced perspective, he was no less educated or refined than were local physicians, and he accomplished more for his patients in many cases.

The Method of Participant Observation

Background reading offered an essential introduction to chiropractic, but the next step was to find patients to talk with and practitioners to query and observe. The signature methodology of anthropologists is usually referred to as ethnography, fieldwork, participant-observation, applied anthropology, or even immersion anthropology. In doing that kind of research we seem most at home in the humanities because it is methodologically somewhat like practicing in-depth journalism or naturalistic observation. Yet, commonly we also design and execute surveys and statistical studies in our guise as social scientists or even specialize in anatomic, physiologic, and genetic research as natural scientists. Eventually, as anthropologists are wont to do, I drew on all three kinds of documentation relating to chiropractic, but above all, my way of learning about chiropractic began as participant observation.

On the surface, this research method is easy enough to comprehend. In doing participant observation you move beyond just talking with people to check to see if what they tell you accurately describes what they actually do and say. You attempt to live your own life with them so that you can experience their feelings and involvements as they do themselves. The findings of field researchers documenting a world-wide variety of human cultures in that way now constitute a library of human understandings with wide and lasting value. Let me illustrate how the method is carried out in practice.

In 1950, when Danish ethnologist George Nellemann and I were fellow students at the University of Copenhagen, we traveled north beyond the Arctic Circle to experience what we could of reindeer herding by Swedish Lapps. A few handmade implements that we purchased on that expedition are still in the collection of the Danish National Museum. Our goal as students, however, was above all to gain a deeper appreciation of Sami folkways by participant observation.

It was a brief trip and we made no attempt at all to learn the Sami language. A few years later Pertti (Bert) Pelto, a fellow student when I was at Berkeley, experienced Finnish Sami (Skolt Lapp) culture more deeply by learning their language, growing his own food as they did, fishing in icy lakes, and tending reindeer herds. He adopted the life practices of that community through all the seasons for over a year and returned again in later years.

Our exploration was necessarily very limited. Even so, squatting with our Sami hosts around the fire in a winter tent, its central smoke hole open to falling snow, we nourished ourselves with boiled reindeer meat and comforted ourselves as frequently as possible with cups of coffee flavored with reindeer milk that was both cooled and sweetened by slurping it, Lapp style, from the saucer over a cube of sugar placed on the tongue. We slept with a family in the intimacy of a small room, warmed with reindeer hide mattresses and blankets. We skied to mountain roundups wearing reindeer skin boots with straw instead of socks and curled up toe pieces that functioned as hooks to secure each ski loosely in position as it hung suspended by a single belt-like leather band over the boot. We shared in the pandemonium of corralling half-wild animals, and learned first-hand how powerful and dangerous those seemingly docile creatures can be if not handled by experts.

Our simple student exercise in Arctic Sweden demonstrated the appeal of this method. You learn more deeply and truly by participating as well as observing. In what follows I will report upon an ethnographic project I carried out a quarter of a century later in the chiropractic profession when I embedded myself as a medical anthropologist.

Pacific States Chiropractic College

You might say that I entered a back door just to get to the back door. It was certainly not my original intention to enroll as a student. I visited the Los Angeles College of Chiropractic and Cleveland Chiropractic College, also in Los Angeles, in March of 1978, but as far as I knew, there were no chiropractic colleges in the Bay Area, so I got started by visiting local chiropractic offices, of which there were plenty. I was always welcomed to talk with patients, receptionists, and the doctors themselves. They invited me to observe them with patients and were long suffering in going over radiographs and other measures of biomechanical health.

It was April 20, 1978, when I arrived at the practice of Ed Van Buskirk, D.C., not far from where our home was located in East Oakland. In our conversation I told him I had become thoroughly confused. Unlike the basic similarities I might have anticipated had I visited a number of medical family practitioners, pediatricians, orthopedists, or rheumatologists, it seemed that the techniques of each chiropractor differed from every other one in dramatic ways. Where were the underlying patterns of uniformity I had learned to identify from as far back as when George and I observed reindeer herding and tent life in Lapland? Or even earlier as a Pharmacist Mate, when I assisted ophthalmologists and ENT specialists?

So I raised that issue with Dr. Van Buskirk. It was during that fruitful conversation that he said a few words that impacted my life. "You know, there's a new chiropractic college not far from here in San Lorenzo. You ought to talk with people there." Pacific States Chiropractic College (PSCC) was located only 20 minutes from the Mills campus. On the other side of the Bay in Palo Alto a second new school had been established just the previous year, Northern California Chiropractic College, but obviously, PSCC was better for my purposes.

Within days and full of hope I found my way to the new PSCC campus. Well, it was a new campus to them but it was old as a cluster of buildings. They were setting up shop in a closed down middle school leased from the city. As hard pressed as they were to get the college up and running, President Leon Coelho, D.C., invited me into his office for a long talk. I also met Len Rudnick, D.C., who was in charge of academic affairs. They arranged for me to view a film in the library,

"Chiropractic Research: A First Report," distributed by the International Chiropractors Association. It described the research of a University of Colorado scientist, Chung Ha Suh, Ph.D., Professor of Biomechanics. I was elated.

Five days later Coelho and Rudnick joined me for lunch at Mills in the faculty dining room. I gave them a copy of my curriculum vitae, showed them the books on chiropractic I had been reading, and talked about my interest in doing research. That led to another luncheon meeting when Coelho introduced me to George E. Anderson, D.C. a local chiropractor, a generous benefactor of the new college, and Chairman of the Board of Regents.

In that luncheon meeting I made my pitch. I explained that at Mills I was expected to spend about half of my time doing research and getting it published. I reminded them that while they were struggling to recruit students, equip classrooms, set up laboratories, create a library, and organize courses, they would also need to get a research program up and running. Without a research program they would not qualify to be accredited and grant degrees. My pitch was that I would design and administer their research program just for the opportunity to do it. My salary would, in effect, be the salary I earned at Mills College.

Two days later they called to tell me that the Board had accepted my offer. In November, 1978, I was officially appointed the first Director of Research of Pacific States Chiropractic College.

During the rest of the month I drove almost daily to my new, though barren, office/laboratory in San Lorenzo. I got acquainted with students and members of the faculty and spent a lot of time in Hayward hanging out in the practice of Dr. Anderson, where he guided me to a better understanding of what it was like to be a successful chiropractor.

The door to chiropractic research had opened wide, but passing through it placed me in a quandary. I met with President Coelho in his office to explain my predicament. I couldn't design and execute research because I still didn't know enough about what chiropractors did. What I had learned thus far left me confused. Anderson was a NUCCA practitioner. Van Buskirk worked in an entirely different way using the Pettibon Technique. Another chiropractor practiced the Gonstead Method. How could I design research when they all seemed so different.

Coelho's response was spontaneous and made eminent good sense. "Why don't you sit in on technique courses with the charter class and learn the basics as they learn them." We agreed on that. A couple of days later I suggested that rather than merely audit, it would make good sense for me to formally enroll so that when the time came to apply for research grants I would be able to produce a transcript to verify that I was qualified for chiropractic research because I had completed basic courses in chiropractic.

Coelho and the Board of Regents agreed. I got a copy of my university transcript to document that I had completed the required pre-chiropractic courses when I was a premed student at Berkeley, and that's how I ended up attending classes as an officially enrolled student in the spring of 1979, a year and a half after I taught my first course in medical anthropology. I had arrived at the threshold of a major *Back Door to Medicine.*

Chapter Three

Student Life as Chiropractic Culture

The Daily Routine

It was a good thing I was highly motivated because my daily schedule was demanding. I taught three courses each semester at Mills, held office hours, participated in faculty and committee meetings, all of the usual things. My family and children were a high priority. Yet I managed to drive the round-trip from Oakland to San Lorenzo once or twice a day to attend chiropractic classes on a trimester system that included summers (when I didn't teach at mills), and also to give attention to my chiropractic research responsibilities.

I always started the day as an early morning student. The program was set up to accommodate those who needed to work enough to support themselves and pay their fees, so classes began early in the morning at 7:30 a.m. and ended at mid-afternoon. On Mondays, Wednesdays, and Fridays, when I didn't teach at Mills, I was able to spend whole days in San Lorenzo. Tuesdays and Thursdays, after my 7:30 a.m. class, I drove to Mills to teach and hold office hours until noon, after which I returned to San Lorenzo for classes that met until 3:20. As soon as the last class on those days was finished I rushed back to Mills to teach from 3:50 to 5:05. Fortunately, I was highly motivated and my wife and teenage children indulged me my passion. It helped that as high school and college students our children had their own busy lives and Edna, as Professor and Head of the Department of Education, was equally committed to work from early to late and on weekends.

Fellow Students

Only rarely was a student already medically qualified as some kind of a doctor before enrolling in chiropractic college. One fellow student was a clinical pharmacologist (Pharm.D.) fed up with hospital practice in which he advised medical doctors on the effects of multiple drug interactions. Another was a new medical graduate severely injured in an automobile accident just a few weeks after earning his M.D. During more than a year of slow, painful recovery he felt he had been helped more by his chiropractor than by medical doctors, so he began his slow comeback by enrolling to study chiropractic. Those two were exceptional. Several others, however, were trained at the doctoral level in non-clinical fields.

The 1970s began a decade when universities awarded more Ph.D. degrees to talented students than they could place in suitable employment. Your car salesman, the cocktail waitress, or a business-person next door proved sometimes to be this type of submerged academician. Five of them enrolled at PSCC while I was a student.

Carrie Holms was one I knew especially well, because she was my teacher before she became a fellow student. Her Ph.D. in immunology was earned in medical school. For about ten years she worked in a well-paid research position at her university, but she was not very happy. Others functioned as the official "principal investigators" who designed and administered research projects. She found herself functioning essentially as a highly trained technician, carrying out complex laboratory procedures which after a time became more work than challenge. Funding became scarce. Her job depended upon the success of professors in securing research grants, and when those didn't come through she found herself out of work.

Carrie knew absolutely nothing about chiropractic the day she walked into our classroom to teach microbiology. She had been told to help students see the relevance of her courses for the practice of chiropractic. Chiropractors do not diagnose visceral diseases or use microscopes to identify bacterial agents, so students understandably wondered why they should study so hard to master a field that seemed irrelevant to their future professional responsibilities. Determined to succeed, Carrie set about reading everything she could on chiropractic. She talked with fellow teachers who were chiropractors. She had no difficulty accepting the chiropractic emphasis on conservative, natural methods of healing and eventually she saw the practice of chiropractic as a way to break out of the trap of long hours and short pay. That, at least, was my understanding of her motive when she showed up in one of my classes on the student-side of the classroom.

After part-time student status for a year or two, Carrie resigned her teaching position to finish up the program in a full-time capacity. She graduated within a semester of me as *a summa cum laude* valedictorian who had studied hard and learned well.

She spoke at times of her plan to move to New Orleans to set up practice. It seemed she wanted to provide quality health care and earn a good living in a different part of the world, and she saw New Orleans as an elegant and exciting place to live. Yet she stayed on at the college. Immediately after graduation she returned to her teaching post. With her new qualifications, the salary was ten percent higher, although still not as large as the work-load.

In joining the faculty some years earlier it became apparent that Carrie had moved into a chiropractic version of the status and identity problems that underlay her discontent with doing research in a medical school setting. She felt less than the complete professional because she did not possess clinical qualifications and was not a professor. Returning as a Ph.D. comma D.C. made a lot of difference to her. The desire for a higher income and the challenge of responding to patient needs were only a few of her personal goals. Self-respect and the respect of colleagues also had importance and for the time being, at least, seemed more important. Especially, perhaps, because by then, she had learned how to justify the relevance of immunology for students of chiropractic: The State Board qualifying examination would include questions on the subject.

Joe Marcus was representative of several other post-doctoral students at PSCC. He entered as a student and then did some part-time teaching as the school took advantage of his qualifications. His Ph.D. in physics qualified him to teach the x-ray physics course. But why did he want to change careers and become a chiropractor?

His was an increasingly familiar story. After graduating with a Ph.D. he failed to land a good job, so he ended up selling life insurance. In addition, he belonged to the sixties countercultural generation, so it was not out of character that he meditated in an American Hindu temple. He was a vegetarian. He believed that health care should be nature-based. Although he was poorly informed about chiropractic theory and practice when I first talked with him, he did know that he approved of the exclusion of drugs and surgery.

As one might imagine, most of the fourteen students in the charter class and those who enrolled later were not educated at the doctoral level. To gain entrance they didn't even need a bachelor's degree as long as they had completed basic courses in the natural sciences, which could be done part time in a community college. All of them were adults who had worked for some years at quite ordinary jobs but developed an interest in natural healing and saw a four-year doctoral program as a potential upgrade in occupational status, community service, and financial achievement.

As additional students enrolled during my four years as a student, I found that most of my fellow students were educational resumers. After graduating from high school or college they worked at a full range of jobs. Two of my close friends were former school teachers, as were two of my instructors. Others had worked in the health-care system as an x-ray technician, a laboratory technician, a nurse, and an orderly. Several were massage therapists who saw chiropractic as a way to build on their experience in body work.

Most had nothing to do with health care. One was a house painter, another a firefighter, and still another the operator of a janitorial service. There was a social worker, a newspaper vender, and a retired postman. A couple of students in my class came directly out of high school by way of pre-chiropractic courses in junior college, but that was unusual. Correspondingly, we students varied greatly in age. Very few were still in their early twenties. Many were between thirty-five and forty-five and a couple were in their fifties, including me.

Now let me introduce Peter Edgeson, a failed premedical student who ended up in the chiropractic class in which I did one of the natural science courses. It is often thought that chiropractic students are mostly failed pre-meds, but that was only the case for one other of my fellow students, but let me write about Peter.

I found it fascinating to compare Peter, as he was when we first got acquainted during his early weeks at PSCC, with Peter, as we talked together three years later when we were both interning in the clinic. His school history was familiar. He completed a premedical curriculum with so-so grades and low scores on the MCATS. He was prepared to go to medical school but was not given the opportunity. His father was a physician, so it hurt all the more that he didn't make the grade.

Frustrated, but not yet defeated, he applied to a medical school in Italy which enrolls hundreds of Americans each year. He was accepted. It was a big struggle to get his finances, transcripts, and visa in order, but he got it all done and was ready to fly off to study medicine when he was informed that something went wrong with the paperwork. A key document got lost in consular red tape. Time ran out before he could make it right and he was informed that he would have to wait one more year before he could begin his studies. Meanwhile, he had begun to worry a lot about studying in a foreign language he did not speak and had never studied.

I no longer remember what triggered his interest in chiropractic as an alternative. I do remember that he easily qualified for admission to the school. We had to have taken the same basic premed courses as he did for medical school - biology, general chemistry, organic chemistry, and physics among others - but with a big difference. Whereas medical schools in the United States look for "A" students, a "C" average will do for chiropractic.

And those C's could represent only minimal competencies. Some, like the house painter, who had no training beyond high school a quarter of a century earlier, required two years part time to complete those requirements in his local community college. I'm sure he learned a lot. Others, however, were encouraged by an admissions advisor to enroll in a so-called experimental college that offered science courses in unusual ways that struck me as superficial and inadequate. No need to devote two years to fulfilling entrance requirements there. That could be accomplished in months, not years, of weekend class work in the natural sciences, all with laboratory supplementation. It was hard to see speeded up courses that no one seemed ever to fail as equivalent to those taken by a premed student.

So Peter easily qualified for admission. In addition, he found that a chiropractic education was far less expensive, would take only four years of study and internship (three for those who did summer trimesters). With a Doctor of Chiropractic degree in hand and passing scores on state and national board examinations he would be ready to practice almost as soon as he earned his degree. If he worked four years to qualifying for an M.D. degree he would still have to complete an additional four to eight years of internship, residency, specialty training, and certification before he could completely escape student status. So Peter resigned himself to modified career goals. He had discovered a back door to medicine. He would achieve his goal by qualifying as a doctor with a limited scope of practice but with excellent prospects for a productive career.

Student Culture

Unlike many of us, Joe Marcus seemed little concerned about status and identity, although, like Carrie when I first met her, he pointedly introduced himself to me as "Doctor." In that he had already come under the influence of the culture of chiropractic wherein the title "doctor" is used and over-used as a psychological weapon of self defense against disrespect in the world of medicine. Chiropractic can be looked at as a culture that defines itself in terms of similarities to, and differences from, the practice of medicine. Students must learn to create professional identities by negotiating a labyrinth of cultural complexity in which the shaping process is one of cultural imitation played off against cultural differentiation, a powerful cultural process I first wrote about forty years ago based on my study of aristocrats and peasants in Denmark (Anderson, 1971: 165-168).

A commitment to natural health care emerged as a dominant cultural theme at PSCC. We sat in terrible chairs designed for young teenagers: smooth plastic seats with inclined bottoms on which it was impossible not to slide off without repeatedly straightening up and pressing back. Sitting hour-after-hour in those chairs was one of the most tedious occupational hazards I have ever endured as an anthropologist doing fieldwork, a reminder of my academic forebears who sat cross-legged in Indian tipis until their knees screamed surrender. Their knees screamed. Our backs screamed.

Uncomfortable seats manufactured for growing children in a middle school contributed to daily rituals for us adults who had become obsessive-compulsive about spinal health. One young husband and wife arrived each morning carrying seat inserts that provided support up to their shoulders. Many brought more modest foam rubber pads, pillows, or automobile seat adaptors. One student spent a hundred dollars for a portable reclining chair that he was allowed to set up in the aisle, where he promptly fell asleep during after-lunch lectures. He worked nights.

He was outdone, though, by an outstanding student who leased a hospital bed on which she stretched out at the rear of the classroom. Her back was seriously injured in an airplane crash and she truly needed special accommodation. Only a chiropractic college would be that tolerant of installing a hospital bed in a classroom. But concerns about personal back pain were consistent with the experience of most of my fellow students who had endured the agony of back pain as well as the benefits of chiropractic care.

Food and drink concerns were prominent in the culture of our student body. The 7:30 a.m. procession of sleepy men and women resembled a work gang as students made their way into classrooms carrying knapsacks crammed with books and notes, but also lugging handbags, cloth sacks, or styrofoam ice coolers stuffed with food and drink.

We did a lot of snacking in chiropractic training. In the absence of a cafeteria, and given our location in a residential area, we all brought lunches. The school repeatedly reminded us that the consumption of food and drink in classrooms was forbidden. At times, after an assembly reprimand or a memo from the president, table tops and lockers would be cleared out for a few days. Then stockpiles would build up again.

Lunches tended to be vegetarian, prepared at home and carted to school to be consumed out of enormous jars and pots which could be capped and taken back each night for washing and refilling. We celebrated the passing months with frequent potluck lunches. As resuming students struggling with the more or less forgotten stresses of classroom life we responded with a supportive camaraderie. Not every student was equally high in health awareness, so the buffet might include a casserole with hamburger from mainstream culture. Most of the food, though, was health-oriented and very flat tasting and uninteresting to one not habituated to the subtle seductions of vegetarian cuisine. Most of us eat too much anyway.

It was never clear to me whether the constant fluid intake represented unusual thirst, nervous mannerisms, or a belief that the gastrointestinal system needs constant flushing. The Coke machine down the hallway - a leftover from public school days - was ignored by the majority, who arranged for their own supplies. In most of my classrooms we all chipped in to maintain a bottled mineral water dispenser. To drink from the hallway water fountain was to raise in question one's true commitment to health ideals of the profession. I drank from it a few times just to shock my friends, since I knew that Bay Area tap water was very pure and healthy. It was a mistake. So few used that fountain that it ran rusty. I quickly learned to use the water dispenser myself.

But water was not adequate for many dedicated health conscious students who repeatedly pulled out thermos jugs of herbal tea or re-used mayonnaise jars filled with natural fruit juices. Cranberry juice was especially in vogue, purchased in large one-gallon containers. If drinks or foods needed sweetening, coarse unrefined sugar might be used but pure honey was preferred. Candy bars were déclassé unless they were sweetened with honey and flavored with granola or cabob.

Practicing the Practice of Natural Healing

As fledgling doctors, a lot of unofficial prescribing transpired, all in the form of natural medications. Desk and tabletops were crammed with vitamins, minerals, and food supplements. In every class, one or two students testified about health cures based on those natural products. They usually kept small pharmacies at their desks and followed complex routines for timing self-medication. On the fringes, factory produced vitamins and minerals sufficed, but hard-core believers argued that manufactured products were ineffective. They might even be harmful. For the hard core, only natural herbal preparations would do. Vitamin C, for example, had to come in the form of rose hip tablets at a third the price rather than ascorbic acid from the pharmacologic industry. Seaweed, ginseng, and other herbs were consumed in various forms. The expense of supplements often exceeded the cost of food and drink.

And yes, fasting was very much practiced. Although fasting is no more a necessary part of the practice of chiropractic than are natural foods, vitamins, and supplements, they all coexist well with the chiropractic set of mind. A couple of my teachers were champion fasters. Dr. Martin, a yoga expert and lacto-vegetarian who carried not one ounce of excess fat, regularly undertook marathon fasts, each lasting a month. It's amazing he didn't harm himself. To the contrary, he always felt wonderful while on a prolonged hunger strike, enjoying an agony of purity in which he visualized a draining out of poisons and toxins that had somehow slipped through the armor of his rigorous diet and exercise program. A year after I graduated, one of my own patients turned out to be an ex-patient of his who presented to him with a painful shoulder and was dumbfounded when he told that she ought to commence a complete fast as a way to start off her recovery.

Some students, it must be emphasized, paid very little attention to the health habits and recommendations of student zealots. They ate hamburgers and French fries washed down with soft drinks as do students anywhere, and hopefully survived to pursue healthier lifestyles after graduation. Almost no student, however, was immune to the seduction of spinal health care practices.

One in particular, Rob Smithson, made his living as a masseur. Three members of the charter class did some form of bodywork, as did others who enrolled in the following couple of years. Rob had been taught a chiropractic technique known as Touch for Health, also known as Applied Kinesiology, an approach to health that focuses on an analysis and treatment of muscle tension in different parts of the body. A license for therapeutic massage is sufficient to legally practice that technique, as long as you don't identify it as chiropractic. Because it is a borderline brand of practice within the profession it is not taught as part of the clinical curriculum, but Rob instantly converted his classmates to value it by bringing a massage table to class and demonstrating how it was done. Before the week was out he was teaching an unofficial noon class to his fellow students, for a modest fee.

He was a magician with his treatment table. He could show you that an arm, a leg, or a rotational movement of the head was detectably weaker on one side than on the other. With a little pressure it would "blow out," that is, give way in total weakness. Then he pressed a bit here and there and lo and behold, that weak place became strong. It was not slight-of-hand or psychological trickery. It really happened. What was not clear is whether it made any difference for one's health, but that is another matter. In our classroom he converted nearly everyone to the idea that they should eventually practice chiropractic in a way that would incorporate Applied Kinesiology, and he helped earn his way through chiropractic college at the same time. Those were wonderfully resourceful students.

Peter, the pre-med whose father was a physician, joined the noon class and became one of the most proficient. He was equally serious and successful in his other technique classes. His conversion proceeded rapidly, but I didn't give much thought to it until we were approaching graduation and I reminded him of things he told me when we first met.

What a transformation in his mindset! "Bob, I would much rather be a D.C. than an M.D." "But Peter," I responded, "you told me you wished chiropractors could legally prescribe medication for patients with diseases like rheumatoid arthritis, since chiropractic alone is often not enough." "Did I say that?" he pondered. "No, I don't remember saying that. Anyway, I wouldn't prescribe even if I could. I can keep that patient a lot healthier with regular adjustments, and he won't be poisoned by drugs." He concluded by insisting that he considers it a blessing that he didn't get into medical school because it is a lot better to be a chiropractor. The first time he said, "I would rather be a D.C.," he crossed an enormous divide from when he arrived conceding that he was compromising his original career goal in medicine.

Peter's dedication to learning manual methods of treatment was fairly typical of chiropractic students. Some were always experimenting with alternative adjusting techniques they willingly demonstrated to friends. At home they reduced the subluxations of fellow students, family members and neighbors, even though it was strictly against the law to practice chiropractic without a license and to do so could serve as grounds for dismissal if they got caught. They tried out techniques from the official curriculum. They applied what they learned on weekends when they found the money to pay for external courses for which they got no school credit.

The weekend seminars came as a surprise. I assumed that in school I would be taught all that was important. It wasn't so. Only certain approved adjusting methods were placed in the curriculum. However, the school sponsored a revenue-producing extension program of workshops taught by well-known chiropractors who encouraged us to commit ourselves to one or another of the many competing techniques for identifying and adjusting subluxations.

Students coughed up a lot of money to pay for those intensive courses. They coughed up even more to buy special tables and other equipment. In their enthusiasm, they spent evenings and weekends - even breaks between classes - rehearsing themselves with fellow students. I have never seen so many highly motivated students keep up their enthusiasm for so long. Even those who were not attracted to seminars on nutritional therapy, meditation, or other alternative health practices got caught up in an eagerness to learn highly touted methods for spinal or peripheral joint adjusting.

As a corollary they experienced a chiropractic version of a typical medical student syndrome. In every medical school, some students studying pathology will anxiously worry that a blemish here or a pain there may be symptomatic of one of the terrible diseases they are learning about. Student health services can predict that a few will show up in fear at one time or another.

But the medical school syndrome is small potatoes compared to that of chiropractic school, where nearly every student sooner or later realized that he had a vertebral rotation or protrusion that was very hard to adjust and needed expert care. Every new technique course or weekend intensive offered an opportunity to get treatment by a hitherto untried technique. It was OK to ask instructors for adjustments, which were freely and willingly given.

The culture of the chiropractic classroom, then, included a lively and enthusiastic interchange of concerns about health care, with an emphasis on chiropractic philosophy and technique. We learned a lot that way outside of formal class hours.

The Enculturation Process

Even during our first days as students a process of conversion was underway for Peter and the rest of us. It was the beginning of a cultural transformation that lasted the entire three to four years. Much of it was carried out as an organized formal program. Just as much took place informally.

The formal program began each term with a meeting of present and potential students. Open-houses resembled the revival meetings of my Uncle Harry, the evangelist. At the first one I attended the president of a chiropractic college told the story of his conversion experience. As a young man he was on his way to M.I.T. where he had been admitted on a full four-year scholarship. (I took that with a grain of salt.) Although still a young man he fell victim to the agony of low back pain. Some years earlier an older neighborhood friend transferred from medical school to complete his studies in a chiropractic college. (I also took that with a grain of salt.) They ran into each other just days before the president was to fly off to M.I.T., and his friend subdued his excruciating back pain with a chiropractic adjustment. That did it. His cure was complete and instantaneous. Like Paul on the road to Damascus, the president realized that chiropractic was more important than engineering. He diverted to Davenport, Iowa, where he enrolled in the Palmer College of Chiropractic as a better place to study than M.I.T.

The next speaker was an "all-American level" football player in college. (I took that with a grain of salt.) He planned to attend medical school until a chiropractor healed his football injuries after medical doctors had failed, a road to Damascus experience that similarly diverted him to a career in chiropractic. As he spoke to us he described a high-volume practice in his own architect-designed clinic where he was assisted by several other doctors and a large staff of receptionists and assistants. (I verified that. His clinic was in a new, beautifully designed building tucked away in its own surrounding garden and parking lot. He made a ton of money.)

Note the basic underlying message of each of these speakers. Every week in a compulsory assembly we usually listened to a field doctor with a similar message. We were being trained to be doctors (cultural imitation). It is better to be a chiropractor than a medical doctor because we provide a more effective kind of care (cultural differentiation). We end up in clinics with white-uniformed assistants (imitation). We are regarded with the high respect due to a doctor (imitation). We will be paid a lot of money for rendering a service to humanity that other kinds of doctors cannot offer (differentiation). The message was very seductive.

In chiropractic technique classes the testimonials continued. Instructors told endless stories of the seemingly miraculous cures of patients in pain who were medical failures but chiropractic successes by virtue of the hands-on adjusting methods we were taught.

The Chairman of the Board of Regents, Dr. Anderson himself, explained to me very early in my apprenticeship at his office that language is important. Medical doctors "diagnose pathology" and "treat disease," physical therapists massage and "manipulate" the spine, but chiropractors identify "spinal subluxations" and offer "adjustments," leaving the innate intelligence of the body ("Innate") to bring about a return to normal health. Remember, not "diagnosis," but "subluxation." Not "manipulation," but "adjustment." Not "pharmaceutical prescription" but "freeing up of Innate." In short, not cultural imitation, but cultural differentiation.

The really basic conversion experience of the student generally took place or was reaffirmed and deepened elsewhere than in public meetings and classroom encounters. Conversions grew out of the influence of one student on another in the daily activities of campus life. When everyone around you is a true believer, you may well find that you become one yourself.

What is Important?

I must confess a prejudice in favor of chiropractic. I liked it a lot that chiropractic opened its doors easily to individuals ready for a change in careers. I applauded how chiropractic colleges offered opportunities for intellectual and vocational growth. I liked seeing minimally educated working people discover they could train to be doctors. I also learned that chiropractors develop healing skills that justify their status as doctors, support them as professionals, and serve a public need.

Chapter Four

Learning to Be a Chiropractic Doctor

Courses on How to Make a Diagnosis

I was excited. We were all tense and excited. A door was opening. We were crossing a threshold. Old self-identities retreated as our lives went on hold, freeing us to move toward a future empowerment, a new status, a different role in society.

Anthropologists have long referred to the process of advancing to a new status in society as a "rite of passage." As an analytical concept it serves well to capture the meaning of our experience (feelings, hopes, fears, realities) as we depart an earlier status - teacher, painter, firefighter, social worker - on the way to achieving a new status - chiropractor, clinician, doctor, consultant (Gennep, 1909). We were entering a critical four-year stage in the ritual process that anthropologists speak of as liminal (from Latin *limen*, meaning threshold). Victor Turner wrote quaintly of liminality as located "in and out of time" in a place "betwixt and between." In that way he described us rather well. Also, in introducing the concept of communitas, he could well have been describing our student culture of pot-luck lunches, mutual prescribing, and school spirit. "Among themselves," he wrote, "neophytes tend to develop an intense comradeship and egalitarianism" (Turner, 1969: 94-97).

For us, the feelings of liminality and communitas intensified the first time we entered the classroom where we would be taught how to diagnose and treat people crippled and in pain.

For me personally, it had been exactly twenty years since I last served as a young Navy medic who scrubbed in to assist in surgeries, used hypodermic syringes to inject clinic and hospital patients, prepped patents for invasive procedures, (and who cleaned up the operating room and clinic after doctors and patients moved on).

I scarcely remembered any feelings or skills from those two years in the military world of medicine. They had receded out of awareness while Edna and I filmed, recorded and published our findings on musical events in Nepal as part teaching my course on ethnomusicology. They were increasingly forgotten as we did ethnographic fieldwork that required us to alternate winter breaks in Mexico with summer vacations in Denmark in order to observe, interview, and compare ceramic artists. That research enlivened my course on ethnographic art. I still have the manuscript of our book, *From Folk Art to Modern Design*, never published, never read, but stimulating to research and write. (The text was OK but we neglected to take the photos needed to illustrate it.)

Now, unexpectedly, I was going to ratchet up and build on whatever remained of that Navy experience. I was going to be taught how to become a practicing doctor. Yes, like my fellow students, I was a little tense but very excited.

Diagnosis courses, in chiropractic college as in medical school, always introduce each new subject with a review of basic anatomy, physiology, and pathology. In that way the basics were drilled into us before we moved on to diagnostic procedures and hands-on experiences. A doctor arriving at a diagnosis is like a detective unraveling the mysteries of a crime. We were taught to be medical detectives. It was challenging. It was difficult. But it was rewarding as the human body and mind revealed their secrets, just as it had been intellectually and emotionally rewarding to gain insights into the lives of musicians and artists. (I really love being an anthropologist.)

Our training was distinctively chiropractic in that the emphasis zeroed in on musculoskeletal disorders. The educational program was organized as an integrated approach, chiropractic and medical, that went beyond strictly chiropractic examination techniques not taught in medical schools to include the standard orthopedic examination based on a widely used medical textbook, Stanley Hoppenfeld, *Physical Examination of the Spine and Extremitie*s.

It was a time for nervous excitement when we entered a classroom to begin our first course on how to work with patients. We had been told to wear gym suits, because we would each select a partner with whom to alternate in the roles of doctor and patient.

The course began with learning how to identify normal ranges of motion in all of the spinal and peripheral joints. Faltering at the beginning, we practiced the uniquely chiropractic motion palpation test as a way to examine the spine from neck to pelvis. Usually while sitting behind a seated patient, the doctor controls the patient with one hand at the shoulder in order to control bending to one side and then the other, backwards and forwards, clockwise and counter-clockwise, all the while holding the thumb of the other hand against each vertebra in turn to detect how it responds to stress. A fixated, misaligned, or loose joint pinpointed the level at which corrective action would be required.

In his transformative encounter with Harvey Lillard, Daniel David Palmer crudely anticipated motion palpation as he ran his fingers along Lillard's spine to locate "a vertebra racked from its normal position." And similarly today, just as Old Dad Chiro "racked" Lillard's vertebra back into position, "by using the spinous process as a lever" we would be taught how to adjust a subluxation for pain relief and restored mobility. As in that historical moment, so in our time, hands on procedures remain the most important skills a chiropractor needs.

The motion palpation test, a few other maneuvers such as Adson's test, and the use of our bare hands for adjusting, those skills and a table are all that is needed to practice chiropractic safely, efficiently, and effectively. You can bet we all paid close attention and practiced hard.

We were also taught how to carry out standard orthopedic maneuvers such as Yergason's test to rule out a biceps tendon injury. There were dozens like that, but we especially focused on spine-related functions. We were taught, for example, that an Adson's test must always be carried out before performing a rotational cervical adjustment. Your patient could suffer a stroke if the subclavian artery that supplies blood to the brain were compromised while you twisted a patient's neck. So we practiced Adson's test on each other and we were tested on each other to confirm that we had learned to do it properly, and that was a good thing, for sure. After a neck adjustment that damaged a vertebral artery, the patient of an unlicensed chiropractor recently fell unconscious, was declared brain dead, and died two days later (Minneapolis-St. Paul Star Tribune, June 16, 2008).

As a major part of the course we were taught how to execute a complete neurological examination that required us to identify which peripheral nerve, spinal nerve root, or central nervous system pathway might deprive some reflex of its normal response, some muscle of its proper function, or some body part of its proper sensation of touch, vibration, temperature, or pain. Between books, lectures, and laboratory exercises it was a lot to learn, but we worked steadfastly at it. It mattered that we were highly motivated.

Even students who had achieved only a minimal pre-chiropractic background in the basic sciences accomplished what we needed to know. Remember, Palmer was educated only to the level of learning how to read and write. It was hands-on skill that mattered.

At the beginning of the following trimester the general physical diagnosis course began with a flurry of cooperative activity as members of the class formed a purchasing group to qualify for price discounts on the expensive instruments we would need. We each ended up with a traditional black leather doctor's handbag (or more commonly, a brief case, camera bag, or even in one case, a small cardboard box). Although we thought of ourselves as future chiropractors, each of us acquired that universal symbol of the physician, a stethoscope, along with an ophthalmoscope, blood-pressure cuff, penlight, reflex hammer, tuning fork for testing neurological pathways, and a pinwheel for evaluating sensation in the skin. Several hundred dollars was involved for each student. That outlay was a tribute to the value our new profession placed upon an essentially medical education, since most students were well aware that they would probably never practice chiropractic in a way that would require them to possess any of those instruments. (Some would end up using chiropractic instruments totally foreign to medical practice, but that was a different matter.)

The goal in this class was to teach us to do a complete medical history and physical examination. Later we would be have to survive a course on how to interpret x-rays, sonograms, and CAT scans, yet another course on clinical chemistry that would prepare us for ordering and evaluating laboratory results. In the end we were taught the fundamental clinical skills a medical doctor must master, but first we took this course on how to interview and examine when a patient presents with a health problem.

Our physical examination instructor was thorough and adequate, even though he lacked experience. With ophthalmoscopes in hand we looked into eyes. Through otoscopes we scanned eardrums. With stethoscopes to chest we practiced interpreting heart and lung sounds. Religiously we were taught to carry out examination procedures, but with one critical shortcoming. We practiced in gym suit sessions on perfectly healthy people, students practicing on students. As substitutes for sick people we listened to audio tapes of heart anomalies and watched video presentations of abnormal reflexes. In written and practical examinations we were required to demonstrate that we understood and could perform the necessary procedures, but it was necessarily superficial.

Later, while interning in the clinic, we were supposed to gain experience from real patients. Although essential for honing chiropractic skills, the clinic never amounted to much for the practice of medicine as such. People who sought care in the school clinic predictably suffered from joint, muscle, ligamental, and tendon pain or dysfunction. For other health problems they sought care from medical doctors and hospitals. We had to do complete histories and physicals on every new clinic patient, but as in our classrooms, it was rare to encounter much of interest.

Courses in Radiology (Spinography)

In 1895, as an offshoot of experimenting with the Crookes tube in his laboratory at the University of Wurtsburg in Germany, Wilhelm Roentgen presented medicine with a wonderfully useful diagnostic tool, the radiograph. Since chiropractors benefited their patients by correcting mechanical misalignments and faulty motion they were quick to see potential diagnostic value in x-ray imaging. Obviously, they would also find prestige in utilizing a complex medical instrument and it would be profitable.

As early as 1910, the founder's son, B. J. Palmer, acquired an x-ray machine for Palmer College of chiropractic. Three years later, when enough electricity was finally available to power the new instrument - we're talking about a country town in Iowa - B.J. produced the first chiropractic x-ray in history. By 1920 he had succeeded in enlarging his imaging capability to capture the whole spine from top to bottom as a single picture, a distinctly chiropractic achievement of uncertain value for diagnosis but impressive for patient indoctrination.

Since the time of B.J., chiropractors have devoted what might seem a disproportionate amount of attention to acquiring roentgenographic skills. We certainly were enrolled for extensive course work to that end, beginning with a theoretical course on x-ray physics. Unfortunately, the physics course was not taught by Joe Marcus, who didn't begin to teach it until the following year.

Our teacher was a chiropractor who short-changed us miserably. First, he was absent most of the time. He set his pace by not showing up for the first meeting. Altogether he missed forty-two of the sixty hours for which we got credit. Students liked him, however, and no one seemed to mind the missed or wasted time. It was preferable to the hard work of attempting to master more physics. Dr. Marcus faced a small student revolt when he inherited the course. He taught it at a university level that overwhelmed his students. By the next trimester the course settled into a compromise that fell between the quality extremes of the first two. Learning radiological physics just did not motivate PSCC students as intensely as the acquisition of hands-on chiropractic skills.

Our instructor, a former junior high school teacher, short-changed us in a second way. He didn't teach much or well when he did show up. He just read from one of three texts. When asked a question he either shouted down the student, making her feel stupid for having asked, or he cut her off saying, "it's something to memorize," because the only apparent reason for the course was to get us through our qualifying board examinations when we were ready to graduate.

He did seem to know a lot about how we should evaluate x-ray equipment and set it up, based, no doubt, on his own recent experience in establishing his practice in a nearby community. If not exciting, that was at least of practical use. He taught us how to adjust kilovoltage and amperage for best results. He also explained practicalities involved in wiring and insulating an x-ray set-up. So, in his course we got some instruction on "how-to-do-it" issues, but nothing about physics beyond what we could decipher for ourselves in the assigned textbooks. Appalling, but true.

The next course was to teach us standard medical procedures for positioning patients in order to view whatever joint or bone was malpositioned. We practiced x-ray setups on each other, memorizing routines for the cranium, spine, and extremities. The purely medical nature of this course revealed itself most clearly as we were taught how to produce standard films of the spine, the only setups we would conceivably ever need, and which would be taught in other courses. The radiographs we interpreted for this course were placed on the view box with the patient's right side to the observer's left, as is always done in medicine. In chiropractic x-ray analysis we always place the patient's right side on the doctor's right. In other words, medical doctors look at x-rays as though they are approaching the patient face-on, while chiropractors look at x-rays as though they are standing behind the patient. That difference goes back to B. J. Palmer when the new technology was first integrated into clinical practice.

As an addendum to our training in x-ray analysis, for chiropractic purposes we received our most pertinent hours of instruction independently of the college curriculum. Every optional course on chiropractic technique - those weekend intensives - offered training and review on how to position patients and measure the position of one vertebra relative to another by penciling in horizontal lines and calculating angles in uniquely chiropractic ways (the one advocated technique differing from the other as each technique booster attempted to convert attendees to his particular style of practice). To that end we purchased measuring instruments totally different from those carried in our black doctor satchels, namely ruler and protractor elaborations of the sort used for high school geometry or by architects. We were taught how to use them for calculating the angles and directions required for adjustive thrusts to reposition vertebrae.

It should be pointed out that research has not demonstrated that small asymmetries measured so precisely are of much practical significance when it comes time to administer an adjustment. Cynthia

Peterson, Meridel Gatterman, and Tyrone Wei would seem to agree: "Occasionally radiographic measurement of the spine offers useful information." Their emphasis is on "occasionally," because they preface that conclusion by stating, "there is a fundamental fallacy in attempting to evaluate biomechanical function on static radiographs." The fallacy derives from universal asymmetries in vertebral anatomy and the related "extremely poor" reliability of inter- and intra-examiner consistency in x-ray marking (1990: 92).

To illustrate that last point, in one small project undertaken in my capacity as Director of Research I reviewed a sample of 300 patients for whom at least three sets of post-adjustment x-rays of the first cervical vertebra (C1) were available in the practice of a single chiropractor. On radiographs recorded by the chiropractor immediately after he had adjusted C1 to the position identified by measurement as normal, only 3 percent (8 radiographs out of 886) measured as completely normal (Anderson, 1981: 267-268). In that test of the theory that the axial skeleton in good health will be aligned to 0° of deviation from precise angles of alignment, the hypothesis failed. In the words of William G. Blair, D.C., "one of our greatest constants is the presence of non-symmetry in the bilateral formation of these structures" (1964: 4).

More than a decade after I graduated from chiropractic college, Dr. Herbert Vear, former president of the Council on Chiropractic Education in Canada, invited me to contribute to a book he published, *Chiropractic Standards of Practice and Quality of Care* (1992). In that I spelled out what research had taught us. "Most patients with acute back pain can be treated in a chiropractic protocol that does not require spinal radiographs." X-rays are only required in patients over 50 years of age, or in those of any age who have recently suffered severe trauma, complain of pain at rest, describe excessive weight loss, or present with certain other relatively unusual signs and symptoms. "In the absence of these factors, the risks of missing serious pathology by not using x-ray evaluation are minimal" (Anderson, 1992: 165-166). It is clearly unethical to expose patients to the dangers of ionizing radiation when the indications for adjusting can be adequately determined by performing motion palpation tests as part a case history.

In the two remaining courses we learned how to interpret chest and abdominal films for respiratory, cardiovascular, gastrointestinal, and genitourinary pathology. Although our instructors worked hard, they were handicapped by a lack of medical education. They showed more competence in reading plain films - the sort chiropractors use in evaluating musculoskeletal complaints - than in contrast studies such as the barium enema, which are never done in a chiropractic office. Chiropractors only see contrast studies, CAT scans, nuclear magnetic imaging, bone scans, or sonograms when patients bring their own records from medical work-ups. In our school years, my class only saw a couple of CAT scans and no MRIs, bone scans, or sonograms. I felt those two courses barely achieved minimal goals.

The medical courses were to prepare us to identify pathology other than what we would treat ourselves. We were given regular reading assignments in the three volumes of Meschan's *Analysis of Roentgen Signs in General Radiology* along with written examinations to confirm our diligence.

We were also rehearsed to follow a strict evaluation procedure: "All Mixed Couples Should Dance Slowly" was recommended as a mnemonic aid. In scanning a radiograph, begin with anatomy (the "A" of "All"): count the ribs, vertebrae, fingers, *et cetera*, to be sure all are present. Then examine the inner medulla (the "M" of "Mixed") of each bone for cysts, tumors, or other lesions. Next check the integrity of the outer cortex of bones ("Couples"). That done, look for misalignments, dislocations, and soft tissue changes ("Slowly'). Only after completing this medical evaluation should you proceed to a chiropractic analysis, which has nothing to do with mixed-couple dancing.

Yet, the law offered a powerful motivation to get this right. If you x-ray a patient you are responsible for identifying any pathology, musculoskeletal or not, that may be visible. You can be sued for malpractice if you miss a tumor, infection, or other problem that should be referred for medical consultation and possible treatment. It takes a lot of supervised training to learn to detect the often subtle signs of serious disease. A chiropractor relying on x-ray analysis is well advised to ask a radiologist, a certified chiropractor radiologist if you prefer, to evaluate films for medical problems that might be missed because of inadequate expertise.

Courses on Therapeutic Techniques

When I decided not to do research on Chinese medicine and for the first time in my life observed chiropractors with patients I was confused because their treatment protocols were all different. Depending on where you look, I later learned that the number of named chiropractic techniques ranges from 15 to 60 to 132 and counting! (Anonymous, 2008; North City Chiropractic, 2007). As trimesters passed, one after the other, the college enrolled us in five technique courses. Chiropractors refer to the techniques we were taught as Diversified, Gonstead, Thompson/Pierce-Stillwagon, Toggle Recoil (Palmer Specific), and Grostic (NUCCA).

D. D. Palmer's archetypal method survives as the Diversified Technique. For each part of the spine the heel of the hand (usually) is used to deliver a precisely placed thrust that often elicits a cracking noise to announce that the targeted vertebra moved. How the patient should be positioned and how hands should be placed to execute an effective thrust differ for different segments of the spine and for other parts of the body. In that sense the approach is "diversified."

And, although it is customary to take x-rays and to calculate angles of thrust based on careful measurements, motion palpation alone can suffice for the kind of excellent results Palmer himself achieved. Similarly, although many different kinds of table are on the market, a simple padded work surface with an open slot to accommodate the nose of a supine patient is all that is absolutely required. Nor does a chiropractor need to rely on special tools such as the Activator, the Variable Frequency Adjuster, the Derma Therm-O-Graph, the Dorsal Blocker, or others. (As I write 30 years later, so many devices have been invented and are now marketed that a free "product magazine for chiropractors" arrives at my office every month as an advertising throw-away.) Because Diversified can be practiced effectively in such a simple way, it is the norm for altruistic chiropractors who contribute their skills in remote villages of the developing world that lack electricity and are difficult of access.

With or without accessories, Diversified Technique is the norm for over 95 percent of all chiropractors, so it was appropriate that we began with it (Anonymous, 2008). And we were unanimously eager to become as proficient as we could with the enthusiasm that enlivened every one of our chiropractic classes from day one.

Communitas reigned. Frequently it led to generous gifts to the struggling new college. Students organized raffles, operated bingo games, solicited donations, and formed work parties in order to provide extra funding for treatment tables and other equipment. They spent substantial amounts of money out of their own limited budgets to pay admissions to special weekend seminars offering instruction in various aspects of practice. They seemed never to run out of enthusiasm for improving chiropractic skills, in contrast to the way many felt about medical knowledge.

A propos that disinterest in medical procedures, eventually we were required to take two trimesters of physical therapy. Many of my fellow students regarded physical therapy as medical and totally unnecessary. The most doctrinaire considered it contrary to chiropractic philosophy and a sellout to the influence of medicine on licensure requirements. Some members of the administration and faculty were in full agreement. Astonishingly, our instructor in these two courses, told us he saw no harm in it, but felt that chiropractors didn't need it and that students shouldn't have to waste time on it.

That instructor lacked experience and proper training. Only months before he taught us he passed the course himself in a different chiropractic college. He took it because it was required for chiropractors like him from another state in order to qualify for a license to practice in California. He read to us from the notes he took as a student in that course. Fortunately, he recognized our need to know enough facts and to be sufficiently familiar with equipment so we would be able to pass the California examination ourselves. We did a lot of memorizing.

The shortcomings of our two physical therapy courses were rectified to some extent later when we were interns. In the clinic we came under a young chiropractor who believed that physical therapy was valuable. He possessed both knowledge and experience. He forced us to practice on each other, and eventually on patients.

The clinic possessed only limited equipment (and the spirit of communitas did not include fund raisers for medical purposes), but we did get some familiarity with how to apply heat and cold, electrical stimulation, ultrasound radiation, and infrared heating. Perhaps the main modality missing, one that I regretted enough to study later in a physical therapy seminar elsewhere, was the use of traction. Basic physical therapy, irreverently referred to by chiropractors as "shake and bake," can ease pain and facilitate healing. I see no reason why it should not be offered in chiropractic clinics, just as it was in ours.

But I digress. The second technique we were taught was that of Dr. Clarence Gonstead. He elaborated basic Diversified by adding extensive instrumentation, beginning with complex methods of x-ray analysis using a measuring device called the Gonstead Radiographic Parallel.

In addition to identifying subluxations on x-ray film, Gonstead developed the Nervo-Scope, a handheld device to record temperature differences between the two sides of the vertebral column. A simple descendant of the neurocalometer invented by B. J. Palmer in 1924, the heat differences were said to identify precisely where "nerve heat" was caused by a "pinched nerve" and should be taken as a sign that an adjustment would be curative, but those claims are purely speculative and highly questionable.

Not the least, Gonstead invented the so-called pelvic table, the knee-chest table, and the Gonstead Cervical Chair along with a remarkable number of new adjustive maneuvers.

Our course on the Gonstead Technique was taught by an inexperienced practitioner and was only so-so in quality, but some students were determined to become expert. They formed a Gonstead Club. In addition to discussion meetings they arranged for weekend seminars by experts. I attended several of those myself. Often in addition to Diversified, about half of all licensed chiropractors use the Gonstead approach (Anonymous, 2008).

Our third technique course, Thompson/Pierce-Stillwagon, was a disaster. The emphasis was on how to use Dr. Clay Thompson's invention, the Thompson Terminal Point Table along with his variations on adjustive maneuvers. The table was big, heavy, and pneumatically powered in five sections, three of which were drop sections that released under the patient when a thrust was administered. It improved accuracy by safeguarding against overadjusting (thrusting too hard). Progress was evaluated by leg check analysis. As measured at the heels, a subluxation was taken to have been eliminated if the patient's legs became equal in length.

Building on the Thompson Technique, Walter Pierce and Glenn Stillwagon replaced the neurocalometer with their own version of it, the Derma Therm 500. It measured bilateral infrared radiation to record temperature differences. Using that combination technique, abnormal spine function was measured in three ways: by x-ray measurements, by leg check analysis, and by thermography. Pierce-Stillwagon especially advocated a very heavy reliance on radiological analysis. "Unless contra-indicated by pregnancy, etc., as soon as it is determined that a new patient is a chiropractic case . . . the doctor immediately takes the following X-rays: Cervical Series (8 x 10's): A-P Open Mouth and Lateral (with additional views optional), A-P Full Spine (14 x 36), Lateral Lumbar (14 x 17)" (Seminar Manual, 1976). That adds up to an extraordinarily heavy exposure to ionizing radiation as routine practice. Thompson Technique as such is as widely employed as Gonstead, but Pierce-Stillwagon is limited to about 15 percent of practitioners (Anonymous, 2008).

I didn't learn much in that course, which was taught by the inept instructor we had for x-ray positioning. He knew so little about the method that he stalled through weeks of class as he waited for the weekend when an introductory seminar was scheduled to be taught by Dr. Stillwagon in person. He expected his students to sign up for it at additional personal cost. In the seminar they got two days of instruction. Those who didn't attend got through the course with a very sketchy and in some ways incorrect training. For those who did, it was still inadequate, a travesty of proper teaching.

Even so, the Thompson/Pierce-Stillwagon method of adjusting (exclusive of their approach to radiology) served me as an addition to Diversified. I developed my skill, such as it was, in six weekend seminars taken over a period of several years, two with Dr. Thompson and four with Dr. Stillwagon. When I opened my own clinic at the Mills College Health Center, it was the Thompson table that made the difference. I never took an x-ray or used a chiropractic instrument. It was entirely a hands-on practice.

The Upper Cervical Technique was developed as a revolutionary simplification of Diversified by B. J. Palmer in the 1930s. His alternative name for it was the Hole in One (HIO). HIO contrasted with the customary practice of adjusting subluxations at different levels, analogously to the way golfers expectably hit their golf balls several times to get from the tee to the green and from the green to the cup. HIO was modified in the 1940s by John Grostic and Ralph Gregory, who founded the National Upper Cervical Chiropractic Association (NUCCA) in 1966.

For upper cervical adjusting B.J. developed a modified technique known as Toggle Recoil. It delivered a low force thrust at high speed in a different way from the traditional adjustment. It took a lot of practice to get it right. NUCCA for its part modified the adjusting technique to become a low force squeezing motion directed only at atlas.

Although the Diversified course was the best taught of the full-spine technique courses, the most competently taught of all were Toggle Recoil (Palmer Specific) and Grostic (NUCCA). They were similar in that only the top-most vertebra (C1) had to be adjusted, because that was always the site of what B. J. termed "the major subluxation." He theorized that all other deviations along the spine would adjust themselves automatically if the major subluxation was normalized, and it would always be located at C1 or C2. Anatomically, CI is also known as atlas, from ancient Greek mythology in which the Titan named Atlas carried the earth high on his shoulders. For "earth" think "head" and you've got the basic structural concept behind B.J.'s revolutionary approach to adjusting.

Can you imagine spending 120 hours in two courses solely to learn how to use the small sesimoid bone in your wrist (the pisiform) to direct a few ounces of force at the atlas for a literal split second, a millisecond in order to shift its position by a few millimeters with the understanding that it will reposition C1 to O° of deviation? Can you imagine teaching that in a millisecond you can potentially initiate the elimination of all spinal nerve root problems below, and ultimately most of the health problems that challenge specialists in internal medicine?

Well, we spent 120 hours that way, and it was not easy, because in addition to other demands it required strenuous physical training. We worked daily on often painful stretching exercises so we could position ourselves in a precise way to bend straight legged at the waist and reach to our ankles to squeeze off an adjustive thrust. At one point in taking the NUCCA course that maneuver left me with a painful lumbago that lasted for a week, in spite of still being an active gymnast in those years.

If you rely on either technique, and believe in HIO, you can forget about the diversified ways in which you might otherwise adjust the spine at any of the 33 different vertebrae. Just position the patient on his side with one ear upward, palpate a bit behind and beneath the ear to put your finger on the transverse process of atlas where it can be felt just below the skin. Place your pisiform against the blunt end of the transverse process and toggle or NUCCA it to sit precisely below the condyles of the cranium. If that is achieved, the theory is that the whole of the spine below will creep back to perfect alignment. According to the National Board of Chiropractic Examiners in a 2005 report, about one in four chiropractors use the Palmer Hole in One technique, which is hard to believe (Anonymous, 2008). (I don't know how many resort to Grostic.) Many chiropractors, however, are skeptics, as was one of the first patients I observed in the office of a NUCCA practitioner.

It was mid-afternoon when a station wagon parked at the clinic door. A man, so in agony from low back pain that he couldn't tolerate riding on the car seat, lay stretched out on the floor. Helped into the examination room he found himself seated under an x-ray machine where the doctor explained that he was going to aim the camera through the top of his head to take an x-ray picture of the bottom of his skull (the foramen magnum) where cranial condyles support the head on top of atlas. Measurements of the film would inform the doctor of how his adjustment would need to be aimed up or down and left or right to reposition atlas to a postulated anatomical normal.

The patient was incredulous. His lower back was killing him but the doctor was only looking at his head and the top of his neck. It got worse. After the x-ray a current version of the neurocalometer was moved down his neck only as far as his shoulders to produce a wavy line that recorded small thermal differences right and left of the central spinous processes. Finally, stretched out on his back, a leg check confirmed that his spine was out of adjustment because one leg was a half centimeter shorter than the other. The lumber spine itself was neither unclothed nor palpated and it was not adjusted. Baffled and still in pain after his atlas adjustment ("it will take a while before the pain eases off"), that patient never returned, but most did.

The practice was very busy and very profitable, which is why we were taught that course in NUCCA. The chiropractor was Dr. George Anderson, who provided huge sums to get the college started and served as Chairman of the Board of Regents. I learned to respect Dr.

Anderson as a splendid human being, but he could offer no scientific evidence to substantiate the bizarre belief that HIO or NUCCA was a valid substitute for full-spine chiropractic.

A therapeutic course on whiplash and spinal trauma unexpectedly served as a capstone for our clinical education. Whereas the course that was supposed to put us through a final review of the whole of therapeutics was a flop, the whiplash course achieved that purpose superbly without announcing itself that way. Starting with musculoskeletal embryology, the histology of tissue injury, and a detailed review of spinal anatomy, the instructor went on to review physics in order to identify on a mathematical basis the mechanism of whiplash. He reviewed the biomechanics of a neck injury. He covered symptoms, orthopedic and neurological testing, radiographic evaluation, diagnosis, initial treatment and case management. He even covered the handling of insurance forms and how to appear in court as an expert witness in a personal injury case. It was a course that taught hard, examined hard, and made you wish you could remember even half of what was covered. So, in spite of the many shortcomings we endured because the school was still struggling to establish itself, by the end of our coursework we achieved what I felt was a sound basis for working with real patients as interns and, eventually, for practicing as field doctors.

Chapter Five

The Culture of Clinic Interns

How it Feels to be a Doctor

In spite of obvious shortcomings, our preparation in the basic and clinical sciences, our training in techniques of spinal manipulative therapy, our indoctrination in the ethics and philosophy of health care, and hundreds of hours in classrooms and laboratories, when taken together, prepared us to be doctors - but without making doctors of us. Only clinical experience would or could do that. Sir William Osler counseled medical students to "know that by practice alone can you become expert. Medicine is learned by the bedside and not in the classroom" (cited in Bean, 1950). For the most part without ever having heard of Osler, we knew the truth of his advice and looked forward to the hands-on training our five trimesters of clinic internship held in promise.

The first time I felt like a physician occurred for a brief moment the first time I walked into the clinic toting a black bag crammed with instruments and wearing a white clinic jacket. It happened again the first time I heard the loudspeaker sound through the waiting room and down the corridor of the treatment area, " Dr. Anderson, your patient is ready. Dr. Anderson, your patient is ready."

It seemed deceptive to me that a student intern should be referred to as "doctor," but for the student it served as a powerful motivator, a reward for months of preparatory study, and an enormous symbolic leap in self-identity. The clinic, consecrated by the pain and fear of patients, served as a stage in the drama of a future doctor's life. The novice actor in her new attire practiced playing her still unaccustomed leading role on a stage-set of clinical props.

It ended up taking a whole trimester for the curtain to rise on that clinic stage. "Clinic l," we soon realized, was still limited to classroom work. We showed up mornings before the first patients arrived in the waiting room, isolated from working interns by the walls of a classroom. (By this time, given my part-time schedule, I had temporarily fallen behind the charter class.) Our supervisor was a newly licensed chiropractor, recently graduated from a chiropractic institution in another state. He was assigned to guide us for an allocated six weeks to review principles of patient care and to indoctrinate us in clinic procedures. He walked us through the patient flow process. We studied the clinic manual. He instructed us on what to do with twenty-eight (count them, 28) pages that we would have to fill out for each patient.

Those forms covered everything that a medical hospital might require, including the "chief complaint" and "present illness," the case history, a review of systems (the intake interview, referred to as "taking a history" by medical doctors), previous hospitalizations, surgeries, and medications. It continued on through the physical examination, moved on to laboratory and x-ray findings and ended with instructions for keeping treatment and progress notes. To all of that were added more pages for recording the findings of the spinal orthopedic and neurologic examinations along with a chiropractic analysis and treatment plan. Chiropractic and medical notes were combined in the contemporary record-keeping method currently most widely advocated in medical circles, the Problem-Oriented Medical Record (POMR) system of Lawrence. L. Weed, M.D. (1969; see Savage, 2001).

Modern health care involved mountains of paper work before computers took over. We were coached on how to arrange appointments, fill out forms, and secure authorizations from our supervisors. We reviewed treatment procedures as such. Our instructor required us to demonstrate competency in four different techniques for diagnosis and treatment, which for me were Diversified, Gonstead, Thompson, and NUCCA. He tested us on our skill with a treatment table powered by electric and hydraulic energy sources and operated with a complex system of buttons and levers to make different segments of the table move, not move, shift, release, catch, or rotate the patient from standing to lying and back again. Did one need a driver's license?

We reviewed chiropractic instruments bearing unusual names, such as the model 500 Therm-O-Graph and others. We re-acquainted ourselves with physical therapy: cryotherapy (a fancy name for ice packs), fomentation (hot packs), ultraviolet and infrared lamps (artificial sunlight), electrical stimulation, ultrasound, and shortwave diathermy.

A bit more than a month slipped by and we were still classroom students holding a rain check for our first on stage performance as physician actors. Then suddenly, it seemed, we were told to appear the following Thursday morning for the big clinic entrance examination. We were told to appear in suits and ties or the female equivalent. Why the formality? Every test during clinic years mimicked those we would eventually have to survive to earn a state license to practice in California. It heightened our anxiety during training, but lessened it greatly when we faced the California Board of Chiropractic Examiners about two years later.

That instructor, whom we all liked and admired, became a monster on clinic entrance-exam day, along with other supervisors who grilled us in oral and practical examinations. Trembling and perspiring we demonstrated competencies on those daunting tables. Our eyes silently implored leniency as we demonstrated we knew when to use a physical therapy modality, what its dangers and contraindications were, and how to apply it to a student recruited as a model. In retrospect it seemed cut and dried, but at the time we were frantically uncertain of what we really were supposed to know and what constituted an acceptable method of practice for the mock patients we treated that morning. Some members of the class flunked the first time and had to repeat the ordeal. I was lucky. That afternoon I was allowed to see my first patient.

Well, he wasn't really a patient. He was my reciprocal patient, and that's different. Before we could take responsibility for walk-in cases we had to practice on another member of the class, so we paired off, alternating doctor and patient roles. It was only a step beyond the technique courses we had survived many times. The difference was that for the first time we were officially permitted to administer a spinal adjustment.

To justify that training, each student had to become a genuine patient in need of care. Strange, but true. My counterpart, Dan, was as sound as a dollar, yet he felt he had spinal problems. For purposes of the official clinic records, because we were enrolled as true patients, his chief complaint was entered as a broken foot. Three months earlier he had fractured a tarsal bone. It healed without incident, but his foot got achy and tired when he walked too much. That was not a bad case for a first patient. A bit of ultrasound and some gentle mobilization made the foot feel better. Although easy, it was doctoring (well, physical "therapy-ing").

What we really wanted, of course, was to treat spinal cases. Through a liberal interpretation of findings, my analysis indicated that Dan had a spinal subluxation as well as a foot problem. More, my patient confirmed that when extremely tired he experienced pain in his neck and mid-back. Marvelous. That was easy for a beginner. Unfortunately, it would be a while yet before I would actually be allowed to adjust him.

I first saw Dan on August 27 (the first week of the fall semester at Mills). I spent most of the afternoon doing his case history, the interrogation part of an examination. My supervisor had to review and approve that part of the file before I could proceed to the next stage. On September 3 I carried out the physical examination. Not until September 10 was I authorized to go to radiology, to position my patient and then step behind the lead screen and zap him to produce a complete set of full-spine radiographs.

On September 14, Dan took x-rays of me. Without exception, every student was found to "need" a complete set of films. Before graduating we interns would have to produce evidence that we could operate x-ray equipment and interpret radiographs. Neither Dan nor I would have been allowed to finish our training and graduate if we hadn't each x-rayed the other.

During our five clinic trimesters we were required to x-ray every patient, often on repeated occasions. I faced an ethical dilemma, since I did not believe then, and do not believe now, that proper chiropractic treatment requires studies except in a small number of patients for whom one must consider the possibility of tumors, fractures, bone demineralization, or some other pathology.

Some ways of practicing chiropractic cannot be done without the use of x-rays. Practitioners of the Gonstead Technique insist that they must have films. So do those who specialize in Palmer Specific or NUCCA. In part for that reason, I followed the teachings of Clay Thompson along with those Henry Gillet (whom I later visited in his clinic in Belgium), and his successor, L. John Faye. I was also much influenced by a French specialist in orthopedic medicine, Robert Maigne, M.D., and a New Zealand physical therapist, Robin McKenzie. The methods of all of these clinicians can be carried out without exposing patients to the dangers of ionizing radiation.

Most of my fellow students accepted without question the need to do x-ray studies of every patient. I was nearly alone in my dilemma. Ethics gave way to expediency. I objected. I argued. I reasoned. I had no success in asking for a waiver of clinic policy. I felt I had no alternative but to x-ray every patient, except when they had been to a chiropractor before and I could submit that doctor's films in place of my own (at a loss of credit for me, of course). I approached the end of my internship desperate for ways to satisfy my final x-ray requirements. It had been a steady concern for nearly two years, beginning when I submitted to x-ray exposure myself in order to provide one credit for my reciprocal, and to justify exposing him to radiation so I could get one credit for myself.

Finally, on September 21, my first set of radiographs had been measured and approved by a supervisor and I was allowed to provide the first chiropractic adjustment of my life. I knew exactly what to do from hundreds of hours of drill and instruction. I maneuvered the table so that Dan was positioned on his back, with his head cradled in my left hand. With trained purposefulness I applied right hand against a precisely selected aspect of the fifth cervical vertebra (C5). Then, shifting my weight while bending and turning Dan's head, I deftly administered a lightening quick thrust.

Thud. No meaningful "click." Just thud. Nothing happened. I got credit for completing an office visit, but it was depressing. After years of study, not to mention twenty-six days of working up my patient, the culmination was a dud. I obviously still had a lot to learn before I would be a chiropractor. Dan seemed uneasy that he would be in my hands for several weeks of follow-up treatment. I was depressed and humiliated.

In order to graduate we were required to record 250 patient visits over the course of five terms. Neither Dan nor I needed spinal manipulation as patients, but we did need experience and credit as interns, so we adjusted each other several times a week. It was disconcerting. An inexperienced fellow student adjusting the neck or lower back could cause pain or hypermobility. To avoid that, we agreed we would approach a less difficult area. The mid-back thoracic area, solidly splinted by the rib cage and shoulder girdle, was less vulnerable. Most people enjoy the feeling of a manipulative loosening up of that area, and we invariable obtained instrumental and clinical findings to justify the treatment, so we went after our credits in a that way. Under the watchful eye of the supervisor, Dan administered so-called anterior thoracic adjustments to me until he could get a reassuring popping sound every time. Half an hour later I did the same to him. Student adjustments of this sort over the next months added up to fifty of the 250 credits I needed.

For every new patient we had to scale a mountain of bureaucratic obstacles. In order for the clinic to maintain close control over each novitiate we were required to wait until a supervisor was able to join us in the examination or treatment room to monitor our work. We were only permitted to carry out a physical examination and diagnostic work-up on the first patient visit. We had to convince the patient that it was worthwhile to return another day and pay another clinic fee before we could take x-rays. In the interim between those visits we recorded our data and got the file signed off as meeting clinic standards.

With pages of records completed and approved, including a review of the x-ray analysis, the intern at last could schedule a third visit for the spinal adjustment. (Emergency patients in acute pain could be adjusted on a first visit, but I never had a patient like that.)

The system of controls, checks, and credits was put in place to ensure that students uniformly underwent a planned minimal experience, but the system worked against itself. One result was that Osler's ideal could not be realized for more than just a minimal few intake examinations and diagnostic studies. As interns, it worked to our benefit to get a patient though the admissions red tape and then schedule that patient for two or three treatments a week for as many weeks as the patient would accept, at one credit per visit.

A schedule of perhaps a dozen adjustments over four or five weeks was consistent with the philosophy of chiropractic that prevailed. Whenever I suggested that a single treatment session might be adequate I was reassured that experience would teach me that it took time and repeated visits for a patient to heal. I was also reminded that field doctors who built successful practices almost invariably scheduled each patient for something like three visits a week for three weeks, and once a week thereafter until a maintenance schedule of once every several months was put in place - forever.

Five semesters as an intern gave me experience in the use of x-ray equipment and the chiropractic interpretation of films. It left me inept in intake examinations and diagnosis. It barely reaffirmed my training in another essentially medical skill, the use of laboratory data.

I only encountered one patient for whom laboratory studies seemed advisable before I proceeded to chiropractic management. My physical examination revealed a somewhat enlarged and tender liver. I ordered tests for liver function, found an elevation in liver enzymes, and scared her half to death when I referred her back to her regular physician. She turned out to be free of liver disease, illustrating that the practice of medicine is as much art as science. I continued to see her as a chiropractic case. For many of my other patients, however, I had to order basic blood and urine tests at the patient's expense. At least, in principle it was at their expense. To that end the ethical issue was not one of harming the patient but merely of adding costs to their clinic bills. I resolved that by paying for their lab work myself. One of my last duties as an intern was to meet the minimal requirements for laboratory work by having blood drawn on several students who volunteered to do that and to pee in cups so I could graduate.

A major shortcoming in my clinical training centered on the problem of getting access to patients. Medical students work on hospital wards or in clinics where they find patients waiting for attention. They are almost immediately sent into an examination room to do a history and physical on a patient who is sick, and from the start they learn how to reason medically, scientifically (and artfully) as they list the possibilities of a differential diagnosis. In contrast, we had to recruit our own patients.

In effect, each of us had to build a private practice within the clinic. Interns spent off-duty hours getting people into conversations in order to convince them that they needed a spinal check-up. The clinic program had to finance itself on the income from those patients, although the student doctor was not remunerated. On the contrary, students paid college fees for the opportunity to work and to learn.

Some students learned very fast how to recruit patients, a skill that would stand them in good stead when they graduated and went into practice. They gave talks in churches, service clubs, and public meetings. They hustled people who waited on them in stores and the people they waited on while working as sales people or restaurant waiters. Neighbors, friends, church members, any contact could be turned to chiropractic evangelism. Other students found it hard to proselytize. I found it impossible. One of my best friends, though, was a champion. A devoutly religious man who seemed to feel as keenly about the importance of chiropractic care as he did about God, soon built up a large following - mostly from his church.

He also had a solid retention rate. His patients kept returning for visit after visit until he finished his training and they were all judged ready for safe discharge. For most of us, however, a patient only arrived at the clinic once or twice before becoming a "no show." For the school, that failure was interpreted as both a financial and a training problem. To help us retain patients the administration restructured the fee schedule and set up a program of recruitment speakers.

I never felt at ease inviting people I knew to make appointments with me for treatment, and my discomfort increased after the fee schedule was changed. Under the new plan, patients could attend the clinic for half-price if they showed up for a Thursday evening lecture on the importance of chiropractic care. After that change I was not only expected to entice people to make appointments with me at the clinic, but also to attend evening recruitment sessions. I found it embarrassing, and by the end of my internship had only recruited seven patients that way.

I was a flop at practice building. As a result, although I put many hours into attendance at the clinic I worked with a very small number of true teaching cases. During the course of five semesters ten of the patients for whom I got credit provided very little "bedside" experience.

Seven were students. Three were family, two sons and one daughter. I got credit for physical exams and lab workups on my children, but not for treatment, since their progress through the clinic stopped abruptly at the x-ray department. Scott and Tom were both high school lettermen in gymnastics. They needed chiropractic care at times. I gave it to them (illegally) at home on a portable table, for which I got no school credit at all.

In all, my learning experience was limited to only six patients. One was a twelve-year old girl transferred to me from another intern. Her original x-rays showed a mild scoliosis. Her mother as a girl suffered a serious scoliotic deviation of the spine. I wasn't sure what to do. We still lacked research to back up the possibility that certain kinds of chiropractic treatment might interrupt evolution of the curvature, so I did what an M.D. would have done. I watched this patient, but not for long, since she came to me just before her family moved to another part of the state.

The five remaining patients had one thing in common. They all had chronic, incurable musculoskeletal disorders that had not gotten better under previous care by medical doctors, chiropractors, or physical therapists.

With every one of them I had identical experiences. Subsequent to the first one or two treatments each demonstrated gratifying improvement. Ms. Smith, with pins and needles down both arms reported that they disappeared and that she felt better for the first time in months. Professor Brown, nearly killed a year earlier in an automobile accident that inflamed the spinal cord in her neck, was thrilled when painful nighttime cramps in her leg eased off. Ms. Green, with a painful sciatica, including numbness in the afflicted leg, reported near normal sensation and easier walking. Ms. Blue, subject to chronic neck and mid-back pain, was completely free of pain for twenty-four hours. Officer Jones, with morning pain and stiffness in his right shoulder, awoke the morning after his first treatment completely free of distress.

Let me tell you it was gratifying to be a successful doctor. I have never experienced anything more satisfying than to provide relief from pain and disability. My patients were ecstatic. I was ecstatic. Perhaps because I was too inexperienced, or perhaps because these patients required kinds of care I couldn't offer, or most likely because of the inherent limitations on what chiropractic can achieve, every single one relapsed. Each returned discouraged. Four simply accept their recurrent pain. They had been disappointed many times before. They felt, as did I, that if they could find relief for a day it ought to be possible to give them lasting relief. But they had not yet found a practitioner who could pull it off. I was no more to blame than the others who failed, and at least I was a lot cheaper.

Officer Brown was tougher on me. Thrilled on the day I "cured" him, he phoned the next morning complaining angrily that he woke up the next day with far worse pain in his arm and shoulder than usual. Ohh! It was bad enough to fail to get improvement, but it was catastrophic to make that patient feel worse. In subsequent visits, nothing seemed to help for more than a few hours. He left my care to return to his regular medical doctor. After that he did better with daily nonsteroidal anti-inflammatory drugs. For him, maybe that was the best he could hope for. Or maybe a far more experienced chiropractor was what he needed.

There you have it, my training as an intern. I saw very few patients, but I put hundreds of hours into it. The daily pace was grueling. Exhaustion was part of the course. I returned home one evening so tired that I could hardly drag myself to the door to answer a timid knock that got me out of my chair. It was a small boy dressed in a Halloween costume. "Trick or treat," he lisped. "What are you doing here? It's not Halloween," I said in a kindly but perplexed voice. Only it was Halloween. I had been too busy to notice. An anniversary slipped by with no chocolates and flowers. It was not forgotten, just postponed. There were personal and family costs in those months of internship.

There were benefits as well. Not the least of the benefits was that I saw a lot of my mother, Stella, who was delighted to spend time with her son. Stella was in her eighties, widowed, and retired. She loved having lunch with me in the Mills Faculty Dining room, and she didn't mind in the least going to the clinic three times a week. It was nice for me, too, except that I had to pick her up at her home in Orinda and return her there since she couldn't drive that far anymore. Part of the reason I was so busy was that I was driving as much as fifty miles a day in order to transport her back and forth between the clinic, Mills College and her home. Each time she got lunch and I got credit for an office visit.

Stella was extraordinarily healthy, with abundant energy. She suffered none of the usual aches and pains of old age. She took no medications. She was always upbeat and smiling. There was simply nothing wrong with her except that she was all wrinkled and very forgetful. Being a senior citizen, she qualified for a very small clinic fee, so it didn't even cost very much to bring her in so often.

To adjust such a patient three times a week could be harmful. Her bones were quite fragile. Heavy manipulation could break a rib or fracture a vertebra. Repeated heavy movement of spinal joints might cause pain. Any chiropractor knows that. I knew that. Under the rules of the clinic, however, I got credit for a visit even when my examination showed no need for an adjustment that day. So I repeatedly brought her in, examined her, reported that she did not require a spinal adjustment that day, and got credit for an office visit. I owe almost half of my required 250 credits to my mother, who signed in a total of 123 times. That added up to 123 lunches, 600 miles of driving, and maybe a dozen very gentle spinal adjustments.

Stella became so much a part of the clinic scene during my internship that everyone greeted her by name. She happily spent hours waiting for me in the large waiting room, talking with other patients, and reading outdated magazines. She never tired of telling anyone within earshot that the "Doctor Anderson" announced over the loudspeaker was her son. She acquired a very bad case of the "my son the doctor" syndrome, from which she suffered to the end of her days. Only very small babies and very old mothers give such unquestioning admiration.

That intimacy with my mother survives now as a sweet memory, even of the time when a fellow student had to stop me in my car on the street to remind me that I was about to drive away and leave my mother behind, forgotten in the waiting room. But while rewarding for a grown son and his aging mother, it didn't teach me much about the chiropractic care of patients. The best students gained wonderful experience in techniques of practice building as well as in the treatment of a large number of patients. I spent time with my mother. Others like me also got very little variety of patient exposure during their intern trimesters. We still felt insecure and uncertain of our skills on graduation day. Osler was right. You learn from your patients. The clinic was our boat on a learning sea, but for some of us it was a leaky boat, and the true Oslerian voyage got underway after we entered practice. I would emphasize, though, that we were well prepared to succeed as practitioners. We knew how to practice safely and effectively. We only needed time and experience.

Chapter Six

Interlude - Establishing My Own Clinic

From Red Tape to Chiropractic Ethnography

Let me start with a red-tape recital in three parts. Part one, getting a diploma: I enrolled in Pacific States Chiropractic College (PSCC) in 1979 and four years later was awarded a Doctor of Chiropractic diploma dated March 1, 1983 from Life Chiropractic College – West (LCCW).

How did I end up graduating from LCCW? The college came under new management on March 13, 1981. PSCC had been struggling. The transfer of ownership offered new hope.

But why didn't I graduate before 1983? Although I personally still had some classes to make up because of my teaching schedule, my class, the charter class, completed all requirements for graduation in December 1981.

As it happened, the last year for the charter class was the first year as LCCW, and it was a year of enormous uncertainty. In February it was rumored as a realistic fear that accreditation might be denied. By spring that uncertainty merged with a realization that even with success, the school could not hope to achieve formal accreditation before 1983. Many in the charter class huddled in stressed-out conversations about possible gains and losses if one were to transfer to the fully accredited mother institution, Life Chiropractic College in Atlanta, Georgia. Transfer students could be sure they would qualify for licensure, but it would be in Georgia, not in California.

As fall approached, the mood changed, in spite of continuing uncertainties, all twenty-one members of the class elected to tough out the uncertainties. More than a year later we got the good news. So at last, in March, 1983, we donned caps and gowns to accept handshakes of congratulation on stage from President Gerard Clum as members of the "Class of March, 1982." Six other classes were lined up behind us as they, too, officially graduated. Finally.

And that brings me to red-tape, part two: getting licensed to practice. No surprises, just some high stakes examinations. The big one was required by the State of California Board of Chiropractic Examiners. Succeeding in that, I was granted a license to practice dated July 8, 1983. I had already qualified by examination as a Diplomate of the National Board of Chiropractic Examiners in 1982, also a requirement. But one more remained. I had to survive a test by the State of California Department of Health Services to be designated a Certified X-Ray Supervisor and Operator. That came through on August 17, 1983. At last I was fully qualified to go into practice. Qualified, but not yet ready.

It would have been easy to join an established practice as an associate chiropractor. I received 26 letters inviting me to interview for that kind of an appointment. But I had never planned to earn my living as a practitioner.

With the last of the examinations behind me it was time to deal with red-tape, part three: setting up my own clinic at Mills College. Poor Steve Weiner, Dean of the Faculty at that time. He had a hard time figuring out what I was up to. A chiropractic clinic in the Mills College Health Center! It would be a national first for an American university or college, but totally lacking in precedent only made it seem wacky.

When I first joined the faculty in 1960 the college maintained a Health Center and Clinic with a fulltime physician on staff and hospital rooms available for indisposed students. But Evelyn Urrere, M.D., had long since been replaced by a nurse practitioner. The absence of a physician on staff left two surgery rooms unused and unneeded. I wanted that space for a clinic where I could gain experience by caring for patients three mornings a week and where I could also set up a research and teaching program in medical and physical anthropology. The initial administrative reaction was as predictable as it was reasonable: anthropology, "yes," but recruiting patients, "you've got to be kidding."

Nonetheless, the Dean relented and gave me the space I needed after we arranged for college malpractice insurance in addition to my own. Early on Dean Weiner came by to see what in the world I was doing in my seminar on physical anthropology, chiropractic style. On that day I needed a model on whom to demonstrate how muscles and joints in the human body react to postural changes. The next thing he knew, we had Weiner in his shirt sleeves and supine on an examination table, surrounded by half a dozen young women staring down at him as I made his limbs and spine contort in ways only a chiropractor could manage. (Thanks, Steve. I don't know why anyone would give up the rewards of being a professor for the hassles of being a dean, but I'm thankful for those who do.)

On Becoming a Slightly Experienced Practitioner

On September 17, 1983, I wrote a strong supporter of my research program, Dr. Clay Thompson in Iowa. "Our on-campus chiropractic clinic is now operational. Every Monday, Wednesday and Friday I am there all morning to see patients. Although I am working very hard, since this is simply added on to my regular duties and responsibilities, we got the clinic started up during the very first week of classes in the new academic year."

Dr. Thompson convinced his very reluctant manufacturer to provide a Terminal Point Table in support of my research program. That Thompson table would have cost as much as a small compact car if I had to pay for it. I didn't need or use a radiology lab. I also didn't have to make monthly payments on a lease or provide salary for an office assistant. In addition, since I provided chiropractic care entirely free of charge, I did not have to cope with business problems at all, but I did need to attract a clientele.

My practice started off very modestly. During four months in the

71

fall semester, from September 5 to December 19, I only recruited 30 patients, 80 percent of them for only one or two visits each. Even when offering free care I was a loser as a practice builder, but I did make some progress in working toward my goal of becoming more competent as a service provider. Then, unexpectedly and to the surprise of the Dean and my other supporters, not to mention Edna, who thought I had finally achieved my purpose, I abruptly closed down the clinic, as I will eventually explain, but not in this chapter or the next. This chapter just offers an interlude.

Director of Research: 1979-1983

I kept my promise to the Board of Regents of the chiropractic college. The research program was lively enough to meet accreditation standards. Actually, by the end of my four years as research director, Life-West surpassed all of the other fourteen chiropractic colleges in the United States in at least one definable way. We had the single most active research department when measured in terms of the number of articles published and papers presented in scientific meetings. I was publishing at a rate slightly in excess of one article per month (Appendix A). I hasten to add that other chiropractic colleges were doing much more important work in terms of quality and value to the profession. As a measure of scientific importance, only four of my publications appeared in non-chiropractic refereed journals, which is a far more important measure of credibility and significance than mere numbers and is not impressive at all.

In terms of my commitment to Mills College, research, along with the on-going growth experience of being a student, energized my teaching, particularly in medical and physical anthropology. So my work in chiropractic justified my paid job as well. I did work very hard to come through on all fronts.

Two main kinds of research occupied those four years. One was an attempt to serve the profession by evaluating chiropractic instrumentation and documenting aspects of spinal biomechanics. Financed by a substantial grant from the Foundation for Chiropractic Education and Research (FCER) we tested an instrument called the Gravity Stress Analyzer and another called the Anatometer. Also, for three years in a row I reported on research projects utilizing hundreds of patient records and x-rays in the annual Biomechanics Conferences on the Spine convened at the University of Colorado. I regret to say that none of those publications and presentations were of more than passing interest.

The other main focus of research was primarily of value for my research and teaching as a medical anthropologist. In evolving from quadruped apes we bipedal human beings ended up with spines highly vulnerable to back pain, so back pain predictably occurs in every society and can be depended upon to constitute a worthwhile research project anywhere in the world. In urban industrial societies, from 18 to 26 percent of the adult population will be experiencing low back pain at any given moment in time (the point prevalence rate). The lifetime prevalence for at least one episode of severe back pain ranges from 50 percent to 80 percent (Anderson, 1999, 333).

In collaboration with Mills sociologist Laura Nathan my research program at Life West in 1984 sponsored a research project designed as public interest anthropology. I had been approached by representatives of an urban transit union in the Bay Area to document what union leaders believed was an occupational hazard. They were convinced that bus drivers suffered more back and neck pain than other kinds of workers. In response to their request, Dr. Nathan and I designed and administered a research project that clearly demonstrated in a stratified random sample of 195 employees of union members that 80.5 percent of the drivers were experiencing back or neck pain at the time I examined them. That contrasted with 50.7 percent of our control group of non-drivers, itself a sizable percentage (Anderson & Nathan, 1984; Anderson, 1992a).

Earlier, as an anthropologist member of the 1982 Medical Expedition to the Himalayas organized by the Johns Hopkins Department of International Health, I pursued my newfound interest in the spine by undertaking a field investigation on the prevalence of back pain among peasant farmers in the mountains of Nepal. For 646 adult villagers examined, the point prevalence rate turned out to be 18.4 percent. Although that point prevalence fell within the range of variation for urban-industrial societies, cultural factors specific to their mountain-peasant way of life implicated a different etiology. In contrast to aching backs from poor posture in sedentary occupations, the people we examined plowed fields with oxen and carried heavy baskets of produce on tumplines as they walked up and down rough mountain paths and across deep gorges on swaying suspension bridges (Anderson 1982).

Why This Interlude?

Remember, when I observed chiropractors at work for the first time I was confused because they differed so much from one another. What I learned in chiropractic college was that basic spinal manipulation could be practiced as a straight-forward hands-on identification of biomechanical causes of pain and immobility and that the those causes of pain can be ameliorated by spinal adjusting. In addition, randomized clinical trials have demonstrated that chiropractic adjusting is more effective than any other known forms of treatment, including those of medical doctors, for spinal misalignments.

I wanted to interrupt my ethnography of a chiropractic education in order to clearly state that what made chiropractic a success among hard-working, accident-prone farmers in Iowa also ensures its ongoing success for people suffering back and neck pain in other societies where the cultures are often very different from those that D. D. Palmer and later chiropractors encountered.

Not the least, I wanted to explain how I benefited by practicing chiropractic ethnography as part of my modest contribution to anthropological research cross culturally on healing and alternative medicine (Appendix B). Having used this interlude to those ends, I return, now, to my education in a chiropractic college in order to describe the rest of our course work. To my surprise, I found that I was, in effect, attending medical school in a chiropractic college.

Chapter Seven

Medical School in a Chiropractic College

The Imitative Reality

I cannot claim to have started my research on chiropractic free of prejudice. I thought the level of education was dismal. My journal from the late 1970s reminds me disconcertingly of how easy it was to confirm that kind of bias. While in a distant city to get first hand information about one chiropractic college I took an evening to visit with a colleague on the faculty of a nearby university. By pure coincidence, as I explained my reason for being in town, he told me that he and several other faculty members in the School of Education were hired periodically to proctor the National Chiropractic Board examinations in the basic sciences. They did not prepare the examination questions. Nor did they correct them. All they did was police the handing out, filling out, and turning in of exam booklets. On looking them over, however, he felt he was entitled to have a low opinion of the quality of their education. "They all arrive with little pillows to sit on," he reported anecdotally, "to take an exam on a level just above that of high school students."

I nodded in agreement and responded with my own anecdote. In one chiropractic school library I looked over the shoulder of a student studying a filmstrip on anatomy that struck me as on a junior high school level.

Additionally, library research gave reason to believe that chiropractic education was very primitive. As noted in *A History of Chiropractic Education*, an official publication of the Council on Chiropractic Education, when Abraham Flexner published his 1910 Carnegie Foundation documentation of how in need of reform medical education was he passed over chiropractic schools as unworthy of his attention and "best dealt with by prosecuting attorneys and grand juries" (Keating, et al, 1998: 33).

In a similar vein, H. L. Mencken wrote in 1924 of recruitment into "this preposterous quackery" of retired piano-movers, out-at-the-elbow Baptist preachers, retired baseball players, work-weary plumbers, truck-drivers, longshoremen, bogus dentists, cashiered school superintendents, garage mechanics, ash-men, decayed welterweights, hearty ex-boilermakers, night watchmen, quacks of other schools such as homeopathy, and "hundreds of promising students . . . from the intellectual ranks of hospital orderlies." In short, Mencken concluded, "Any lout with strong hands and arms is perfectly equipped to become a chiropractor" (Mencken, 1955, 148-153).

Mencken was read for laughs as well as for challenging opinions. He stressed the extreme rather than the mean. Yet, chiropractic education was very limited in those days, and at its extremes was very much as Mencken said. "As the old-time family doctor dies out in the country towns, with no competent successor willing to take over his dismal business, he is followed by some hearty blacksmith or ice-wagon driver, turned into a chiropractor in six months, often by correspondence" (Mencken, 1924, reissued, 1955). The reference to correspondence schools was distortive, not because they didn't exist – they did – but because they were resisted by the profession and were dying out by the time Mencken wrote (Keating, et al, 33-34).

Morris Fishbein, a contemporary of Mencken, trumpeted the same tune in his widely read book, *Fads and Quackery in Healing*. He wrote of Carver Chiropractic College in Oklahoma City that they admitted illiterates if they could pay the tuition, illustrating that claim with the following supposedly authentic exchange of letters.

From a woman in Texas, the school was said to have received this application: "Sirs, Mister Kirpatic School. I want to rite letter and see if I can be kirpatic dr. if you can make a kirpatic dr. for how much money I got about 2 thousend dolers that my husband got when he died from the insurance company. . . ."

To that inquiry the college reputedly offered this more literate but grammatically impaired response: "Dear Madam: Chiropractic is a profession based upon a science. While your education may be limited you have the intelligence and the determination and sufficient education to understand the English language you would have no difficulty in getting a knowledge of this subject so that you could go out and practice and be efficient. You can enter at any time and in eighteen months, upon making your grades, can be graduated" (Fishbein, 1932: 104-105). Keep in mind that Fishbein was a physician, not a professional historian, so one must wonder how he documented the authenticity of the Texas woman's letter.

The curriculum was very different by the time I applied to "kirpatic school." It had become a four-year program with a two-year pre-chiropractic requirement. It was still open to the intellectual ranks of hospital orderlies or any lout with strong hands and arms, including an ex-Navy enlisted man lout like myself. But we were only graduated if we had completed required courses in accredited institutions of higher learning. No exceptions were made to those requirements.

And that brings us back to the medical school curriculum in a chiropractic college that I have described so far only as it related to how we were taught how to diagnose musculoskeletal disorders. We also pursued course work in chemistry, anatomy, physiology, pathology, and public health.

Chemistry

I will never forget the first exam I sat for in a medical science class at PSCC. It was organic chemistry. My fellow students typically invested their energies in chiropractic courses and minimized the time, energy, and interest they devoted to medicine-related subjects. Remember, many of them worked part-time to support themselves. I decided that I, too, would only study enough to get by, not for lack of interest, but because of other heavy demands on my time and interest and anyway, as an embedded ethnographer, I was there to experience what they were experiencing.

So I arrived on that unforgettable day to write my first chemistry exam, having merely looked over the assigned pages the night before. I passed the exam, but I couldn't live with just getting by and besides, science is fascinating and the opportunity to delve more deeply was irresistible. From then on I studied hard and ended up with the highest grades in my class, graduating *summa cum laude* and honored as the designated class valedictorian.

I didn't feel right about giving the valedictory address at graduation, so I wrote the following to President Clum: "Thank you for honoring me as Valedictorian of my class. Your warm, supportive letter will be kept to show my children and grandchildren, for it makes me very proud. I must decline the honor, however. As a professional scholar, a member of the staff and faculty of LCCW, and a professor at Mills College, it is simply not fair." So it went to a student with the very high grades, and her commencement address suited the occasion perfectly.

In all, we completed five courses in chemistry for a total of 420 classroom hours: organic chemistry (60 hours), biochemistry (120), clinical chemistry (120), nutrition (60), and toxicology (60).

For two years in a row the instructor who taught organic chemistry and biochemistry was voted the most outstanding teacher in the college. It was not because he was easy on students. His homework and examinations were up to the standards of the books from which he taught. For biochemistry, that was a standard medical school textbook, R. W. McGilvery's *Biochemistry: A Functional Approach*. Organic chemistry, not usually taught in medical schools, was fully up to university standards. The clinical chemistry course, with a laboratory component, guided us through the application of chemical principles in laboratory analysis. We learned how to order laboratory tests, how to interpret them, and how to perform laboratory procedures ourselves.

Nutrition was limited to a single course. It was so highly appreciated that we marched on the administration to demand a second course. Student culture nurtured a pervasive interest that derived from personal habits and from knowing that counseling on nutrition was legal under a chiropractic license. In addition, we felt our instructor, who "practiced what she preached," had a lot more to teach than could be crammed into sixty hours. We were steered competently through the biochemistry of food metabolism while at the same time gained practical knowledge on how to identify and prepare foods that contribute to a healthy diet. We were given assignments in a standard textbook, *Cooper's Nutrition in Health and Disease* by Helen Mitchell, and others, but the course went far beyond that both in the theory and practice of nutrition, paced by a skilled teacher.

Unfortunately, the overall success of chemistry was less than complete because one course, toxicology, proved to be one of the most miserable classes I have endured anywhere. The rationale for it was miserable to begin with. We were told that as chiropractic physicians we could expect to see patients who were suffering the toxic effects of medicines prescribed by medical doctors, as though we would learn pharmacology by learning how prescribed drugs could be harmful or deadly. Knowing about those "poisonous" side effects was taught to help us succeed with our patients, so we needed a course on poisons.

What nonsense. The subject encompassed in our textbook, Dreisbach's *Handbook of Poisoning: Prevention, Diagnosis and Treatment*, instructed mainly about accidental, agricultural, industrial, household, animal, and plant poisons. It included very little on medicines because that section was limited to accidental overdoses, which did not include the problematic side-effects of normal prescribing.

Toxicology presumably substituted for a course on pharmacology. It apparently represented an effort to incorporate the medical topic of poisonous reactions without teaching the iconic medical practice of prescribing pharmaceuticals for their curative benefits. For us, toxicology was ill chosen and should have been replaced by a real course on pharmacology.

In the hands of a better, more knowledgeable instructor, the course might still have added to our basic science repertoire. Unfortunately, we were subjected to rambling, anecdotal lectures that contributed almost nothing to an understanding of the masses of data we had to memorize. Worse, we were assigned a book meant to serve as a reference to pull off the shelf when you need to look up a particular poison. It was not designed to function as an aid in teaching the subject. We fought our way through that sticky encyclopedic morass, miserable, but sustained like soldiers fighting terrorists, by a camaraderie (communitas) that grew out of fear and disdain.

Anatomy

One of the most expensive and challenging tasks for the senior anatomy instructor as he prepared for the first year of classes at PSCC was to set up a teaching laboratory for anatomy, but it turned out rather well. Our instructors were uniformly well trained and they paced us mercilessly to memorize seemingly numberless details they anticipated we would need to know if they were not to get into trouble by failing to survive the National Boards. That was all well and good. Medical school anatomy courses, although better supplied with human cadavers and body parts, are equally demanding.

We were assigned the standard medical school textbooks for histology (60 hours), embryology (60), dissection (72), the central nervous system (60, the peripheral nervous system (60), regional anatomy (40), mycology (40), genesiology, angiology, splanchnology (60), spinal anatomy (60), osteology, arthrology (60), and special senses (60), a total of 420 hours of classroom and laboratory work.

Those aspects of anatomy most relevant to the work of chiropractors were highlighted. We were taught to correlate the physical anatomy of joints, muscles, tendons, and ligaments we explored with our fingers in anatomic dissections with what we experienced with our fingers when doing motion palpation diagnostics relating to the spine and peripheral joints. It was a great way to learn.

Physiology

We sat through a lot of class hours in physiology: systemic physiology (60), cell physiology (48), neurophysiology (60), muscular and cardiovascular physiology (36), renal and pulmonary physiology (60), endocrinology (60), and a laboratory course on correlative systemic physiology (60). Total, 384 hours.

Again, excellent textbooks were assigned: A. C. Guyton, *Textbook of Medical Physiology*, E. Frieden and H. Lipner, *Biochemical Endocrinology of the Vertebrates*, and C. Avers, *Cell Biology*. The level of teaching was up to that of the textbooks with the unfortunate exception of the laboratory course on correlative systemic physiology.

Those lab sessions were under the direction of an instructor who was totally unqualified in physiology, except that she was a recent graduate of a chiropractic college herself. Her bachelor's degree was in music. I give her credit for working hard to get us through a series of experiments, but they ended up being trivial. It contributed to the shallowness of the experience that the laboratory as such was not fully equipped yet.

That was the second time I had bad luck in a lab course in physiology. I also got little out of a physiology lab when I was a premed student at Berkeley. In that lab students worked in pairs, and it was just my luck and his that my partner ended up being on the track team while I was on the gymnastics team. We both had to hurry through lab exercises in order to show up on time for team workouts. In retrospect, I still think we had our priorities right. He was a P.E. major and went on to a career in coaching. I was a nerd, so athletics provided some balance in my life. In my senior year I was elected captain of the gymnastics team and ranked fifth in national collegiate (NCAA) all around gymnastics competition, but I barely squeezed a "c" out of physiology.

Pathology

We completed 468 hours of coursework in pathology: general pathology (96 hours), neuromuscular and skeletal (60), hematopoietic and lymphatic systems (60), cardiovascular and pulmonary (60), gastrointestinal (36), genitourinary (35), microbiology (72), and psychiatry (45). Except for psychiatry, those courses proceeded chapter by chapter through Stanley Robbins, *Pathologic Basis of Disease*. I was fascinated by every chapter. We also read Eugene Nester and co-authors, *Microbiology*, and Leroy Hood, et al, *Immunology*.

In all of those courses we were required to master materials at the level of the texts. The quality of teaching for the most part was barely satisfactory. I was disappointed that instructors only occasionally showed film documentaries and almost never used slides, the two audiovisual aids widely used in those days before video documentaries and Microsoft PowerPoint presentations.

The most knowledgeable in pathology was an English medical doctor retired from active practice. He sporadically enlivened his lectures with brief comments based on years of clinical experience. "If you examine the inner cheek of a sick child and see Koplick spots, tell the parents the child will break out in a rash in the next two days. When the measles appear they will think you are a marvelous diagnostician." "You must know the basic facts about pheochromocytoma, but you will probably never see one in your office. They are very uncommon." For the most part, however, he just sat in front of the class and read to us from the assigned readings, one sentence monotonously after the other. We could just as well have read to ourselves. A lovely man, but a boring teacher.

Something of the quality of those pathology courses was captured in our experience with genitourinary pathology and microbiology. Both were taught by the same instructor, one who had earned her Ph.D. in immunology. She taught microbiology quite well. However, she was assigned to teach the GU course in spite of protesting that she had no background whatsoever in anatomy and physiology, not to mention pathology as such. She confessed that the first time she taught the course she thought the kidneys were located somewhere near the back pockets of a pair of jeans. She had not moved much from that level of ignorance when I sat in her class (since I had missed it the first time around).

Her way of coping was to take two textbooks, that of Robbins along with an equally encyclopedic book, William Boyd's *A Text-Book of Pathology: An Introduction to Medicine*, and interweave sentences from the two in a typescript from which she read aloud in class, sentence after monotonous sentence. Where the two authors differed, we listened to conflicting statements that were not reconciled. Where the authors were unclear she was helpless to elaborate.

We wrote furiously, trying to get all of the detail down accurately. Those were aggravating and difficult hours until she consented to let us Xerox copies of her notes. Then we could read along as she read aloud. Better, but still boring. Also, confusing. But, as with all of the other instructors in pathology, she subjected us to very difficult tests, so we acquired a lot of information on GU disorders.

Psychiatry was taught by a recently graduated chiropractor who had taken some psychology courses at the university where he earned his bachelor's degree. He had been a junior high school science teacher before enrolling to become a chiropractor.

He ran a loosely organized class that was heavy on discussion and weak on assigned readings and organized lectures. The classroom was a place to talk about one's personal feelings in life encounters, about aberrant individuals we had encountered, and above all about Freud's concept of human sexuality. Freud's fascination with the libido, however was just about the extent of the theory that was taught and, of course, Freud was a psychoanalyst, not a psychiatrist as such. No effort was made to help students develop analytical and treatment skills. Neither the instructor nor the students took psychiatry very seriously.

Public Health

Public Health, consisting of Public Health I (60 hours), Public Health II (48), and Emergency Care (24), turned out to offer a review of immunology, virology and bacteriology from the perspective of epidemic disease control. The instructor for PH I held a Ph.D. in microbiology from one of the finest universities in the United States, which should have qualified him reasonably well. However, he was consistently imprecise and uncertain about his facts. That raises a whole separate issue about how some Ph.D. programs are organized in the United States, but we won't go into that.

He was the most ignorant individual I have ever had to associate with in an academic institution. Fortunately, he was dismissed after two trimesters, but unfortunately for me, I had a course from him in each semester (the other course was toxicology).

In Public Health I we spent our time re-reading the text we had already studied in the microbiology course taught by a different instructor. We learned that he became absolutely furious if we questioned any of his statements of fact, and I had to put a lot of effort into protecting myself from his misinformation and inaccuracies. I used to write into my notes some of his atrocious utterances, just so I could entertain Edna with them when I got home.

He referred to himself in the third person, and that regal attitude reflected a capacity for self-centered anger in the classroom I have never seen equaled. On the first day of class he introduced himself in the third person: "Dr. Soandso took his doctorate at Suchandsuch University and then went on to work at . . . ." He spoke in passing of the reflex "arch" (arc), then got mixed up on the role of high and low density lipoproteins in the etiology of atherosclerosis, and went to speak of "dilastolic" (diastolic) blood pressure and the value of the "water pill" (diuretics) to bring it down. He told us about chicken "pops" (pox), "Borella recurrents" (*Borrelia recurrentis*), Streptoccocus "pie-oh-jeans" (pyogenes), and the "blue bonnet" (bubonic) plague. What was truly objectionable was when he moved beyond course objectives to wax poetic on how much he personally enjoyed the ecstatic thrill of an organism. Very unprofessional, to say the least.

His teaching was so terrible that sometimes I had to laugh, but very discretely, because he was easily upset. As I said, his contract to teach was terminated, but it wasn't soon enough for me. We counted the weeks until we had finally struggled through his extremely difficult exams and could put the course behind us.

Public Health II was a sleeper. It put us to sleep. But it was also a sleeper in that we learned a lot about subjects we had never studied before. It was hard for chiropractic students to accept the stated importance of knowing so much detail on community water supplies, waste disposal, housing, food protection and pollution control. We also had to memorize tedious details relating to community, state, national and international health services. As a student I felt side-tracked and bogged down in rote memorization. As an educator, I witnessed the threat of exams as a kind of intellectual cudgel to make us apply ourselves when no other motivation prevailed. But as a social scientist, I was rewarded in getting acquainted with a body of knowledge and a point of view unfamiliar to me.

Emergency care was taught by a chiropractor who formerly worked as a nurse anesthetist. He taught basic first aid and cardiovascular resuscitation (with assistance from the local fire department). If emergencies showed up in our chiropractic offices we would be able to handle them as Red Cross certified first-aiders.

Where Medical Literacy Fell Short

We completed thirty-four medical science courses taught by fourteen instructors qualified either by a Ph.D. (7 of them), an M.A. or M.S. (2), an M.D. (l), or a D.C. (4), including one D.C. who was also an R.N. On paper, they apparently passed muster as far as accreditation committees were concerned. Yet eight of the courses (almost one in four) were badly taught, six of them because the instructors were asked to teach in areas for which they were not trained. In those courses they coped by reading aloud in class from the textbooks, often with incorrect pronunciation. They possessed virtually no capacity for explanation or elaboration.

That kind of poor teaching did not reflect upon the instructors, but upon administrative demands. Faculty were asked to teach too many hours a week (a minimum of fifteen, in contrast with the 9 hours a week I taught at Mills College, itself a heavy load long since reduced to 5 by Dean Weiner [bless you Steve]). They were required to teach too great a variety of courses (often more than six different subjects), and to teach subjects remote from their fields of expertise. In addition, they were poorly paid, received few benefits, and were given no job security. Instructors did their very best, not simply because they could be fired, but more because they were dedicated to their work. In all, it was a marvel during those first years of the institution that the level of teaching ranged from satisfactory to excellent in three-fourths of our courses.

I acquired enormous respect for the young woman who taught five of the courses I took. In addition to the nutrition course I lauded above, I had her for embryology, central neuroanatomy, the anatomy of special senses, and cell physiology. Every one of them was taught competently. Students loved her because she was caring, even though she was tough on exams. I sat in awe of her capacity to master such a wide range of subjects so thoroughly.

With some exceptions, other teachers ranged from outstanding to mediocre-but-adequate. The real teacher, though, was a system, not a person. It was the anticipation of National Board qualifying examinations. Every course was geared to presenting materials we needed to know for those eventual multiple-choice questions, much as has been true in high school since the 2001 No Child Left Behind Act pushed teachers into preparing students to pass high stakes tests at the cost of educating them in the broader academic curriculum (Anderson, 2008).

It followed that many career-oriented students were totally uninterested in any lecture that wandered off on purely intellectual pursuits, but that was rare. Instructors themselves were hard pressed to cover the mass of information that might potentially be required for exam questions. Courses that were well taught were those that helped us in that direction. Courses that were poorly taught necessarily became self-teaching enterprises. One way or the other, we mastered basic sciences on the level of medical textbooks. Every student eventually had to meet at least minimum standards on that level.

Almost half of the students from the five chiropractic colleges in the State of California at that time failed on their first attempts. Most, however, eventually succeeded. It was not an exciting system. It had some dreadful drawbacks. But it did enforce the achievement of a minimal level of competence in thirty-four courses on the basic medical sciences (except for pharmacology).

As an educator, however, I want to argue that the program almost completely failed to teach what is most important about a medical school curriculum, the inevitable consequence of "teaching to the test." What is most important is not what you know of a factual nature, it is how you think. It is not concrete knowledge, easily forgotten (and easily re-learned, usually), it is the scientific mind-set. That alone can sustain a doctor ten, twenty, or more years into the future. In my experience, chiropractic course work provided starvation fare for nurturing the scientific mentality.

And equally, for medicine as such, we had no access at all to the kind of "teachers" who are essential for transforming students into doctors: patients in their beds to whom students minister as they apply their textbook knowledge under the guidance of expert supervising physicians. Never forget the aphorism of Sir William Osler a full century ago! "He who studies medicine without books sails an uncharted sea but he who studies medicine without patients does not go to sea at all."

Chapter Eight

Public Policy and Scope of Practice

The Labyrinth of Cultural Complexity

Why in the world did we have to complete so much coursework in medicine? Students were not deceived into thinking it was more than tangentially relevant to the way they eventually would practice their profession. It threatened the possibility of eventually flunking the National Board examination. It was costly for the college. It seemed to make no sense.

The explanation is complex. Medical courses were not in the curriculum a generation earlier when Dr. George Anderson, founder and chairman of the Board of Regents, qualified to be a chiropractor based on a high school diploma and an eighteen-month course "that was mostly chiropractic philosophy," as he once told me. In fact, Dr. Anderson founded Pacific States (later Life West) because his philosophy was opposed to what he perceived as a mistaken emphasis on medicine in other schools of chiropractic. Yet, we had to survive all of those hours on medical topics. It seemed to make no sense, but it can be explained.

The explanation is exceedingly complex, which is why I felt it appropriate for this chapter to re-use the title of my recent book on public policy for failing high schools, *The Labyrinth of Cultural Complexity* (2008). It is not just that the shaping forces were multiple, diverse, and inconsistent. It is also that movement in the direction of medicine was nonlinear. It varied from year to year, from state to state, and from school to school. Its history constituted a metaphorical labyrinth of philosophical disputes, political battles, economic dilemmas, psychological distortions, and postmodern conundrums. It constituted a labyrinth of blind alleys and false starts.

We're talking about a policy issue here. Public policy as an academic discipline emerged out of a growing trend toward interdisciplinary research taking place during the last three decades, which is to say, very recently by academic standards. Nothing like that was even thought of when I matriculated in chiropractic school.

I will not presume to define the discipline of public policy here except to mention that it emerged by means of interdisciplinary incursions into several social science fields, including anthropology. As a founding pathfinder, Aaron Wildovsky wrote when the field was still quite new, "Explorers bearing the ensign of policy analysis seem bewildered by this scramble for territory. They expropriate lands claimed by political scientists decades ago and more recently by planners and public administrators. They skirt the edges of economics, law, organizational theory, and operations research." In brief, the field of public policy was established as "a discipline in the interstices of disciplines already distinct" (1977: 386).

It will help in trying to understand how policy decisions impelled chiropractic schools to become significantly medical if we reconstruct in detail how policy was created and enunciated, the process of policy design (see Roe, 1994; also, Dunn, 2008: 46). As concerns educational policy in chiropractic, that process will challenge us to navigate a baffling labyrinth of cultural complexity.

Begin with Chiropractic Philosophy

Policy design began with the founder himself. Daniel David Palmer practiced chiropractic by adjusting subluxations using his hands only. No instrumentation. No healing modalities such as physical therapy. No medicines. Just bare hands and a table. (Note that D.D. abandoned magnetic healing, the therapeutic modality he earlier advertised as a cure-all. Keep this in mind for later reference.) Those who practice in the founding tradition of Old Dad Chiro are known to this day as "straight" chiropractors. I was a straight chiropractor in technique (but not in philosophy) for those short two-and-a-half months when I was in practice.

Straight chiropractors are still considered straight if they add instrumentation, but only if the instruments are limited to facilitating the hands-on adjustment. Daniel David's son, B.J., was a super-straight chiropractor, even though he introduced the three major innovations described in Chapter 3, (radiography in 1910, neurocalometer readings in 1924, and the Hole-in-One technique around 1930). Most chiropractors then and now have been critical of B.J.'s inventions and innovations. Craig Kightlinger, a prominent chiropractic educator and politician at that time, abandoned the straight alliance after B.J. started leasing the neurocalometer, insisting that chiropractors would serve the public better "by discarding all mechanical devices that tend to lessen the efficiency of the palpater" (1925, cited in Keating, et al, 1998: 58).

My earliest sponsor and mentor, Dr. Anderson (no relation, by the way), was a straight chiropractor completely in the style of B.J., except that his instruments were technologically more up-to-date. That was what chiropractic philosophy was about in 1968 and 1969 when he was a student at Palmer Chiropractic College in Iowa and it was the philosophy he personally explained to me during my initial visits to observe him at work.

B.J. was disdainful of chiropractors who adopted medical practices, and scornfully referred to them as "mixers." In the twenty-first century, more than four-fifths of chiropractors are mixers, more or less. Although spinal adjusting remains central, they combine it with a variable assortment of other modalities suggestive of medicine. Physical therapy or therapeutic massage is commonly incorporated. Very commonly they recommend and sell nutritional supplements, vitamins, rubbing ointments, lotions, liniments, and even homeopathic remedies. They often offer nutritional advice and counsel (which fits well with what they learn informally and formally as students). They may organize teaching sessions in meditational or yoga techniques. A growing number now qualify by state licensure to treat with acupuncture, or with acupressure, which does not require a special license.

In short, any drugless approach that does not require a license to practice is likely to show up in the offices of mixers. Straights hated that openness to medicine. Ernst DuVal, founder, president, and dean of the Canadian Chiropractic College, when admission to the 12-month program required only an "ability to read and write," declared in their 1922 catalogue, "We have no course in Photography, Chemistry, Bacteriology or any other 'Bug-ology' that take the time, waste the money, and tax the energy of our students" (cited in Keating, et al, 1998: 31, grammar as in the original). (Note that CCC is no longer a straight college.)

But for policy design the labyrinth of cultural complexity is not adequately negotiated by a simple dichotomy of straights versus mixers, because radical straights do, in fact, claim to offer a broad scope alternative to conventional medicine. Yes, broad scope comparable to the scope of practice of a medical doctor!

According to chiropractic philosophy, radical straights grudgingly agree that medicine and surgery can be beneficial for many conditions, but they insist that conventional medicine and surgery can also be harmful for health problems for which chiropractic is better suited. They would include many respiratory and gastrointestinal problems, heart and circulatory conditions, liver and kidney diseases, viral and bacterial infections, and even deafness. Deafness?

That straight chiropractic is not only an alternative to general medicine but superior to it was first articulated by D.D. himself, and it is central to the philosophy of extreme straight chiropractic. In 1910 he put it this way, "Disease of every organ or portion of the body may, and do arise from defect in the nerve centers rather than in the organ itself" (1910, cited in Gatterman, 1990: 379, grammatical errors in the original).

To understand how Palmer came to that conclusion let us return to that iconic moment when the first chiropractic adjustment cured Harvey Lillard, not of back pain, but of deafness!

I was in Denmark with Edna in 1981 on a self-imposed blitzkrig ethnographic assignment additional to our joint research on the arts of modern design. Since I have Danish relatives and friends, I can get a lot done in that country during the weeks of a summer break. In those years we kept an automobile for summer use, packed with sleeping bags and a tent, stove, and typewriter, thanks to George Nellemann who, with our Lapland adventure long behind us by then, was in a position professionally to store our car through freezing winters in a slightly heated museum garage in which prehistoric Viking ships were preserved.

My goal that summer included to learn more about Danish chiropractors, and especially about medical doctors who practiced chiropractic. As it happened, that spring a Los Angeles newspaper published the emphatic statement of a surgeon who ridiculed chiropractors for believing that Palmer had cured the deafness of Harvey Lillard by adjusting his spine. His was not a sneak attack. Medical experts had long insisted that Palmer's claim was impossible, because auditory nerves are located entirely inside the cranium, with no spinal nerves involved. That anatomy is not in dispute. Chiropractors were at a loss to offer a counter-argument. They just knew that "chiropractic worked," and that made them seem simple minded.

A Danish physician was the first I knew of to provide anatomic credibility for Palmer's claim, and he was no backwoods family doctor. He was Paul Bechgaard of the Faculty of Medicine of Aarhus University, who happened also to be one of the first Danish physicians to add chiropractic spinal adjusting to his armamentarium. Among his patients was a fifty-four-year-old man who suffered from lumbago. In treating that condition Dr. Bechgaard manipulated the whole spine. The back pain cleared up. To the doctor's surprise, so also did his patient's hearing problem.

Much like Lillard, that man had suffered a hearing impairment for years subsequent to an incident in which he made a sudden turn of his head. Following that experience, Bechgaard began to look more carefully for changes in the hearing of other patients. In all, he identified six similar cases (personal communication).

How can hearing improve after a spinal adjustment when the auditory nerve never leaves the skull? Bechgaard speculated that it might be caused by interference with blood supply to the organ of Corti as a result of pressure on sympathetic nerves that do emerge from the cervical spine. Adjusting the spine in such cases could improve the tonus of arteries to the inner ear and thus improve the quality of hearing.

Perhaps Bechgaard had been influenced by Henry Winsor, M.D., who offered evidence that thirteen visceral diseases ranging from heart and lung to prostate and uterus appear to have resulted from "vertebral curvatures of the same sympathetic segment as [the] visceral trouble" (1921: 1-7). Almost four decades later, Burkhard Franz and Colin Anderson now offer clinical evidence, again in a medical journal, that sympathetic enervation "may be irritated by cervical injury and become dysfunctional" in ways that could contribute to Meniere's Disease, which includes hearing loss (2007; see also Murphy, 2008).

In all events, the fact of improved hearing is beyond dispute. Another Danish physician offered additional support for the claims of Palmer and Bechgaard. Torben Prip, who for years taught manual medicine (chiropractic technique) to interested doctors, spoke with me on that issue over coffee in his suburban home and clinic. He confirmed that after hearing Bechgaard speak he, too, began to take note of the hearing problems of his back pain patients. He recalled that over more than a quarter of a century his busy practice produced four or five cases of unilateral deafness that responded to spinal manipulation. That, he argued, was far too little to justify what he characterizes as excessive claims on the part of chiropractors, which brings me back to chiropractic philosophy, "philosophy" rather than "science," because not much is based on clinical trials.

Life Chiropractic College (now Life University) and Life Chiropractic College-West are straight institutions. We were taught that many diseases involve nerve interference, sometimes from entrapment by muscles and connective tissue, but mostly from narrowed openings where spinal nerves exit the spinal column. We memorized which sympathetic nerves led to which organs of the body so we could know which level of the spine to adjust in order to dilate bronchioles for respiratory disease, to speed up heartbeat for heart failure, to increase intestinal motility for constipation or obstruction, and even to delay emptying of the bladder for incontinence (Freeman, 2004: 313-314; Wiles, 1990: 379-396).

All of which brings us to a philosophical subtlety of considerable importance. In a 2008 publication, David Koch, D.C., Professor of Philosophy at Life University, wrote about "Chiropractic Myth No. 1:

Chiropractors think that they, or that chiropractic care, can cure anything and everything. " Koch credits Palmer with a conceptual breakthrough in his realization that "chiropractic adjustments weren't then, and aren't now, a 'cure' for anything! He began truly to appreciate that it was the body that 'cured' itself" (2008: 60). Remove the nerve interference and you do not cure the ailing organ, but you restore normal nerve function and that releases the body to heal itself.

That explanation goes back to Old Dad Chiro, who gave up magnetic healing, but not its explanatory theory of vitalism. The importance of vitalism dates from a 17th century belief that our health is less a product of physical and chemical forces than of a mystical energy, a life force; what the French referred to as *élan vital* and Palmer termed the innate intelligence of the body. Innate, as it came to be called, had to flow freely in the body for good health. Building on his father's teaching, B.J. went on to explain that spinal adjustments to remove nerve interference did not cure disease, but they did release Innate, which allowed the body to heal itself. That's the point that chiropractic philosophy Professor Koch is making in discrediting "myth number one."

Unfortunately for radical straights, vialism was discredited by a famous chemical experiment way back in 1828, when urea was synthesized from ammonium cyanate in a laboratory experiment to demonstrate that organic compounds were not produced by an inexplicable vital force, but could be forthrightly created by objective chemical reactions. But old Palmer apparently had never heard of the urea experiment, which was published half a century before his time. On the contrary, his thinking evolved into what Joseph Keating characterizes as a kind of bio-theology, whereby he conceptualized Innate as an individualized extension of the universal intelligence of all existence, that is, of God (Keating, 2002).

As concerns bio-theology, Dr. George Anderson explained to me once that God created the human hand with a sesamoid bone (the piseform) in the wrist where it is perfectly positioned to fit snugly against the end of the transverse process of the first cervical vertebra. Hence the Creator insured the effectiveness of a carefully calculated upper cervical specific adjustment, NUCCA style, to remove nerve interference and permit Innate to heal the body.

For a moment in that conversation, the chiropractor had become a priest, but only for that moment. Straights prefer to think of themselves as doctors. The ability of a chiropractor to release a pinched nerve, and thereby to liberate Innate, inspired one chiropractor in Oakland to identify himself as a "nerve doctor." He was not a neurologist, but he was very straight. He liberated Innate from nerve interference.

However, mixers go beyond knowing that spinal adjusting sometimes benefits or cures visceral diseases, as when Palmer, Bechgaard, and Prip cured a few cases of deafness. Mixers added medical and even surgical techniques to their scope of practice as they expanded their capabilities in the direction of becoming general practice physicians. But, while their philosophy of practice was open and receptive, powerful political and legal opposition limited their ambitions and shaped policy design profoundly.

Complicate with Politics and Legislation

Most chiropractors in living memory have been mixers, but nowhere have they been more "mixed" than in Oregon (Keating, 2002). In that state, in the past and even now, a chiropractic physician can be licensed to practice minor surgery (laceration repair, excision of a lipoma, removal of a sebaceous cyst) and proctology (treatment of the colon and ano-rectum using electro-surgical and minor scalpel procedures).

To qualify for minor surgery and proctology in the 21st century postgraduate program at Western States Chiropractic College requires only a distance learning tuition fee of $450 (in 2005) and completion of a 36-hour home-study course, plus 25 supervised surgeries. For an additional fee one can also qualify for obstetrics (midwifery). And not the least, $65 will purchase a 4-hour home-study course on the basic principles of pharmacology and toxicology as preparation for providing counsel on over-the-counter (non-prescription) drugs, complete with contraindications and potential side-effects, of course.

That advancement into medico-surgical terrain began a century ago. Estranged from the Iowa school and his usurper son, in 1908 Old Dad Chiro established the D. D. Palmer College of Chiropractic in Portland, Oregon. In competition with regular doctors, naturopaths, osteopaths and others to define a niche for chiropractors, Palmer declared, "A Chiropractor should be able to care for any condition which may arise in the families under his care, the same as a physician; this we intend to make possible in a two year's course." Surprisingly for the originator of straight chiropractic, Portland students in their second year were instructed in "First Aid, Minor Surgery, Surgical Diagnosis and Obstetrics . . . [including] Special cases, as Cancers, Tumors and Epilepsy. . . ." (cited in Keating, 2002: 21, 45-46, grammar as in the original).

Political and governmental circumstances favored a broad scope of practice, perhaps in part because so few medical doctors worked in rural Oregon a century ago. In addition, those early chiropractic educators were politically agile. They succeeded in lobbying for the passage of a very broad scope of chiropractic statute in 1915.

Under that first statute, some aspects of surgery and medicine could be legally taught in chiropractic colleges along with medical science courses. But, given the claims of chiropractic philosophy, why so? What made D.D. decide to become such an extreme mixer? The answer is concealed in a labyrinth of historical uncertainties, but a major reason was that the medical establishment was campaigning to eliminate chiropractic as unscientific. Their strategy was to mount a nationwide attack on chiropractic education.

Coming under attack, chiropractic schools felt pressured to demonstrate that they taught a basic science curriculum comparable to what was offered in medical schools. For example, as early as 1915, Pacific Chiropractic College (PCC) at La Grande, Oregon, required students to master anatomy, dissection, osteology, histology, cytology, sphlanchnology, neurology, angiology, bacteriology, chemistry, and physiology, along with options to add minor surgery and obstetrics.

The claim for equality was made explicit in a pamphlet, "Medical Education versus Chiropractic Education," that chiropractors distributed nationally in 1927. It listed courses said to be required for the practice of medicine in all 48 states, along side of which they listed equivalent courses taught in the 38 states in which chiropractic at that time was regulated by law. In that chiropractic example of political spin, the two professions appeared to be the same for most of the basic courses (anatomy, physiology pathology, hygiene, obstetrics & gynecology). For medical courses not taught in chiropractic schools, equivalents were listed. For example, the course equivalent to their "pharmacology &

therapeutics" category was listed as "diagnosis or analysis, including x-ray" (Keating, et al, 1998: 47, 51).

But as concerns policy design, the medical strategy was more complex and devious than was evident on the surface. Arguing that the basic sciences were essential fields of knowledge for practitioners of any of the healing arts including chiropractic, which was a dubious and insidious assertion in itself, the true purpose in proposing basic science legislation was to position themselves to deny practice rights to chiropractors, naturopaths, and other drugless practitioners. They anticipated that only medical graduates would be well enough educated to pass licensure examinations. The threat to non-medical graduates was all the more serious insofar as the qualifying examinations were to be graded by medical doctors.

And as expected, "Basic science examinations wrought havoc on the chiropractic profession and its schools." In seven states between 1927 and 1932, only one chiropractic graduate out of four was able to pass the basic science examinations. A politically influential mixer of that time, John Nugent, recalled in 1949, "Basic science laws threatened to shrivel the ranks of the profession, to dry up student enrollments and to force costly curricular changes. . . ." (cited in Keating, et al, 1998: 52-53).

The laws were especially offensive to philosophical straights, who considered medical courses a waste of time because they distracted students from learning as much as possible about the healing power of Innate, what Dr. Anderson learned in his eighteen months of training "that was mostly chiropractic philosophy." Taking the lead in collaboration with naturopaths and other drugless physicians, chiropractors used their political clout to get an amendment that authorized independent licensing authorities for non-medical professions.

As an example of how effective that strategy was, in 1933 the Oregon state legislature passed a new basic science law that regularized the curriculum pioneered by PCC at La Grande. Oregonian chiropractors at the time knew that it was a hostile maneuver engineered by the medical establishment to disqualify chiropractic graduates. In response, the chiropractic leadership, with the support of drugless physicians and naturopaths, used their political clout to work for an amendment that would authorize an independent licensing authority for each health care profession (Keating, 2002: 56). Under that kind of authority, chiropractors rather than medical scientists would grade the state licensing examinations and new graduates would predictably not fail in huge numbers.

However, the chiropractic amendment was defeated. It was vigorously opposed by a medical offensive energized by "wholesale falsification, slander, libel, and wanton calumny," according to William Budden of Western States Chiropractic College (cited in Keating, 2002: 56).

It was also resisted by straight chiropractors who turned a labyrinthine corner to join the medical opposition. Advertisements in newspapers statewide announced that B. J. Palmer, "America's Leading Chiropractor," agreed with medical authorities in urging voters to reject the amendment. Under attack by that unlikely alliance of medicine and straight chiropractic, the amendment failed. But, although the amendment failed, chiropractic colleges ultimately succeeded in teaching well enough to succeed in producing graduates who were able to pass state examinations and qualify for licensure (Keating, et al, 1998: 54). Eventually, a chiropractic board of examiners was put in place.

As Keating concluded from his historical research, "Budden and his faculty were adamant in their determination to produce well-educated 'chiropractic physicians'" (Keating, 2002: 55). Other states, including California, also adopted science requirements under pressure from political medicine, which was a big part of the reason why we had to struggle with medical courses at PSCC/Life West. There were other reasons, too, as we shall see.

But first, an addendum. Note that at PSCC/Life West we were not given the opportunity to qualify for surgery and obstetrics. Based on its history in Oregon, extensions of that sort had no appeal in most states, and certainly not in California. For those who might be interested, surgery was regarded as an unrealistic aspiration. It is notable that Oregon chiropractors of the 21st century almost never add minor surgery and obstetrics to their scope of practice, even though it is a legal option. The reason is that to do so would make them highly vulnerable to malpractice lawsuits. Because they are not as well qualified for surgical procedures as medical doctors, malpractice insurance with that inclusion is prohibitively expensive. In that indirect way, the ultimate force limiting their scope of practice in Oregon is economic. Ah yes, economics adds additional twists and turns to the labyrinth of policy design.

Confound with Economics

Think of this. If I had established my clinic in an Oakland neighborhood with the hope of supporting my family from full-time practice, I would have been in deep trouble. I would have needed to earn enough to pay for my housing and family expenses and to put my children through school. We would have needed medical insurance and life insurance. Some sort of retirement plan would have had to be put in place. And not unreasonably, I would probably have wanted to make it into a high-income bracket that would elevate us into upper-middle-class comfort and luxury.

In addition, it costs a lot to manage a business. Even minimal overhead expenses would have included investment costs for treatment tables and furniture, a lease, monthly telephone bills, minimal advertising outlays, and the overhead of laundry, utilities, janitorial service, and probably a receptionist/office manager.

So how much could I hope to earn from each patient for spinal adjustments? Well, it would rarely be enough, even if my practice building skills miraculously improved enough to create a busy practice. I would be under enormous pressure to consider legitimate ways to increase my income beyond what I might earn from spinal adjusting alone.

I might be tempted to add radiology as a diagnostic tool. Multiple x-rays of every patient, as we were taught to require by Pierce and Stillwagen, would bring in a lot of additional money. Regular follow-up x-rays as part of the NUCCA protocol we studied would unquestionably increase profits. X-rays can be used effectively for patient education, including to demonstrate the need for follow-up appointments. I was told that the full-spine radiographs routinely taken and repeated by practitioners of the Toftness Technique are needed solely as "teaching aids," since measurements inscribed on them are not factored into the practitioner's treatment decisions.

Admittedly, x-rays can be helpful in some difficult cases, including fluoroscopic imaging (or the new digitalized equivalent) to reveal how joints are moving in real time. I would certainly have to calculate how much my income might be enhanced by some reliance on radiology after I had invested in expensive equipment.

Nutrients, supplements, vitamins, and liniments can be profitable as easy tack-on sales. They probably do no harm (unlike x-ray), although they are of questionable value for many or even most patients. I would be able to boost my income significantly by those sales, however, and the placebo effect alone might make their sale defensible. Other items for sale could include neck braces, lumbar supports, knee binders, and arch supports that can be demonstrably beneficial for some patients.

Best of all is to keep patients returning for check-ups and additional care. Virtually an industry standard now is to apply the dental model to chiropractic practice. To that end every patient would have to be convinced that regular check-ups constitute preventive care. Once every six months is a dentistry practice now advocated by many chiropractors. Routine lifetime visits make good sense medically for the health of your mouth. It has never been justified scientifically for your spine, but it can move a chiropractor into the upper-middle class financially.

Another proven money-maker is family practice. Get the kids to come in for checkups, even if they are symptom free and not pre-scoliotic. Just over the horizon when I was a student, but big time now, is pediatric chiropractic. We were taught that even the newly delivered baby needs a chiropractic examination and adjustment because the neck gets subluxated as the head twists and bends through the birth canal. Since I graduated, pediatrics has become a major subspecialty. Parents are warned that every baby, toddler, and growing child needs occasional spinal adjustments, even when their vertebrae are still mostly pliable cartilage rather than bone.

I would also be tempted to advertise non-medical, non-surgical, Innate-mediated prevention and care for headaches, respiratory diseases, heart conditions, and even hearing loss.

With the right combination of add-ons to straight chiropractic adjusting, I might build a practice so big that I would need to hire new graduates to work for me as associate chiropractors. Their contracts would entitle me to a percentage of all of their patient billings. Add a physical therapist, an aroma therapist, an acupuncturist, and I could end up making it big time.

But as an alternative plan, I might have tried to build a practice without being a mixer. A straight practitioner can make a lot of money if she is able to adjust a different patient every five or ten minutes. To facilitate that, I would need to hire assistants to guide patients in disrobing and onto the treatment tables, while I would just move from one patient to the other, thrust, thrust, thrust as my cash register says ding, ding, ding.

As still another labyrinthine zigzag, I must add that one reason many chiropractors are so popular is that they resist the temptation to increase income by moving rapidly from one patient to the next. On the contrary, what is often most important to patients is that their alternative practitioner spends more one-on-one time with them than their medical doctor. (Keep in mind that medical doctors, also under pressure to make money, may have to schedule only 10 minutes for each consultation.) That caring relationship can be therapeutic, but it is not a money-maker.

Many if not most chiropractors locate themselves somewhere along a continuum between small practices earning small incomes at one end and huge practices with big incomes at the other. But wherever I might have chosen to locate myself, my style of practice would not succeed if I could not pay expenses and earn a livable income, which is the ultimate bottom line for any profession.

Not the least, pride in oneself and a self-identity of professional worth would have to be part of my payoff for becoming a Doctor of Chiropractic, which adds yet another labyrinthine issue that impacted policy design.

Tweak with Identity Theory

A bit of anthropological theory will guide us through one more twist in the labyrinth that was leading to a medical school curriculum. Some decades ago my main field of anthropological interest, like that of other cultural anthropologists in the 1950s and 60s, was to document and understand peasant culture. In that pursuit I was challenged to understand how two contrasting subcultures coexisted on shared terrain in historical Europe, the subculture of peasants with the subculture of aristocrats.

What challenged my interest was the extent to which the subcultures (habits of work, housing, clothing, social customs, values, beliefs, dialects, recreation, what have you) were similar in underlying ways for peasants and aristocrats but, in other ways were remarkably different. Moreover, the ways in which those subcultures differed was experienced as very, very important to the populations involved because they symbolized contrasting identities based on a dichotomy of wealth, status, and power.

The result was a seesaw process of imitation and differentiation. Aristocrats lived as though it was very important that their way of life should symbolize their superiority and dominance. That identity was experienced as threatened if any peasants or burghers (townspeople) adopted aristocratic cultural practices with their symbolic subjectivities.

Permit me to illustrate with an obvious example. Aristocrats differentiated themselves in their styles of clothing. For the most part, peasants couldn't afford the fancy clothes of "their betters," which were also very impractical for farm work, so it was rarely an issue of contention. But occasionally a wealthy villager or burgher could. To stop imitation in styles of dress, the ruling caste in some places imposed sumptuary laws, making it illegal and punishable for a non-aristocrat to wear clothes made of silk, for example. Where such laws were not imposed, fashion designers assisted the process of differentiation by inventing expensive new styles, leaving old styles to lower status individuals and their imitative impudence (Anderson, 1971, 29-34).

For analytical purposes, we can take medical doctors and chiropractors as analogous in coping with identity issues. Chiropractors resorted to both differentiation and imitation.

Differentiation was extremely important to the chiropractic identity. In competition with medical doctors they attracted back pain patients by letting it be known that they adjusted subluxations rather than prescribing analgesics and bed rest the way medical doctors might, and chiropractors got better results.

Yet it also suited their purpose to imitate, so they expected to be addressed as "doctor." Many (not all) also referred to themselves "chiropractic physicians." They established "clinics" with waiting rooms, reception desks, and treatment rooms in the style of medical doctors.

In them they wore white clinic coats and advertised themselves as "Dr. Smith," for example, rather than as John Smith, D.C.

Not the least, they may have let it be known, as D.D. put it, that "A Chiropractor should be able to care for any condition which may arise in the families under his care, the same as a physician. . . ." In the straight tradition, in place of frightening surgeries, evil-tasting decoctions, painful injections, and expensive hospitalizations, the straight chiropractor offered hands-on treatment scarcely more frightening than the ministrations of a massage therapist. Mixers, for their part, extended their chiropractic adjusting with a medley of remedies, all of which were "natural" and therefore gentle and harmless.

And not the least, after the introduction of medical science courses in a four year course of study, a chiropractor could display a diploma to signal that her training was very much the same as that of a medical doctors (imitation), except that she was trained to identify a cause of disease missed in medical diagnosis (differentiation) and cure it with adjustments that medical doctors were not qualified to provide (differentiation).

But whereas one can generalize about the diagnostic and therapeutic practices of medical doctors as conforming rigorously to legal, professional, and ethical requirements, the same is not true of chiropractors. That is what flabbergasted me when I first explored my anthropological interest in chiropractic and observed that no two doctors followed the same protocol as far as I could see (differentiation where I had expected imitation).

Early in my career I framed my narrative of peasants and aristocrats by means of a theory of culture that put the emphasis on homogeneity in each society. Conceptualized that way, it was easy to fall into stereotypes and the sins of essentialism.

By essentialism I mean the assumption that each society would expectably demonstrate a more or less well-integrated ensemble of cultural traits that characterize every member of the society equally, allowing for obvious variations related to gender, age, physical health, and psychological normality, with deviant individuals as unimportant diversions. The statement I just made about medical doctors all conforming to basic standards of practice totters frighteningly on the edge of essentialism. Do keep that in mind.

The way we did cultural analysis as a carry-over from the 1950s and 60s left me wondering how I would ever manage to identify the similarities I assumed must underlie such extensive variability among practicing chiropractors. Fortunately, between the decades of my earlier work on community studies (including peasants and aristocrats) and my more recent work on chiropractors and medical doctors, we anthropologists learned to be much more subtle, or perhaps I should say sensitive, in how we describe heterogeneity within a society. We are analytically better equipped now to cope with the labyrinth of cultural complexity as it impacts chiropractic. We have departed the older so-called "modernist" assumption of cultural homogeneity by introducing postmodern subtleties.

Sort Out with Postmodern Analysis

In the modernist mode we thought of cultures homogenously or functionally as "designs for living" (Kluckhohn & Kelly, 1945: 9), as "patterns of culture" (Benedict, 1934), or even quite recently as "learned and shared human behaviors and ideas" (Miller, 2002: 388). But in the present postmodernist era, we tend to view cultures in much more reflective ways. We no longer theorize them as largely homogeneous. The same is true of professions. On the contrary, we now conceptualize any cultural or any professional inventory of ethical practice as filled with options one may activate or ignore, as constraints one may conform to or resist.

"At any given moment," Lawrence Hirschfeld writes, "the cultural environment which an individual inhabits is fragmented, fluid, noisy, and negotiable . . . comprised of multiple, contesting, competing subcultural environments" (2002: 615). Given that complexity, I find it helpful, taking my lead from Ann Swidler, to think of "culture as a 'tool kit' . . . which people may use in varying configurations to solve different kinds of problems" (1986: 273). Culture being that open to choice, it should not be surprising that chiropractors differ greatly from one another in how the practice their profession. That's why I was so baffled by my earliest observations.

So, why in the world did we have to complete so much coursework in medicine, especially given that ours was a straight school? Our medical training was a product of educational policies that emerged from a baffling labyrinth of cultural complexity. The labyrinth of sharp turns, dark tunnels, blind alleys and sudden pitfalls faced our professional ancestors with competing chiropractic philosophies (ideologies), confrontational legal and legislative maneuvers (power and conflict), economic needs and wishes (costs and benefits), psychological needs and challenges (symbols of identity and self-worth), and above all, postmodern ambiguities (latitude to choose).

By the time we came along, we had no choice about the courses that were required. We were forced to complete a substantial medical curriculum. But we could make choices about the extent to which we invested ourselves in the half of all subjects that were basically medical. Some minimized their attention to them. Yet, even they had to learn enough to pass state imposed examinations. Others of us mastered the subjects thoroughly, even when the teaching was extremely poor and we had to teach ourselves from assigned textbooks. The most regrettable shortcoming was that our training did not include supervised work with hospitalized patients.

Chapter Nine

Chiropractic as Medical Practice

Legitimacy at Last

Chiropractic and osteopathy originated within a couple of years of each other and only a few hundred miles apart in the Midwest. Each independently of the other challenged the hegemony of medicine in a similar way. Both advocated spinal manipulation as superior to medicine and surgery for back pain and the entire array of musculoskeletal disorders. Both saw spinal manipulation as a way to release impaired spinal nerves and thereby to cure visceral diseases by freeing the body to heal itself (compare Freeman [2004: 315] with Northup [1966: 64]).

It is also important to remember that both began to compete with conventional medicine during the last decade or so of "heroic medicine," when medical doctors prescribed often worthless or harmful drugs and weakened or even killed patients with vomiting, blistering, and bleeding. It was not until between 1910 and 1912 that a patient had better than a 50 percent chance of getting better by seeking care from a doctor (Henderson, cited in Ingefinger, 1978: 945). It was a time when chiropractors and osteopaths were safer and more effective than most medical doctors. It is quite understandable, then, that each believed that his profession, the D.C. for one and the D.O. for the other, should be licensed for a full scope of practice, just like an M.D.

Bear in mind that chiropractic began as a "straight" cure-all that replaced magnetic healing for D. D. Palmer, an intelligent but uneducated man. He enrolled his first students in the Palmer School & Infirmary of Chiropractic in 1898, coaching them in spinal manipulative techniques. Without anticipating long term consequences, by the turn of the century he began to move in a medical direction by teaching anatomy and physiology in an attempt to explain why pain subsided, infections healed, fevers broke, and hearing was restored after spinal adjusting.

By the time he arrived in Oregon he had added minor surgery, obstetrics, and treatment for cancers and tumors. As the years passed, medical courses were added as we have seen. But chiropractic schools stopped short of fully replicating medical schools, in part because their standards of teaching were inferior, and in part because they were not able to add bedside training in hospitals to provide at least a rough equivalence to the full medical education of an M.D.

Why, then, did Morris Fishbein, speaking for the American Medical Association, rank the D.O. higher than the D.C. when he wrote, "if osteopathy is essentially a method of entering medicine by the back door . . . chiropractic by contrast is an attempt to arrive through the cellar" (1925)?

The answer, I would suggest, is that osteopathic education rapidly improved to outperform chiropractic in teaching standards and to more fully mirror the medical model. Andrew Taylor Still (1828-1917) began his career as a rural doctor, well qualified in his time for the practice of medicine. He repudiated the methods of heroic medicine for good reason, but he did not renounce medicine as a profession. On the contrary, when he was granted a charter for the American School of Osteopathy (ASO) in 1892, the articles of association stated that its objective was "to improve our present system of surgery, obstetrics and treatment of diseases generally, and place the same on a more rational and scientific basis. . . ." In the words of George Northup, "from the first [ASO] was considered to be a school of medicine embracing all of the arts and sciences of medical practice" (1966: 16-17).

For fifty years osteopaths struggled to gain federal acceptance as completely the equivalent of medical doctors (Gevitz, 1982). Finally, in 1966, the Department of Defense officially accepted Doctors of Osteopathy as fully qualified to serve as physicians and surgeons in the armed services, completely equivalent to Doctors of Medicine in status and role.

As for California, the American Medical Association spent millions of dollars in 1962 to support Proposition 22 as a statewide initiative to make the practice of osteopathic medicine illegal. The initiative passed, with the understanding that in return for eliminating osteopathic competition the California Medical Association would exchange M.D. degrees for D.O. in return for a symbolic gesture, which was to attend a short seminar and pay a fee of $65. That transformed equivalency into a legal non-issue. (In 1974 the state resumed the licensing of D.O.'s as such.)

Chiropractors did not attain the level of equivalency accorded to osteopaths, but they did achieve a substantial degree of acceptance within the medical community. I did become licensed as a practicing doctor of sorts.

Chiropractic as Medical Practice

On the level of doctors, the three leading health care professions rank in descending order as medicine, dentistry, and chiropractic when measured by the number of doctors in each profession. So I made it into one of the three main medical professions. In terms of professional and social ranking, they also rank in that order, with dentists intermediate and chiropractors at the bottom.

Remembering what it was like as recently as 1979 (which happened to be the year I enrolled in Pacific States Chiropractic College), Scott Haldeman, D.C., Ph.D., M.D., wrote how the profession rapidly gained professional stature during the 1980s.

> Chiropractors are no longer isolated in their private practice or excluded from government and privately funded health care institutions and facilities. Chiropractors are increasingly included within large multidisciplinary clinics with medical and osteopathic

physicians, surgeons, and specialists. They are included in Medicare, Medicaid and other government-funded health care systems and participate in health maintenance organizations (HMOs) and preferred provider organizations (PPOs). Increasing numbers of chiropractors have hospital privileges and all now have access to medical specialist consultations (1992: xi).

Integrative Chiropractic

As an example of the new status Dr. Haldeman refers to, I give you Matthew Davis, D.C., whom I have never met. Dr. Davis practices in a primary health care facility in the countryside of Townshend, Vermont, 70 miles from the nearest major medical center (Davis, et al, 2007). The Otis Health Care Center (OHCC) includes a small hospital (19 beds and an emergency room), two outpatient clinics, and a retail pharmacy. Dr. Davis is on staff with six primary care physicians, a psychiatrist, four nurse practitioners, a physician's assistant, five physical therapists, four occupational therapists, and a speech therapist. He refers to his contribution on the medical staff as practicing integrative or complementary chiropractic (see Meeker, 2000).

The chiropractor's responsibility on the OHCC team is to function as a specialist for the diagnosis and non-surgical management of musculoskeletal conditions, about 90 percent of which involve back and neck pain, including tension headaches. As a doctor, he practices with portal of entry status. He ministers to his patients as their primary provider, but with a distinct advantage. In triage at the front desk, the nurse on duty will have already queried for "red flags" to divert those who should be seen and evaluated by a primary care physician in order to rule out serious health conditions that require medical or surgical attention. Fever, chills, or unexplained weight loss, for example may alert the triage nurse to the possibility of infection or cancer. A red flag may suggest the probability of an autoimmune disease or an inflammatory rheumatism.

Coordination among medical specialties ensures better clinical outcomes and higher levels of patient satisfaction, which is one expected benefit from an integrated practice. It is especially important for the chiropractor. In non-integrated settings medical practitioners are often wary of making referrals to a chiropractor, being unsure of how to identify a capable practitioner. They can be confused, just as I was originally confused, by what Dr. Davis himself refers to, as "the wide variation in techniques practiced by chiropractors and the lack of standardization among its practitioners" (Davis, et al, 2007: 700; see Coulter, et al, 2005).

A medical doctor attending to a medical or surgical problem may discover that her patient is also suffering from back pain or tension headaches. At the Health Care Center it is convenient for that doctor to make an in-house referral to a chiropractor because she knows and trusts her chiropractic colleague. Similarly, physicians on duty in the emergency room or those caring for hospitalized patients feel comfortable about the requesting consultative care from Dr. Davis when appropriate, which can include arms, hands, legs, and feet, for which the chiropractor is not the portal of entry.

Not the least, integrative medicine benefits economically from including a chiropractor on staff. Whereas about 10 percent of the American adult population will have sought treatment from a chiropractor (lifetime prevalence), in rural areas that number reaches 15 to 17 percent, which is consistent with what anthropologist Thomas McCorkle described in 1961 (Eisenberg, 1998; del Mundo, 2002). Having a chiropractor on staff in a rural area allows OHCC to profit from that potential revenue.

It is a given that the M.D. is still positioned at the top of a totem pole of prestige and importance. Even the D.O. ranks socially (but not professionally or legally) a bit lower, and the dentist, somewhat lower still. And with them I give you Matthew Davis, D.C., a health care provider on the level of being a practicing doctor who occupies a position of prominence on the totem pole, a specialist among specialists, each one uniquely competent in his own field of expertise.

Coda

Of course it would have made no sense for me to resign as a professor of anthropology in 1983 in order to practice chiropractic, because I enjoy my work as an anthropologist. But I did make extensive use of my (limited) clinical skills to further a research agenda that I have continued to pursue until as recently as 2004-2005. During that year Edna was employed as a consultant to the Minister of Higher Education in Afghanistan and on holiday visits I was able to document the work of a traditional bonesetter, an Afghan *shekesta band*.

But I haven't explained why I closed down my chiropractic clinic and laboratory at Mills after maintaining it for only a couple of months. The reason was that I unexpectedly departed Mills College on a two-year leave of absence to attend medical school.

PART II:
MEDICINE AND SURGERY

1984

"The most recent data reveal the presence of 96,605 FMGs [Foreign Medical Graduates] in the United States; as of 1979 this count was 21 percent of all physicians [during my years in medical school]."

> Stephen Mick & Jacqueline Worobey
> "Foreign Medical Graduates in the 1980s"
> *American Journal of Public Health*

1985

"Larger and larger numbers of US nationals are studying medicine abroad . . . seeking to enter the US health care system."

> Thomas Dublin, M.D., DrPH, et al
> "Where Have All the Students Gone?"
> *Journal of the American Medical Association*

1985

Review of *Bad Medicine*, (Twentieth Century Fox): "While the film deals harshly but humorously with the inadequacies of some foreign medical schools, it salutes those individuals who want to practice medicine so much that they will endure the shortcomings of such schools so they can eventually become physicians."

Welles Propper, M.D.
American Medical News
December 13, 1985.

Disclosure

I describe the university medical school I attended in Mexico as it was twenty-five-years ago. My observations should not be taken to represent the school as it has become in the twenty-first century.

Chapter Ten

Across the Border to Medical School

The Tenacity of a Childhood Dream

Human memory for the most part is Google-like in permitting us to recall bits and parts of the past, usually as sound-bites that speak to us somewhat the way radio talk shows rattle on while we drive. In that immensely broad and deep universe of a narrative self softly spoken, only scattered fragments persist as sharply illustrated videoclips in the mind.

One videoclip is clearly visible to me, though only for seconds at a time, like a shooting star across a black night sky of before-and-after empty space. It flashes back to the day I graduated from Life West. We were putting on caps and gowns in a classroom when Bill, a tall, muscular, non-cerebral guy, turned to face me as I startled at his rhetorical, somehow challenging question. "Well Bob, I guess now you'll go on to medical school."

In my mind's eye I can still see him looking at me with that taken-for-granted prediction. When I retrieve that scene it comes in a mental snapshot album with others. A much older one pictures me as a boy looking across my Dad's sickbed at Dr. Newton and wishing I could be a doctor like him. Another old one recalls my Uncle Fred when I graduated from High School and he told me I should move on to a job instead of premed studies. Yet another, as a student at the Sorbonne walking by the medical school and suddenly imagining what an adventure it would be to study medicine right there in Paris, if only I didn't have family responsibilities.

I don't remember having talked about medical school with Bill, but somehow I clearly triggered his question. I was not planning to enroll in a medical school, but I do remember two kinds of wishes that he must have picked up on, and neither was solely about youthful dreams of social status and self-identity. One emerged from how books and courses on medicine and the medical sciences had captured my interest, beginning with a particular book and a moment in time that I recorded as a kind of poetic reflection shortly after I began my studies at Pacific States. Unlike a mental videoclip or memory sound-bite, that recall was neither visual nor auditory, and it was not nostalgic. It was inspirational.

The summer sun, a gentle tonic for the spirit when it shines on the California coast, can be a demon when it catches you on black asphalt in an inland town. I ducked into an air-conditioned café to escape and lugged along the enormous book I had just purchased, still in shock that I had spent so much for a book I would probably never get through. It was a quiet time. No one would care if I lingered over my new acquisition.

In a lifetime you can count on your fingers those momentary flashes of clarity when, like a statue's heart of Jesus, you catch a glimpse of a deep reality within yourself that almost instantly covers over again. Such moments are always few and widely spaced. I was certainly not expecting one to appear that afternoon as I struggled through a first few pages of densely packed prose, one sentence at a time.

A medical student would have scorned my growing excitement. It was an arm-breaking 1595 page tome called *Robbin's Pathologic Basis of Disease*. Yet, for the first time I became aware of how I could learn in detail about all of the diseases inflicted on humankind. Most of us never see the books that doctors learn from, nor sit in on lectures in medical schools. Tears threatened the corners of my eyes as that door opened onto an ethnographic continent I had not expected to explore.

There was a lot of medicine in *Robbin's*, and a lot more in *Cecil's textbook of Medicine*, and in a small library of other books. I felt foolish that I had taken so long to make an obvious discovery. At that moment I became aware of an empty room deep inside myself. It had been dark and airless from when I was a teenager. I had forgotten it existed. But it was there. It was a room set aside in the expansive dreaming of adolescence for being a physician, for knowing about medicine. It was meant to accommodate a knight who would joust against pain and death.

The light that flooded that room so unexpectedly that afternoon wiped out in an instant the amnesia of that young student. I realized I still wanted to fill that room, to open it out to other parts of my life. I wanted to know medicine. Only a youth dares to hope for more than he can possibly achieve. No longer young, I was shocked at my daring and naïveté. I could no longer focus on what I was reading. I could only think – no, not think. It was more of a feeling. I could only feel that I was not going to quit this life without knowing medicine.

Medical studies at Life West greatly satisfied that desire to explore but I yearned to continue on to Osler's bedside if I could, to experience hands-on learning with hospitalized patients, a kind of clinical participant observation.

The other suppressed wish emerged even more directly from the anthropological me, from the intellectual stimulation of doing comparative work, as when I moved from a year in a Danish maritime community in the process of becoming a suburb (*The Vanishing Village*) to the following year in a in a French village, also transforming into a suburb (*Bus Stop for Paris*). I find intellectual satisfaction in experiencing how cultures can be both alike and different. Having done participant observation as a student of chiropractic, I urgently wanted to compare that with participant observation in becoming a physician and surgeon.

"No way am I going to medical school, Bill," I shot back. "Even if I wanted to, it wouldn't work out. I was really lucky that Life West was only twenty minutes from my office, with a teaching schedule I could work around. Now I need to take advantage of what I have learned here so I can become a better medical anthropologist and a more interesting teacher." And that's where the videoclip stops abruptly.

The truth is, I thought about applying to medical school from time to time while I was studying chiropractic, but always as an impossible ambition. Even to apply for admission to medical school stopped me cold. It was demoralizing. I couldn't face the prospect of cramming to earn the high score on an MCAT test that every American medical school requires. It would sidetrack everything else in my life for months with absolutely no promise of payoff, no certainty of scoring high enough to gain admission.

As thousands of other would-be doctors have done, I looked into alternatives. On one trip to Denmark when I was interviewing a 45-year-old physical therapist about back pain I learned that she was working part-time towards her medical degree at the University of Copenhagen. Anyone with the prerequisite course training is admitted, she told me. Unfortunately, she added, you need to be a Danish citizen to be eligible, and it takes fifteen years of residence in Denmark to qualify for that. I didn't even attempt to verify her facts. I was too discouraged, since I love Copenhagen and speak Danish.

Every avenue I explored was like that. There was always some reason why it wouldn't be feasible. Not the least of the impediments was that I would never want to give up being a professor at Mills and working as an anthropologist in order to practice medicine. I wanted the experience of attending medical school as an embedded ethnographer, just as I had done in chiropractic college, after which I would want to integrate what I learned into my life as an academician. It was a luxury I could ill afford. My prospects seemed hopeless.

Now, mind you, I didn't go through the days and weeks thinking about medical school. I was busy teaching, doing research, writing and enjoying my family. I was even seeing patients three mornings a week at the college health center. I had many other things on my mind.

A Chance Encounter as Transformative

I had other things on my mind until a chance encounter became a transformative event. It happened on Monday, November 14, 1983, eight months after my Life-West graduation. I spent that morning seeing patients in my chiropractic clinic. At noon Barny Coil, Ph.D., met me for lunch in the faculty dining room to talk about chiropractic in third world countries. He unexpectedly brought a friend, Cameron

Ainsworth, Ph.D., M.D. Cam came to talk with me, because he had some questions to ask about developing nations. He thought he might want to combine medical practice with humanitarian service and adventure abroad.

I was fascinated with Cam. He had enjoyed a successful career as a Professor of Chemistry at San Francisco State University until he went through a kind of male menopause at the age of fifty-seven, left his fully tenured position to earn an M.D. degree, and then re-started his professional life as a physician in private practice.

He picked up on my latent interest in medicine and surgery as we talked, leaving Barny to listen as silent witness. Cam convinced himself and me that I should do exactly what he had done. He got himself admitted to an advanced standing program in a Mexican university where he was able to earn his M.D. degree in two years because they gave him credit for the scientific training involved in earning his Ph.D., a legitimate side door to medicine in the United States, where it is referred to as a PhD-to-MD Program.

I would have been very suspicious of that American side door remodeled as a back door through Mexico had not someone I respected told me that you really could get your medical training that way. But there was Cam, who had done it himself. That evening I wrote in my journal, "I got lots of information from him and he is going to send more. He thinks I should do the same, although he feels that if I had not met him and if he did not write a letter for me they would never consider me because of my age and my doctorate in anthropology. The program is for Ph.D.'s, but in the hard sciences."

Two days later we spoke on the phone. He gave me the address of the medical school, and I wrote for information. I also came across the address in an advertisement published in *Science* announcing an "Advanced Standing Admission Program" at the University of Ciudad Juarez, School of Medicine (in Spanish, *Universidad Autonoma de Ciudad Juarez, Instituto de Ciencias Biomédicas*). The requirements were a Ph.D. in a basic medical science or a doctoral degree in dentistry or veterinary medicine. It specifically added, "Individuals with a professional degree in Chiropractic . . . [or] Osteopathy . . . [or Podiatric Medicine, as I learned later] are not eligible for advanced standing."

That was important to know, so I only submitted transcripts from the University of California.

A week later my brother Stan came to town. It was my first opportunity to show him the still new lab and clinic. I told him I had applied to a medical school. His instantaneous response came right from the heart, "You are stark raving mad." He was right, of course, but it didn't matter. Edna knew it was important to me and encouraged me "to follow my bliss," as Joseph Campbell might have put it. Later, Dean Weiner agreed to give me a leave of absence (without pay) for two years, but with a firm reminder that I would have to resign my professorship if two years did not suffice.

Red Tape in an Exponential Dimension

In mid-January Edna and I flew to spend three days in El Paso, Texas, just across the Rio Grande from Ciudad Juarez. Early that afternoon I spoke by telephone with two members of the present class, one a clinical psychologist and the other a Doctor of Veterinary Medicine with a Ph.D. in endocrinology. As noted in my journal, "they think the program is terrific."

On instructions from them, we crossed the river to visit the medical school, including the building housing the Advanced Standing Program. The following day I had an interview with Sr. Gomez, the Dean in charge of admissions. "It went well," I recorded, and we returned the following day, hoping to get an acceptance before returning to California, but instead I got tangled up in red tape.

Red tape, or more aptly, red flag number one: Dean Gomez said there were two problems, age and field (which is exactly what Cam had anticipated). Age he seemed able to accept, since he found me fit and said I didn't look like a 57-year-old man.

But cultural anthropology remained a problem. They have never accepted a Ph.D. in anthropology and were concerned about how it would be interpreted by the American authorities. He promised to get a committee decision for me in a week. I left feeling hopeful because he let me carry off a $200 six-month correspondence course without paying for it on the spot. I was supposed to mail my self-administered tests to him by May 15, in time to start summer classes in Mexico.

Edna – with a woman's greater intuitive sensitivity– cautioned me to be prepared for rejection.

The next morning in Oakland I went over the box full of Xeroxed study materials for the basic science exams I would have to master during the coming four months, since I was getting a late start. I found it was all stuff I had been examined on before in Life-West courses, National Boards, and State Boards. But I could see that it would require an enormous amount of review to get back on top of complex mechanisms such as the Krebs cycle in biochemistry. For the rest of the spring I devoted an hour or two every morning to studying and writing answers to those test questions.

I wrote in my journal, "Overall, my biggest response is to appreciate that going to medical school in a chiropractic college taught me far more than I appreciated. A Third World medical school is about the same, and certainly no better. What was missing, however, was the hospital experience, and we will begin that in the fall."

Red Flag number two. Almost a month went by with no word, so I phoned the clinical psychologist to see what he could tell me. He told me I made a mistake in not getting an acceptance before leaving Juarez, although I felt I had pushed as hard as I could at the time. He told me I may have to fly back to have another face-to-face interview.

Also, in stark contrast to our first conversation, he sounded very down on the program. "You will hate all of your fellow students," he told me. What a shock. From Life-West I would have anticipated communitas. "Why?" "Because you spend nine or ten hours a day with them and they get on your nerves, but I am gutting it out." In the coming year I learned that "nerves" was code for serious confrontations, devious hostilities, and fearful bodily attacks.

Then he added another downer. "It will be virtually impossible to do clerkships in California, but I'm going to stick it out, even if it takes several years, because getting the M.D. is the most important thing in the world to me."

I didn't have to fly back for a second face-to-face meeting with Gomez. The next day Cam intervened for me. He phoned the Dean, who told him a letter had been mailed three or four days earlier. I was on the alternate list. Anthropology remained a red flag. Cam was told that in about a month they were to be inspected by American authorities, and they didn't want me because anthropology was not a qualifying degree, even though I had explained that the American authorities knew that anthropology could be a biological science and that I was well qualified in biological anthropology. I had even recently published in that subfield.

I reminded Cam that I told Gomez that the University of Miami accepted anthropologists into their PhD-to-MD program, although that was a mere guess on my part. Right after talking with Cam I phoned the University of Miami and they confirmed, "Yes, anthropology is an acceptable degree." I immediately phoned that back to Gomez, leaving it as a message with his secretary, including the phone number I used to talk with the Miami admissions department.

Two days later, on February 16, in my office at Mills, I got through to Dean Gomez in Mexico before walking across campus to teach a class on human evolution. That evening I wrote a happy journal entry in capital letters, "I AM ACCEPTED TO MEDICAL SCHOOL. Knowing that anthropologists are accepted at the University of Miami was what did it. He still has to get the committee to approve it (which just meant his brother Dr. Gomez [the program director]) but I am in. Fantastic." I totally did not anticipate that there would be a Red Flag number three.

A week later I phoned Mexico, but first, let me put that conversation into perspective. The economy of Mexico at that time was in deep trouble. It was almost impossible for families to live on wages weakened by an annual inflation rate of 50 to 100 percent per year. Those in positions to do so scrambled after additional income in illegal ways. Bribery and extortion were a way of life in the mid-1980s according to *Time* magazine (August 6, 1984: 30).

To illustrate, on being accepted into the program I found myself billed for two items beyond the $6,000 tuition fee. I had to write a separate check for $200 to pay for that "correspondence course" we were required to complete prior to arriving in Ciudad Juarez. It was a money making scheme that required us to purchase absolutely useless study materials. Much of it was just photocopied from textbooks. Some had been hastily slapped together by earlier foreign students as their way of satisfying the requirement to perform social service in Mexico.

Two-hundred dollars is not much, though, if it puts you within reach of an M.D. degree. We all paid it.

To further illustrate, another separate check for $600 was required to pay for a special course in Spanish. That seemed a good idea. Gomez collected $14,400 from us that way. After we arrived he hired a Spanish instructor for only $300 to meet with us for an hour a day during part of the summer. The instructor was gifted. She helped some students who were willing to put some work into it. I was the only one who arrived already able to speak and understand the language well enough to limp along without needing her introductory course (based on four years of high school Spanish and two at U.C. Berkeley). She excused me from wasting my time with beginners, but the $600 was extracted from me all the same.

Still more on graft. While I was getting certified bank checks to cover those fees I had that phone conversation with Gomez mentioned above, one that raised a third red flag. He told me I should add one more separate check for $2,000 as a "donation." That's where I drew the line. "A donation! For what?" "Well, it's not really a donation," he said. "It's a late filing fee." "No," I argued, "That's unreasonable." I will say this for the Dean, he tended to be reasonable in his own heavy-handed way. We haggled over the "late fee" for several days, and finally agreed it would be $500. I phoned Cam afterwards. He was also nicked for $500, but that was four or five years earlier. I was lucky it wasn't $5,000 by the time I applied. The photographer who took my picture for the visa application at the Mexican Consulate in San Francisco told me that some of those who came to her paid that much under-the-table to get into Mexican medical schools. So, in fact, $2,000 was reasonable and $500 was a bargain. "So I am in," I concluded. It was just a question of the size of the bribe. Five-hundred dollars is not much if it puts you within reach of an M.D. degree.

Meanwhile, I dealt with a lot of red tape that was merely tedious and time-consuming. I arranged for a two-year leave of absence from my job as well as for Ann Metcalf to replace me as a visiting professor. I was advised to try to arrange for clinical clerkships in California right away, because they were harder to get than when Cam did the program, so I hustled around on that. I had to get notarized transcripts from Berkeley and take them to the Mexican Consulate in San Francisco to have them certified. To qualify for a visa I had to go to our bank to get a statement ensuring that I could afford to live without a salary for two years. It was such a strange request, really. So unusual, in fact, that I had to compose the letter for the bank vice president. I even typed it for him on his stationary. I also had to get a letter from Kaiser certifying that they had given me a physical examination and found I was "in a good state of health." The Consulate wanted a letter from the Sheriff's Department certifying that I did not have a criminal record. When I finally got my visa as a "non-immigrating student" I learned that my official name in Mexico was Robert Thomas Anderson Hansen. I rather liked having my devoted mother's name added, but it did come as a surprise. I also purchased certified checks to pay my tuition. Not the least, I spent a couple of hours every day reading and memorizing study materials over morning coffee at McDonald's as I worked on the "correspondence course"

By the beginning of April the time was approaching when I would need to move to Mexico, because the program was scheduled to begin with an intensive summer review of basic sciences leading up to a comprehensive examination at the beginning of the fall semester. It seemed I had cut through all of the red tape. I would wrap up the semester at Mills by mid-May.

Suddenly, a red tape disaster struck! Gomez sent a registered letter to return my tuition checks and inform me that I was expelled. "Expelled" was the term he used! What a shock! I felt so degraded. But he did add that I could reapply for the following year. His explanation was that I had not gotten the last tuition check to them immediately, even though he knew it was coming by registered mail. He added that there were other "issues" as well, including that California teaching hospitals were no longer accepting foreign medical students for clerkships.

The only real issue, of course, was that I had not sent him $500 as a late application fee, never mentioned in any letters but discussed by telephone. When I was billed for tuition, the Spanish course and the correspondence course, the $500 was not listed. I decided I could get away with not paying it. That's when things moved fast for the first time. I got that registered letter of expulsion from the program. The next morning on the phone I humbled myself. I would send the "late fee," I told him. He hesitated. "We don't want you if you're going to be trouble-maker," was his response. "Oh, you can count on me. I won't make trouble." I felt like vomiting. What groveling! But I "ate shit" as the only chance I would ever have to qualify in medicine. It paid off. He gave me permission to re-submit the checks, along with the additional one as my "donation." I heaved a sigh of relief. I thought sure he would increase the donation back to $2,000. At that point, $500 truly did seem like a bargain because it put me within reach of an M.D. degree.

So I returned the checks with an added $500. He said he would recommend me to the committee, but actually, the decision at that point was entirely his. After hanging up I walked to Edna's office to tell her about it, partly because her phone was busy, but also because I was so agitated.

There was another red tape obstacle that didn't amount to much, but was very upsetting at the time. On May 16 I got my grades for the seventeen tests I had submitted for the correspondence course. I was not so much upset by my low scores as I was puzzled.

I quote from my journal: "I was surprised that they got them corrected and returned so soon, but it looks as though many that they marked wrong are correct. That's very hard to cope with, since I can't argue with them. The result is I only passed three of the seventeen subjects, and those were with very low grades. Pedagogically, to create that feeling of hopelessness is a disastrous way to get a student started. [And it was inexplicable, because, as was permitted] I had all of my books open to answer those questions. In fact, [Professor] Darl Bowers, who teaches the subject, worked with me on the embryology section, which scored only 58 percent (75 percent is a minimum passing grade). Similarly, [my daughter] Kris, [who was a Mills senior in biochemistry] did the biochemistry test with me. My score on that was still a flunking grade, only 68 percent." It puzzled me, but it didn't matter. The grades made no difference in my acceptance or later success at the school.

I was also dealing with emotional issues, as attested in my journal entry for May 19. "Awake most of last night, tossing and turning, wondering how I could have decided to risk our beautiful life together in this wonderful environment, driven by an irrational need to qualify myself in medicine and surgery."

Confronting the Emotional Challenge

Three days later Edna and I drove off to a new world of frightening uncertainties. Our car was filled more with medical books than with clothes and household items. Edna added only one small suitcase to last her for a month in Washington, D.C., where she was scheduled to work in the office of Congressman Tom Lantos.

I would have preferred to live in Ciudad Juarez, but Edna convinced me that I needed access to a swimming pool for my daily swim and an American telephone connection for easy communication with her and the family - and it only took fifteen minutes to drive across the bridge to Juarez from the mint new apartment she found for me on our second day in town. Before she left she had me settled in with good second-hand furniture and the promise that she would visit me in El Paso on her way back to California in July.

After our last morning together and I had watched her plane fly over the horizon, I journaled, "it will be so much harder for me to succeed without her to give meaning to my days." The next day I was paralyzed with deep anxiety and depression. I didn't eat. No appetite. I couldn't think. I could only sit mindlessly with tears dribbling down my face as expressions of an emotion of revolting self-pity. Perhaps Stan was right. Maybe I was "stark, raving mad" to purposefully abandon my inner-self in this dark existential cave of unforeseeable challenges and lonely isolation. I felt so utterly alone.

And it was all the worse, because at that point there was no turning back, in spite of devastating news. On March 13, 1984, I came across a headline from the San Francisco Chronicle that hit me right between the eyes: "State Toughens Foreign Medical School Policy." What followed in the first paragraph read, "The state watchdog agency that licenses California physicians adopted new regulations yesterday designed to require students in foreign medical schools to undergo their practical training only in hospitals approved by California Authorities." It continued,

> Investigations by medical authorities in 15 states have
> uncovered hundreds of cases – 300 in California alone
> – where graduates of some schools abroad have obtained

falsified diplomas, or have been certified by their schools without practical training in hospitals.

What had I gotten myself into?

Chapter Eleven

Students in a Medical No Man's Land

Welcoming Formalities

I guess I read every book of memoires ever written about the experience of being a student in medical school before I enrolled myself. One in particular described the first day of classes. All of the new students gathered in an auditorium for a ceremonial ritual. The Dean at a podium on stage formally welcomed them. They were warned that it would be difficult. They were told what their schedules and activities would be in the coming weeks. They were urged to keep their eyes on the stars as they struggled to achieve a noble purpose.

My first day in Juarez Medical School proceeded rather differently. At first nothing at all happened. Because of strict warnings over the phone that we must be there on Friday, the first of June, I arrived two hours early for the opening meeting, only to learn that it was postponed until the following Monday. That false start gave me a chance to meet two graduating students, however.

The two I encountered were in town to pick up their transcripts and degrees. They had spent the previous year in the United States doing clinical clerkships (rotations), just as Cam Ainsworth had done a few years earlier. The dominant one told me he did all of his at University of California affiliated teaching hospitals. They had been successful. Now he was back to take professional examinations administered by the Mexican authorities and soon would be off, M.D. degree in hand, to start his internship year as a PGY-1 (Post-Graduate Year One) at a teaching hospital in the United States and eventually on to a medical specialty, in his case, probably internal medicine.

It was very comforting to be told that you really could get through the program in two years. After the weekend I met members of my own class when I walked into the room assigned for our initial meeting. Some students seemed already acquainted with one another. Most, like me, were subdued and somewhat withdrawn. We took our seats, and waited. We waited some more. Some wondered if we were in the wrong room. We chatted quietly with whoever was nearest, sharing banalities.

After more than an hour I noticed that a few students were conversing intensely with someone just outside the door. Gradually I realized that a man was materializing towards the front. We were meeting our first instructor. Without formalities, he simply lectured for an hour on anatomy and left, to return for an hour each morning for the rest of the week. He was supposed to teach for two hours, but at least he showed up each day for one. No one else met with us that week, no other instructor and no one from the administration. During the second week, a couple of other faculty members materialized to convene classes, also without formalities.

A full month and a half later – yes, six weeks after classes began - Dr. Gomez, the Dean responsible for our advanced placement program, visited our classroom for the first time, unannounced. A few of us were in our places. It was noon and hot. We were supposed to be in class, but nobody expected the instructor to arrive and most had taken off to get some lunch, or had slipped away for the rest of the day. Suddenly, strangers in clinic jackets pushed the door open and entered. Among them was the Dean, his white nylon jacket bulging a half-empty pack of cigarettes and playing peek-a-boo with his bare hirsute chest. He beach-headed on the speaker's platform to command our attention. We were in trouble. Where were the others? Attendance was mandatory. A lunch break was not scheduled. Were we serious students?

Runners slipped out to find whom they could. Eventually half of the class was back in the room. The Dean began. He took it for granted that we knew who he was. We did, even without having seen him before. He spoke to none of us individually. He needed to talk about problems in administering the program, so he had come, after weeks of false announcements that he would show up to answer questions. "I wish I could have welcomed you earlier," he muttered without conviction. "But we have a lot of work to do. There wasn't time. I was on vacation. Now I am here, but I can only stay briefly." It was clear that on an individual and collective basis we were nobodies. And that was it, which was as close to a formal welcome as we got.

Basic Science Teachers

The seventeen basic science courses for our program were condensations of regular courses taught in the medical school. We were admitted on the basis of having already completed a substantial number of the science courses normally offered during the first two years of an American medical school. The underlying justification for an MD-to-PhD program was that we were already highly qualified as scientists and should be able to acquire additional skills rapidly.

The twelve instructors who taught courses for us, mostly in the summer, some in the fall and spring, were all physicians, with one exception. Only the non-physician biochemist (with a master's degree) was trained as a scientist. Not one instructor engaged in research.

Fewer than one-third of the courses (five of the seventeen) were taught by individuals who specialized in the subjects they taught (biochemistry, histology, psychiatry, public health, and biostatistics). But in reality, most of our instructors did very little teaching, so their expertise proved far less relevant than that of members of our class who lectured informally based on their professional backgrounds as scientists.

Individual classmates were well qualified in about half of the required science courses. Most were professional research scientists. Someone in our class had taken at least one course in every required subject. A few had actually taught a number of the required courses in American universities. For teaching ourselves, we were strongest in biochemistry, anatomy, dissection, pharmacology, physiology, microbiology, and statistics. We were weakest in nutrition, genetics, pathology, psychiatry, and public health. But weak, strong, or adequate, core members of the class routinely lectured on topics that were poorly taught by members of the faculty, which was most topics.

Clinical Science Teachers

The quality of our eight clinical courses ranged from excellent through satisfactory, with a couple that were terrible and one that was a travesty.

To start with excellent, our course on surgical methods was offered by two experienced general surgeons assisted by three teaching assistants. Four hours each morning, six days a week for a month we were skillfully trained in basic surgical techniques. We learned preoperative evaluation and patient preparation, including how to rank patients in terms of risk and how to strengthen their resistance to a maximum. Then, in a throwback to Boy Scout days, we practiced tying surgical knots, with the difference that we had to do them equally well with either hand and even at the bottom of a Styrofoam cup. In one of the surgical suites we were put through mock surgeries to practice sterile procedures and gain familiarity with instrumentation.

Finally, we were ready for the dog lab. I was not happy to exploit those animals. When my mentor Cam Ainsworth was a student they worked on sad looking old greyhounds from the nearby racetrack, but that had changed. We were required to bring in dogs ourselves, and we managed to do it as humanely as possible. One of our veterinarians and I showed up at the municipal pound early enough in the morning to rescue a couple of dogs from scheduled euthanasia. We treated them kindly, messed up my car transporting them to a local veterinarian to be housed and shaved for surgery, incised them only under anesthesia, and sent them to their inevitable deaths without pain. We learned the basics of surgery in dog lab in a way that mock procedures cannot equal, but I obviously had misgivings.

Our final exam was comprehensive over two days. We had to demonstrate suturing skills and an ability to intubate a patient using a rubber mannequin. The final exam on how to manage surgical patients was demanding. That useful course was followed by two more on surgical diagnosis, thirty-five hours on general surgery followed by another thirty-five on orthopedic surgery.

Shifting from excellent to merely satisfactory, the anesthesiologist who taught seventeen hours of his specialty was friendly and supportive, but course content was thin and not very challenging. The first hour summarized the history of anesthesiology, beginning with God as the first anesthetist (because He put Adam to sleep when He removed a rib to fashion Eve), which was good for a laugh. His slide illustrated lecture was adequate, but not so fascinating that I wanted to go through it twice. However, since only half a dozen of us showed up for the first meeting he chose to repeat the whole lecture on our second meeting.

At the failure end, dermatology was taught by the dermatologist who was to become our bete noir. He seemed to be available to teach any course that was needed, and he always did a rotten job. We burned out on him early when he gave us anatomy, neuroscience and physical diagnosis, but we felt he might have one good course to give, since he was asked to teach his specialty. Some of the students had visited him in his private office, where he limited his practice to diseases of the skin. Surely he would do a decent job in that area.

How wrong we were! He showed up the first day with a tray of slides picturing patients who had come to him over the years. He brought that same tray every day for the whole course. It appeared from those slides that he mostly saw cases of teenage acne. In all events, he told us that acne was what we mostly would see in general practice, so, day after day we looked at front and side views of pimply-faced teenagers.

He got mean. It became increasingly apparent that we found him trite. He was wasting our time. He taught by asking questions in puerile imitation of the Socratic method. We hated his questions, since no matter how we answered we were wrong. Unless, that is, it was the one student he seemed to favor. That student was never wrong. We got sick of it, and that was his best course!

It was ironic that my coursework on techniques of clinical practice in chiropractic college was superior to what we were taught in medical school by the dermatologist. My chiropractic instructors lacked experience, but they were thorough and adequate. In each school the same textbook was assigned: *Bates' Guide to Physical Examination and History Taking*, revised by Lynn Bickley.

Apparently to conceal his failure as a teacher, when we took the final exam the dermatologist told us our grades would not be turned into the Dean's office until later in the year. In that way, if a student did well in clinical rotations he would be assigned a good grade, but if a student did poorly, turning in a very low grade would mean it could blamed on the student and not on his teacher, the dermatologist.

But I want to end on a high note. Perhaps the best clinical course we had was on endocrinology. The instructor, after earning his medical degree in Mexico, did his residency at Columbia University in the United States He was intellectually as sound as a dollar and came to us out of years of daily experience as a specialist.

He lectured from slides prepared for his regular medical school course and was up to the minute in terms of current literature. He explained well, answered questions thoroughly (in English) and was respected for balancing a supportive classroom manner with ferociousness on the exam. We heard through the grapevine that seven student flunked his final the preceding year. Some had to repeat his makeup exam on a monthly basis before they finally met his high standards.

Fellow Students

Our class consisted of twenty-four expatriate students, ten men from developing nations (Nigeria, India, Turkey) and the rest, American born white men and one woman. All of us looked very good on paper. We were all trained and experienced at the doctoral level. We had been admitted because we were high achievers, and eventually it became clear that eighteen of us really were. One of the most remarkable was Jim Bateson.

Jim was in the program because he had a Ph.D. in anatomy. What a break, since we were scheduled for an anatomy course and the dissection of a cadaver that is part of every medical student's first year ritual.

I liked working with Jim. When I asked him where he had been employed he answered obliquely that he didn't work as an anatomist. He was in business. I assumed he was one of many well-trained Ph.D.'s in the United States who hadn't been able to find employment in teaching or research. It was a full week before I discovered who he really was.

Jim did have a Ph.D. in anatomy, but he earned his living as a physician and surgeon in a large city in Oklahoma. That was his "business," and there was nothing phony about it. He had been working as a practicing doctor for thirteen years. In order to be free for two years in the Mexican program he placed his thriving practice in the hands of an M.D. who had just finished a residency in internal medicine.

Unlike most of us who rarely left town, Jim flew north every Thursday evening because he was also a commander in the medical corps of the United States Navy. As the medical officer in command of health facilities at certain naval installations he had to be on duty on some weekends. He was hoping to earn a fourth gold stripe for his epaulette. Between looking in on his practice, serving in uniform as a reserve medical officer, and keeping up with the rest of us in medical school, Jim was a driven man. But why was he going through medical training for a second time? What impelled him to make such personal and financial sacrifices in order to struggle along with us? Did it make any sense?

He had a ready answer. He was an osteopathic physician (D.O.). He could be licensed in any of the fifty states with all of the practice rights of an M.D., including eligibility for a commission in the medical corps. He could not, however, practice medicine abroad where the D.O. only qualified in a limited way, like a chiropractor, for spinal manipulation. He and his wife wanted to serve as medical missionaries for a year or two in South America, so he was with us to learn to speak Spanish and to earn an M.D. degree that would qualify him to practice somewhere in the Southern Hemisphere. His explanation was patently false and unbelievable. He was no saint. Why the deception?

Jim and I hit it off well outside of the classroom. Like me, he was older than the others and he liked to have a smoke and a beer or two while I swam in the pool that was part of our apartment complex. We found occasions to chat in the late afternoon while I let the sun dry me off. Over time, the real reason for being with us came out with strong certainty. He wanted to be an M.D. because no matter how successful he was as a physician, he could never be sure in either his social or professional life that the next person he encountered would not say or imply that as a D.O. he was not really a doctor.

First encounters with strangers frequently came off badly, Jim told me. "What do you do?" I'm a doctor. "What kind of a doctor?" I'm a physician. "What kind?" An internist. "Oh," with obvious respect and interest, "so you're an M.D.!" No, I'm a D.O.

At that point, nine times out of ten, their high appreciation of his status would tumble. All of the subtleties of verbal cues and body language would communicate that his claim to be a physician was pretentious. It should be noted that Jim graduated from osteopathic medical school shortly after 1966. Most people for decades to follow either knew nothing about osteopaths or still thought of them as more or less like chiropractors, whose work resembled that of physical therapists. All three were valued clinicians, to be sure, but not truly qualified as "doctors" or "physicians."

As late as 1984 when members of my class applied, the Juarez program still discriminated against osteopathic physicians, chiropractors, and podiatrists. None were eligible to apply. Jim gained entrance because he had a Ph.D., as did I.

A very hard man to stop once he set a goal for himself, he enrolled in anatomy courses at the university after medical schools turned him down. As one year merged into the next, he moved up the ladder in the graduate program in anatomy until he finally qualified for his doctorate. Medical schools continued to turn him away. Without knowing much about osteopathy, he gained admission to an osteopathic school just as their role in medicine and surgery was finally legitimated for all fifty states. It was a second choice for a man who didn't think of himself as second class. He did well, though, except in spinal manipulation classes, which didn't interest him in the slightest. He and a dozen others like him learned just enough manipulative therapy to get by, and joked among themselves about what they thought of as an obsolete survival from a more primitive time.

As I think back on my fellow students, Jim is a good one to begin with. In his case it was unequivocally clear how important personal identity and social status could be for medical school aspirants. Every one of us demonstrated a need to validate status and identity by enrolling in the Juarez program. For most of us there were other reasons as well. For Jim it was the only reason.

Hugh Thompson, D.V.M. can be taken to represent seven members of my class who were licensed in fields on the edges of medicine: four veterinarians, one podiatrist, a clinical psychologist, and a chiropractor (although nobody in the class knew that). Except for myself, they gave clinical and/or financial ambitions as reasons for detouring into medical school. The explanation that Hugh gave was a real and true one that shaped his determination to borrow from two brothers and move with his wife and two infants to Mexico. The practice of veterinarian medicine was not as fulfilling as he had expected.

Although his private practice in Tennessee was successful, he felt he worked much harder than his brother who was an M.D. Yet he earned only a fraction as much. Where he lived people were not willing to spend large sums of money on medical or surgical care for pets, he told me. Further disillusionment grew out of the limited scope of his day-to-day practice. He had mastered complex procedures as a student. As a practitioner he learned that people rarely brought pets in for challenging surgery or difficult medical care. He spayed a lot of dogs and cats, removed skin tumors, sewed up lacerations, and gave rabies shots. He medicated for worms or skin disorders. It was limited and repetitive.

Hugh tried to break out. He returned to the university to qualify as a board certified specialist in veterinarian internal medicine. As a specialist he faced the harsh reality that veterinarians only rarely referred patients, preferring to treat every case on their own. He still found himself mainly treating worms and common skin conditions. He wanted more.

For four years before coming to Mexico, Hugh pursued still another way to make his professional life more satisfying. He joined the staff of a medical school as the veterinarian in charge of laboratory animals. He worked on the fringes of research and practice. The work was not demanding. The pay was modest by medical standards. He was still not challenged, but faced more directly than in private practice the way he felt about being a clinician who was not an M.D.

Hugh was not personally conscious of status needs until I explored his feelings with him. His conscious decision was his need for greater challenges in patient care and his desire to earn a better income. With probing it came out that even for this gentle, modest man it hurt to be something other than an M.D. in a medical environment. Thus it was for eight members of our class who were clinicians.

Ten other members of the class, all with Ph.D.'s in the medical sciences, were there for reasons essentially similar to Hugh's. They worked in medicine, but wanted fuller involvement with better pay and higher status.

The remaining six members of the class, also with Ph.D.'s and all from developing nations, were with us because they wanted to qualify as medical doctors in the United States. They were frequently absent and participated only minimally in class activities. I will have more to say about them later.

On Communitas and Classroom Survival

Because our needs as advanced placement students were unique, all of our courses were set apart from the normal school curriculum. They were planned as a highly condensed three-month overview of the standard two years of medical science studies. Time was short, so we were scheduled for an intensive summer of 7 a.m. to 5 p.m. classes five days a week, to culminate in comprehensive examinations at the end of July. We were told that subsequently we would be assigned to a series of fall and spring courses, but most of the academic year would be dedicated to clinical clerkships in the municipal hospital. The second year would be accomplished entirely in teaching hospitals accredited to medical schools in the United States.

We had our own classroom in a small building in the heart of Ciudad Juarez. It wasn't bad. Our class of twenty-four was small enough to be easily accommodated in rows of two-person tables with padded swivel desk chairs, thank goodness. When Edna and I peeked in the window in January it looked as though we would be sitting on the kind of slippery plastic chairs that were such a torment in chiropractic college. (After the first four weeks, all of our classes were moved to the main campus, where we did sit on plastic bucket-seat chairs, and it was torment all over again.)

That inner-city classroom served as our "home room," with a refrigerator in one corner and a washroom in the other. No other students used it. The medical school proper was located on the university campus at the edge of town where some of our afternoon classes convened even during the first part of the summer.

In order to be able to demonstrate to American authorities that the total number of class hours added up to the required number, our classes followed one after the other with no time set aside for lunch or to drive between the two parts of town. That turned out to be no more than a minor frustration. Real as opposed to official class periods - in anthropological jargon, the "real" versus the "ideal" - were capricious, with daily late starts, frequent early dismissals, and numerous no-shows. Capricious also meant that we got into trouble on some days for stopping to grab a bite to eat while speeding between our little campus and the main one.

Capricious timing was evident that very first day, when our Friday convocation was rescheduled to Monday. On Monday it was capricious again that we spent our first hours as a class by ourselves, waiting for something to happen. It was capricious that Dr. Chavez was our first instructor instead of Dr. Piña as announced. It was capricious that our first class consistently started late and dismissed early.

None of us was very surprised at those fickle flip-flops. We had all had been briefed by one or another of earlier foreign students we had talked with, including those who were in town just then to take care of formalities and pick up diplomas after their year in American teaching hospitals.

Communitas in Our Central City Homeroom

Except for Spanish, from which I was excused, our only courses until Tuesday of the second week were two classes a day with the dermatologist who was an incompetent teacher. That introduced us to the program, so let it serve here as an introduction to the whole program as well.

The announced ("ideal") topics were anatomy and diagnosis. The first lecture ("real") was atrocious. In a blend of Spanish and English the dermatologist announced his topic as "orientations," which turned out to mean bilateral symmetry. It was delivered in a meandering, unclear way on such an elementary level that grade school pupils would have understood it if taught properly. Perhaps, as a specialist in diseases of the skin, anatomy and general diagnosis were inappropriate subjects for him to teach. Be that as it may, from that hour alone one thing was clear to us as a class. His courses were going to be a total waste of time. We would have to teach ourselves anatomy and how to conduct a physical examination.

That impression was further confirmed the next day, when the dermatologist used a defective out-of-focus opaque projector to show a handwritten set of notes that we could not clearly see, much less decipher. Continuing the previous day's lecture on gross anatomy, he again demonstrated that his teaching was going to be very incomplete, totally unsystematic, quite elementary, and largely unintelligible, especially since by this second day he gave up on English and lectured entirely in Spanish. He brought his daughter to translate, but she never said a word. She should have been able to do a good job. She was a second year medical student at a university in Texas, home on summer vacation.

She offered no help when he lectured on arteries of the abdomen. He had the right gastric coming directly out of the celiac trunk, along with the right gastric-epiploic, completely leaving out the intervening hepatic and gastro-duodenal arteries. As noted in my journal that evening, "Oh well, those of us who understood also know the correct anatomy. We do study hard."

After our first class it became clear that I was the only student in the room who understood everything he said that was intelligible, and only two or three got bits and parts of it. Most of our class had no background in anatomy, diagnosis, or Spanish and felt very threatened by what they did not know.

On Monday of week two, when the full 7-to-5 teaching schedule was supposed to begin, we sat for anatomy and Spanish in the morning, but otherwise were stood up for every class but one in what was supposed to be a crowded day of intense teaching. It was not an enormous surprise. We all brought books to study. But it was a bit tough to hang around so much. We decided to start bringing sandwiches so we could eat in the classroom. Even though instructors might not show up, we had to be there in case they did.

The one who did show up in the afternoon was Dr. Montes, an orthopedic surgeon. Young, handsome, and clearly very knowledgeable, he was extremely stern. He started his course on dissection with questions that were so threatening and done in such a put-down manner that we were all shaking in our boots; and remember, we were seasoned veterans who had survived doctoral programs in the past.

Montes taught in excellent English, but the problem was, he wanted answers we couldn't reasonably be expected to provide. He asked one victim to draw the brachial plexus on the board. That student had not yet been taught any anatomy at all, so Montes succeeded, I guess, in what may have been his purpose: to let us know that he was not intimidated by a professional adult with a Ph.D. Later he put another student down for identifying anconeus as an extensor muscle of the upper arm, which is what Chavez seemed to have taught that morning. It does have its origin in the upper arm, but Montes correctly emphasized that it is an extensor because it has its insertion at the back of the lower arm, which it serves to straighten. Next, another member of the class was put down for speaking of extension and flexion of the arm, as I just wrote. Only joints move, Montes announced scornfully. That bit of pedantry was completely uncalled for, of course, but we clearly got the message. Whatever he said was to be repeated back as God's truth. The surgeon as God or prima donna is not an uncommon stereotype in American medicine.

The next day was not much different. Each hour I bet a penny with Wally that the next instructor would not show up. I won 4 cents. I would have won more, except that Dr. Tobias, a pathologist, walked in to teach histology. Unlike Chavez, he wanted a translator. Our entomologist Ph.D. volunteered to provide a running translation, but soon floundered. He actually did very well, since he had only studied Spanish for a year. I took over and surprised the class because I had no trouble translating rapidly and accurately. They felt a heavy burden melt away, and from that moment on we fell into a routine in which I always sat at the front left corner of the room where I could turn easily from facing the instructor and blackboard to translate over my shoulder to fellow students.

In order to translate that way I needed to know the subject, in that case, histology. The following morning before driving across the bridge I reviewed staining techniques over cups of coffee at McDonald's, knowing Tobias planned to review them. As a result, my running translation was flawless. I would have faltered on stains had I not prepared in advance. So that established my summer study routine for courses taught in Spanish, which was all but one. It was my contribution to communitas.

Before the second week was over communitas became systematically organized as we got our own teaching program in gear. In fact, Tobias told us he would only come when he could and we should teach ourselves. (Eventually, all of our instructors told us that.) Tobias assigned topics for each of us to teach (others left assignments entirely up to us). We didn't mind, because we were also told we could write the questions for him to choose from for our final exam.

When my turn came to teach the class I covered the material in just twenty minutes, but we agreed I should continue since we wanted to seem busy in case Tobias looked in on us. So I started responding to questions and ended up spontaneously explaining Charcot's joints, tabes dorsalis, syringomyelia, and spina bifida. My classmates were rather surprised that I could lecture spontaneously on these topics. No one knew I had graduated from chiropractic college.

A couple of weeks into our course on diagnosis, the dermatologist asked one of his patients to come to our class to provide us with our first experience in doing a history and physical. He told us we would be asked to work the patient up as a collaborative endeavor. The patient arrived on time. Chavez was half-an-hour late, so while waiting, Hugh Thompson and I agreed to start the diagnostic process, which always begins with questioning the patient about his experience of symptoms before moving on to the physical examination. (As a veterinarian, Hugh would have done that with the pet's owner.)

I had a terrible time taking the case history, and small wonder, because the patient was handicapped with a severe speech impediment. He finally managed to communicate that everybody found it hard to understand him. So I missed one key component of his medical history, as I shall explain. Turning to the physical exam, I began by checking his cranial nerves and found that part of his right mandible was missing with evidence of surgery on that side of his neck. I found some impairment of Cranial VI on the right and an area of reduced sensation in the jaw. When Chavez finally showed up we learned that what I had missed in taking the history was that the patient's face had been partly chewed off by a large vicious dog.

Continuing the physical examination, Hugh and I proceeded to partially disrobe him and we learned other things, such as evidence of an old surgery for internal hydrocephalus to relieve intracranial hypertension and severe headaches, also missing from the history. In reviewing our findings I drew attention to findings additional to hydrocephalus that added up to a diagnostic pattern: the patient's skin was covered with café-au-lait spots, we identified cerebellar symptoms visible on checking his gait, he demonstrated visible atrophy around the shoulders, and overall reminded me so much of a case described in De Groot & Chusids' *Correlative Neuroanatomy* that I felt confident in offering as my diagnostic opinion that he suffered from neurofibromatosis of von Recklinghausen, which is not a presentation obvious to a veterinarian (since they deal with fur and feathers) but would have been well-known to a dermatologist such as our instructor, since dramatic skin lesions constitute the most obvious feature.

Well, I was right, which made me very happy and totally surprised Chavez, as well he should have been, because the disease is rarely seen even by dermatologists. Frankly, as the first workup for our class, the patient chosen was a teaching blunder. We would have been challenged enough to elicit the medical history from a Spanish-speaking patient with an uncomplicated disease who enunciated clearly. And we were too early in our training to profit from throwing in a red herring that had nothing to do with the chief complaint, a face partially bitten off by a dog.

But we had more to learn from that patient when he was returned to class the following day because there was a second red herring. The dermatologist demonstrated that the massive asymmetry of his face was not simply the result of being mauled by a dog but was even more a product of Romberg's Disease (congenital agenesis of the face), which includes respiratory and GI problems. I totally missed that and it taught an important lesson. You must always keep in mind that a patient may present with more than one significant medical condition.

That patient constituted the beginning and the end of learning diagnostic procedures from patients in the mode of William Osler. The diagnosis course deteriorated into straight didactic lectures with no patients to examine and no opportunities to practice on each other with our doctor's black bags of diagnostic instruments. We just sat and listened. It was nearly useless.

In contrast, we taught ourselves at a rather sophisticated level. While waiting for the dermatologist one morning, one of the veterinarians asked if I would review how to examine the head. I soon had the whole class in attendance as I went over the testing of the cranial nerves, clarifying some things left unclear by our instructor and going on to others he had not mentioned. That included demonstrating how to perform a fundascopic examination and how to test for fields of vision. Don, a Ph.D., asked if anything being taught was new to me, and I said no, it's all review. (Hey, I completed medical school in a chiropractic college.) It amused me to speculate on what the American authorities would have thought had they known that diagnosis in the Juarez program was partially taught by a chiropractor!

But I digress. As concerns communitas, my most distinctive contribution was to serve as translator, and that needs to be put into perspective. We were a class of highly trained and well-skilled individuals. Others contributed far more than I to the success of fellow students, especially in teaching from their own expertise as scientists.

For example, pharmacology was not taught, inexplicably replicating a deficiency of my chiropractic education, but we did quite well by working it into the pathology course on our own initiative. One of the veterinarians, the podiatrist, a biochemist and the osteopathic physician shared in teaching a first-rate course (as did a university instructor in the fall when, in response to our complaint, a formal course was added to the curriculum). The ability of fellow students to provide excellent teaching was also evident in the first class we took on the main campus.

Communitas on the Main Campus

During our first week on a full schedule the temperature hit 100° F. Fortunately, our classrooms at the medical school as well as at the PhD-to-MD teaching center were air-conditioned. Unfortunately, that was not true of the dissection laboratory, but it could have been worse. The cadaver was preserved with very little formalin, so it was just barely embalmed. The smell was not as overwhelming as I had experienced in other places and we did not find ourselves coping with tissues exuding toxic chemicals.

Eight of us walked into the dissection amphitheater where we were scheduled to work as two separate teams of four each, one on each side of the cadaver. The door opened to reveal a dead man on a gurney, naked, his penis facing the open hallway door, clearly visible to anyone who happened to walk by. Needless to say, we received no introductory admonition to show respect for the dead. But that was a quarter of a century ago when such sensitivities were still somewhat new in the States and around the world.

Because the whole class had to get their experience from a single dead body, our turn arrived only every fourth day for two hours at a time. Those sessions were exhausting. Dissection by its nature is slow, hard work. Even with six teams sharing responsibility the process seemed to take forever.

The actual teacher was Dr. Pedro Guerrero, a resident in surgery and a very nice man. He reviewed us every time on whatever we were doing. Dr. Montez, a very busy orthopedic surgeon, only dropped in once or twice throughout the whole course to give us twenty-minute oral quizzes and then depart. He was not pleased with class answers to his questions, so we were worried sick about the eventual written exam, and not without reason as we eventually learned.

On the first day for my team, Montes started us off by having us open the upper arm as far as the team of the previous day had dissected before they sutured it back together for the night. (For the record, in my dissection courses at U.C. Berkeley and Life-West we covered exposed areas with wet cloths between lab sessions, so it struck me as an unexpected cultural variation to sew instead.) We were then quizzed on exposed tissues in the dissection that we had never seen before. (I'll say this for Montes, he was consistent in his quizzical ways.)

We were then told to continue the dissection well into the brachial plexus. To cut that far was more than could reasonably be expected of neophytes for a single two-hour session, but we got it done in exactly two hours. Our team was destined to be a winner. My teammates included Gordon Graham, the entomologist who had taught human dissection courses himself at his university. The other two were experienced surgeons, accustomed to doing veterinarian surgery on a daily basis. Two fourth year students from the regular medical school were assigned to supervise and help, and they were very supportive.

In spite of all, the other teams also succeeded quite well in my view. Our class had recruited two other veterinarians, a podiatric surgeon, and even a general surgeon with a private practice in Oklahoma (the Doctor of Osteopathy). Moreover, as a class we were supportive of one another.

During uncommitted hours in our homeroom the six teams willingly reviewed and clarified what we all needed to learn from dissecting the naked man on his gurney. Communitas rather than competition shaped our class ethos for those who were faithful in attendance. Half a dozen students almost never showed up.

To have a chiropractor doing some of the explanations in our program would surely have disgusted the American authorities, and perhaps some of them would have been quite disgruntled had they known that our osteopathic colleague presented what we found to be an excellent series of lectures on pharmacology and patient management.

On Monday, June 25, we had our first exam in anatomy from the dermatologist. It was very difficult. In contrast to his lectures, which capriciously skipped, hopped, and jumped, Chavez's exam questions required an incredible memory for the details of what we had studied in the textbook.

That afternoon after the exam, Hugh Thompson and his sophisticated wife invited the whole class to their home to celebrate getting through the first exam. They lived not far from where we had our classes in a very comfortable townhouse with a maid. It was a high point in communitas, a first and last carryover from our days in previous more traditional doctoral programs in academic disciplines.

The Comprehensive Exam in Medical Sciences

The basic sciences part of the program was largely completed by the end of that first summer. It culminated in a day of comprehensive examinations in which we were given separate examinations for ten different subjects. In truth, for a dozen of us, the whole ten only took about two hours instead of a whole day. Strong members of the class sailed through those exams because the questions were all taken from a list of approximately two-thousand practice questions in the study modules we had acquired at the beginning of the summer. About half of our class had the whole two-thousand memorized, so it was the most non-stressful set of exams some of us had ever encountered.

But it was highly stressful for some of the others, which brings us to a catch-22 and to the incompleteness of communitas.

Chapter Twelve

Corruption and Conflict

Medical Ethics

To prepare ourselves for certification in the United States we taught each other, we taught ourselves from books, and we spent endless hours on study modules distributed by the Educational Commission for Foreign Medical Graduates (ECFMG). I studied for an hour and a quarter every morning at McDonald's before crossing the bridge. I found it hard to study at the medical school sitting in an uncomfortable plastic seat, but like everyone else I opened my books and modules whenever we had free time. I was worn out when I got home at the end of a typical day. A vigorous swim revived me and kept me healthy. Even so, it required self-discipline to hit the books for a couple of hours after dinner. Eighteen of my fellow students were equally self-disciplined. We were the good guys.

Curiously, six members of our class did not share our work ethic and were frequently absent. We wondered how they could expect to graduate if they were not as committed as the rest of us. They were to become our introduction to corruption and discord. They were the bad guys.

A short fifteen-hour course taught by our nemesis, the dermatologist, was supposed to introduce us to the history of medicine and ethics. Since the course emphasized Mexican history, most of those hours dragged on about pre-Columbian history that had nothing to do with modern medicine. As his sole source he relied on a simplistic brochure, *Medicina Indigena* (*Numero* 4, 1978) handed out by the Searle Pharmaceutical Company of Mexico. The cartoon illustrations got passed around to orient us. A few odds and ends of European history found their way into the last days.

Accuracy was not his strong point. He told us that Hippocrates prescribed quinine for malaria, which would place it about two thousand years before European physicians first learned that Indians in Peru treated the disease with bark from the cinchona tree. He liked simplicity, as when he summarized the complexity of nineteenth century medicine with the pronouncement that only two kinds of doctors practiced in that century, homeopaths and allopaths. We were beyond disputing him. Jim, the osteopathic physician, didn't say a word about osteopathy in that century.

In Mexico, as is the case in many parts of the world, the dermatologist as a young man advanced directly from high school to five years of medicine. Unlike American physicians, who complete four years of university before enrolling in medical school, he had never taken a course in sociology, history, philosophy or any other liberal arts subject. So it is, perhaps, understandable that he had no sensitivity at all for evaluating scholarly sources or organizing a perspective on complex historical materials.

Toward the end of the course he instructed us in medical ethics. Nothing about the enormous body of thought and concern for this philosophical problem reached us through him. We were given no opportunity to discuss the complex issues involved. We simply listened as he read aloud from that ancient Greek document, the Hippocratic Oath.

Without comment, we memorized it. We learned that as physicians we should not do surgery for bladder stones. We were to promise not to have sex with patients of our own gender or of the other. We were to swear we would not perform abortions. The oath asked us to pass the craft on to our sons and the sons of our teachers. We were even to share our income with our instructors, ensuring their well-being if they were in need. I never realized before how many archaic concepts the Oath included along with the sound admonition that we should practice for the benefit of our patients.

Above all, we learned that the Hippocratic Oath enjoined us to practice in purity and holiness. Just how pure and holy we were to experience immediately. As was his custom, the dermatologist crucified us on the examination. Characteristically we had no way of knowing how he arrived at the grades he assigned. He wrote no comments or corrections. He simply penciled in a number.

The last time he decimated our class, each person in trouble went individually to his office, paid a "re-examination fee" directly to him and took an "oral exam," which seemed to consist mainly of him telling them what their new grade was. It was very irritating because laggards in the class ended up with grades in the nineties, much higher than the eighteen of us who were diligent students.

This time, however, one of the good guys who was from a Third World Nation and had learned how to handle negotiations of this sort in his homeland collected five dollars from each failed student to present as a class "gift." Meeting discretely in the doctor's private clinic, he handed over the money together with the names of the contributors. We were told that the instructor counted the money in a matter-of-fact way and took the list of names. Our "bag man" negotiated the revised grades. The dermatologist thought five dollars was only worth a seventy-five. Skillful bargaining got a ninety. It was not wasted on any of us that in the course to instruct us on the purity and holiness of medical ethics, the teacher operated a "pay for grade" scheme.

The problem in attempting to function within the informal system was that it was not well understood by Americans, especially not by Will Benson (Ph.D. in biochemistry). He almost became a class outcast as a result. Will was a born-again Baptist who under no circumstances would do anything dishonest or deceptive. He also believed in the inherent goodness of all people, even deans and professors. He paid the fees and assessments to be admitted along with the rest of us. The purchase of study materials, the assessment fee for language instruction, and a late filing fee were costly, even exploitative, but could be considered legitimate. However, when it came time for those who flunked anatomy to settle with the dermatologist in his office, only Will did not assume he would have to pay for his passing grade.

It is relevant in this regard to recall a conversation with a student of a couple of years earlier who dropped by to visit later in our school year. He told us that the dermatologist never demanded bribes while he was a student. My mentor, Cam Ainsworth, said the same. As far as they knew, no one had ever given him a peso. But we didn't know that at the time.

Will, dedicated to living as a Bible-believing Christian, was willing to flunk out rather than pay a bribe. Most of the others in the class thought he was dim-witted to assume he could get through our program with that kind of inflexible attitude. He became a social isolate. Even though he had a Ph.D. and was obviously highly skilled in biochemistry, many thought he was not bright enough to understand that the morality of the United States wouldn't work in Mexico. Personally, I never thought of him as dim-witted and often enjoyed his company on walks to stretch our legs. I did think he was culturally naïve. To pay five dollars as a "re-examination" fee seemed to me at the time to show acculturative sophistication. I advised him to pay, but he was stubborn. It shows how wrong I could be.

Things moved slowly. One by one, students made their way across town to confer with the instructor. Silently they handed over five or ten dollars. They answered an easy question or two and saw their grade elevated. Five or ten dollars is not much if it puts you within reach of an M.D. degree.

A couple of weeks drifted by and Will finally took his turn in the dermatologist's office. He discussed his grade, but offered no money. The instructor discussed his grade, hemmed and hawed a bit, but never mentioned a payment. In the end, Will got a passing grade. He refused to consider it anything other than a customary conference of a professor and a student. The instructor may not have utilized an objective system for assigning grades, which is a pedagogical failing. He was obviously willing to accept money from willing contributors, which is scarcely admirable. However, he did not actually insist that failing student pay for a passing grade.

Through the class grape vine we all knew within hours of the outcome of what we thought was Will's folly. Surprisingly, the lesson wasn't learned. In subsequent months, the number of flunked exams increased with each course. For months, the academic losers pitched in to pay off their instructors. Their grades demonstrated a startling capacity to jump from an F to an A until the dermatologist tortured us with his deplorable course on pulmonary diseases By then, everyone was fed up with his abuse. No one made the trek to his office. No one took up a collection. No one got a decent grade, but no one failed to pass. And no one gave Will credit for figuring out the system before the rest of us.

It was possible, we now know, to succeed in our school on the basis of formal regulations. Unfortunately, we were never fully aware of that at the time. One of the most egregious failings of the university as concerned our special program was a complete inadequacy in maintaining open communication between the administration and us.

Formal and Informal Administrative Practices

Dr. Gomez, the Dean whom we met for the first time half way through the first summer, subsequently met with us as a class only four more times. It was not enough. The next in the chain of command supervised the academic schedule: which classes we would take and when. I didn't even know he existed until halfway through the first year. He met us for the first time in a joint meeting with the Dean just two weeks before the end of that year. He turned out to be a distinguished physician and a kind and responsive educator in the main program, but he had no time for us.

The third in command was the Assistant Dean. His office was located next to our classroom, which he passed every day at 10:30 or 11:00 a.m. when he went to work. Not once in the whole year did he drop in to see how we were doing. Not once did he meet with us to discuss changes in schedules, problems in course-work, mix-ups on clinical rotations, or the failure of instructors to meet classes as scheduled. He was not happy to have individuals from the class intrude into his quiet spells in the office. Communication and interaction scarcely existed.

Finally, at the bottom of the hierarchy two typist-clerks managed the office of the Assistant Dean. On instructions from their superiors, they made out daily schedules. They phoned potential instructors to arrange for classes. They told us of changes, usually by telling any student who happened to drop in. Since that student frequently failed to pass on the information, more often than not we learned of changes either by finding that we were not where we should be or that we had showed up where nothing was happening. It was small wonder that our rumor mill was very active. It was the only consistent supply line available for information.

In the final weeks of the year some of us began to understand that we could do something about those failures. We assumed that we would get into trouble if we complained. In actuality, when we did finally complain we found a willingness to correct deficiencies. By the end of the year our major problem was that instructors left us hour after hour sitting in our empty classroom. We never said a word. In silent collusion, we accommodated what we thought was the informal system. We failed to understand the workings of an informal system with which we were inexperienced. Our lone anthropologist – that's me – should have figured it out, but I was as culturally naïve as my classmates. Much of my fieldwork had been in Denmark.

The Delinquent Six

The absence of communication brought other consequences. We were subject to minimal discipline. Some instructors took the roll, but absences never seemed to keep anyone from getting class credits. Many instructors kept no attendance records. Examinations were often very easy to pass. Even in clinical rotations later on in the hospital, preceptors didn't seem to notice or care whether or not a student showed up.

For eighteen members of the class – the good guys – failure of discipline had only minor consequences. Those students were unusually mature, with high capabilities for self-motivation. For the six others – the bad guys – it encouraged sloth. They apparently were seduced by the informal system to completely neglect the study of medicine. Imagine! Medical students who did not study medicine. What did they do with their year?

We did not realize at first that the slothful six were lazy, because absenteeism and non-participation was assumed to be rational. It appeared to be a way to cope with a dilemma, a Catch-22. Medical school authorities expected us to involve ourselves fully in courses, examinations and rotations. Yet, to qualify for licensure in the United States we had to study in a totally different manner to prepare for American examinations, the "FemGems" (Foreign Medical Graduates Examination in Medical Sciences). Cam Ainsworth warned me when I applied that I would be caught in that double bind. He recommended what was done in his class. Cut classes part of the time to study for the FMGEMS, but attend enough to keep up with the university schedule. So, some doubled the university schedule by being enrolled simultaneously in the Stanley Kaplan course being taught across the Rio Grande River at the University of Texas in El Paso. Kaplan is a private business that coaches students for examinations in a number professional fields. To take advantage of the Kaplan course you needed to spend hours each day listening to tapes in their teaching center, so you had to cut medical school classes in order to study medicine. It was, indeed, a Catch-22. Even the best students maintained uneven attendance records as they tried to balance those conflicting demands.

I was fortunate, because for me medical school was largely a review and expansion of what I had recently been taught in chiropractic college. I studied hard, but I was not tempted to turn over more than a thousand dollars to Kaplan. My attendance record at the University was excellent, but not perfect, because even I flew back to California on several weekends to be with the woman I loved. That year of fieldwork (autoethnography) played hell with my family life.

Those like myself who usually attended class felt ill used. We maintained the integrity of the formal system of education. Because of frequent instructor absenteeism we spent hour after hour hanging around, but we put the time to good use by arranging our own teaching sessions or by studying. When instructors did appear, which was more often than not, we were there to establish the presence of a class. In retrospect, I feel that we learned a lot of medicine in the classroom, in spite of some classes that were a waste of time. Often, however, I would gladly have stayed away to study. We assumed that the absent six were away to study, but excessively so since they were almost always absent, leaving the rest of us to maintain the mandatory presence.

Cutting classes possessed an additional logic for the laggard six. They never learned to converse in Spanish, so they couldn't understand lectures unless I was there to translate. The FMGEMS were entirely in English. Although none of the six spoke English as their home language, all were fluent enough for examination purposes. We could understand their preference for Kaplan rather than for the *Instituto de Ciencias Biomédicas.*

Some instructors forced attendance by taking the roll. Then the six would appear at the back of the room where they read books almost defiantly. They resented pressure to learn Spanish, never acknowledging that they were enrolled in a Mexican program taught by Mexican doctors. They displayed their resentment most vividly during examinations, when they cheated flagrantly. We could see them consulting crib notes. They copied from neighbors. They even talked over their answers and became amazingly brazen as the weeks passed. When caught they smiled and lied. They always got away with it, a tribute to Mexican tolerance of foreign students who were not much liked and certainly not admired.

For most of the year I assumed that in spite of their deplorable methods they were simply being practical. They seemed to function successfully in the informal system and managed to get by in the formal program. I wrote off behavior that disgusted me as my problem, an attack of ethnocentrism. Others in the class were quicker to pass judgment. I, too, finally realized that cultural relativity in their case had stretched into an ethical dilemma. Everyone of them expected to end up practicing medicine. They all hoped to be licensed in the United States. Yet, we knew them to be completely incompetent.

They were not learning medicine. Worse, they never gave any reason to believe that they were even mildly curious about medicine. Both in class and on hospital rounds, their ignorance remained profound, even at the end of the year. Asked in class what a lump on the neck of a child might be, one guessed it was an aortic aneurism. That's on a level with locating Mexico somewhere in the middle of Great Britain. Another of them, when quizzed by our supervising physician in obstetrics after we had added clinical rounds to our days, was asked to name the three signs of pre-eclampsia (toxemia of pregnancy). Instead of rattling off edema, proteinuria and hypertension, as any third year medical student should be able to do, he admitted that he had never heard of eclampsia. In that instance the preceptor told him to get off his service and not come back until he had studied basic obstetrics.

As we moved into the last two weeks of the year, our orthopedics instructor provided a public demonstration of their lack of involvement. One after another, before beginning his announced lecture on disorders of the spine, he called those delinquent students to the board. Each in turn was asked to draw a side view of the curves of the spinal column. Without exception, they failed dismally, even though each took a very hard look at a skeleton hanging in the corner, searching wildly for clues. One drew a bump of a curve halfway down the back. Another settled for as straight line that inclined towards the front. A third drew the three basic curves, but backwards. The worst placed the foramen magnum where the spine attaches to the head at the back of the skull instead of directly underneath. Finally, one of the good guys was called to the board. He got it right.

We serious students shook our heads in embarrassment over that episode after which we were subjected to a diatribe by the instructor expressing his contempt for those who never came to class and never studied. "You don't care, so I don't care," the teacher said, alluding to his own frequent absences. "You think you can learn medicine by studying old copies of the American examinations," he went on, "but medicine requires more of a commitment than that." He charged us with only wanting a piece of paper, a diploma, and quietly but firmly signaled his disgust, after which he began his lecture for the day.

What a pity that the delinquent six didn't understand Spanish. They had no idea what he was talking about, and I didn't attempt to translate during that interlude. Those who understood were not the objects of his scorn. (By the end of the year, all of the good guys had developed at least minimal capabilities in conversational Spanish.)

From Communitas to Discord

The six were lazy. We finally realized that they were not using their absences to create study time. One of them was off for weeks at a time in New York where his family lived. Others were not seen for equally long periods. We don't know how they used their time, but it was abundantly clear that they were not learning medicine. They seemed to have only one concern: to get a degree in Mexico and a license to practice in the United States.

At the beginning of the year we did some foolish things as a class. We had been told by students from the preceding year that we needed to elect a class representative. The Assistant Dean told us the same. He didn't want to talk with us individually when problems arose, but he was willing to meet with a spokesperson. I'll say this for the Assistant Dean: he was a consistent minimalist. Throughout the year he worked an amazingly short day apparently with very few demanding responsibilities.

Most of us did not want to divert time and energy from our studies, so it was relatively easily for the six to elect their ringleader, Morarji. He is the one who spent much of the year in New York. All we knew then was that he was tall, nice looking, and spoke with apparent sincerity. He was willing to do it, so he won hands down.

What followed was several months of intense negotiations. Morarji was rarely in class, but frequently in the offices of the Assistant Dean, of instructors, or of higher medical school authorities. With strong vocal support from the rest of the six, his first goal was to get credit for more than the twenty-four months we would be in the PhD-to-MD program.

Remember, the Assistant Dean sold us that stack of modules we found so useless. We were supposed to receive them six months before classes began in Mexico. Most of us got them much later. I had mine only four and a half months in advance. We were to pursue self-study for half a year, and then on arrival in Ciudad Juarez, sit for a comprehensive examination based on the modules. To be sure we didn't flunk out in the first week, we were given the questions in advance. Working together, we managed to figure out the correct answers and proceeded then to memorize 1500 questions and their answers.

We went through that farce of a correspondence course even though the school discovered they had to abandon the attempt. The rector of the university concluded that it could be considered fraudulent to give medical school credit for study done at home. He refused to sign diplomas for the graduating class the previous year until the six months was removed from their transcripts. Despite that, the politicized six, led by the class representative, continued to insist on credit for study done prior to entering the university. The first meeting with the Dean during the summer was called partly to settle that issue. The Dean and Assistant Dean became frustrated to the point of anger when they realized that our representative intended to continue to harass them on this and other issues. As the year moved on, their frustration grew exponentially.

The next major class issue originated with a ringleader among the six who insisted that to qualify for the medical board in his state we had to have at least eight months of hospital rotations. He wanted our basic science courses cut short so we could begin rotations earlier than originally intended. Again, our class was represented as pursuing this objective until the administration gave in. Basic science courses were precipitously terminated, and suddenly we were notified to show up in whites to begin clinical training.

Some months later, the six were convinced that our transcripts needed to show a wider variety of courses. Again, they negotiated behind closed doors. The rest of the class was not party to any discussion. Yet, suddenly we learned that hospital rotations were terminated and we were to start grueling ten hour days in the classroom. Ironically, the six rarely attended. Once again they had gotten a decision by exploitation of the informal system.

Long before that the class voted to "depose" our "leader." Despite the advice of earlier students and the wishes of the Assistant Dean, we preferred to get along without an elected leader. We did, but it didn't change things much. The conspirators continued to manipulate behind the scenes. I still don't understand why the administration was always so responsive to them, except that they were willing to meet student needs. They obviously had the same low opinion of the six as we. Yet they let them have their way.

The biggest issue of the year was the subject of rumor and stress until the very last days of class. Should we accept our degree at the end of the second year and become the last class to attempt to get licensed in the United States on the basis of a two-year medical school program? Or, should we extend our studies so that we could qualify on the basis of three years. Many states were still willing to license graduates of foreign two-year PhD-to-MD programs. In phone calls to representatives of the medical boards in Alaska, Arizona, Nevada and New Mexico, for example, Gordon was told that we would be fully eligible. New York, Oklahoma and Tennessee, on the other hand, now required at least thirty-two months. The regulations for most states were not known to us.

The class split on this issue as on most. Personally, I had no choice. My leave of absence only gave me two years, and I had no wish to give up my professorship at Mills College. I was in medical school, in fact, in order to function better as an anthropologist at Mills. Others also felt their best interests were served by the two-year program. The administration never wavered from their commitment to let us finish as had been agreed when we came south. They were willing, however, to allow those who were so motivated to design a three-year program.

The conspirators were afraid of the two-year plan, but not willing to commit to three years. Understandably, they wanted to keep the extended program option open until the end of the second year. The administration for their part wanted a decision at the end of the first year in order to meet university, state and federal requirements. Each of three meetings turned into shouting matches as the conspirators continued to insist upon an agreement the Dean could not make. It was frustrating. It was monotonous. It was unreasonable. it left us uncertain of our status at the medical school.

To me, the endless maneuvering was also sad for another reason. In those discussions, administrators spoke of the need to have more coursework on our transcripts and more time in clinical rotations. But whether the administration or the conspirators, the discussion was always entirely about appearances. Only Will, in his unwelcome frankness, broached the issue that ought to have been central. The only time he ever showed a capacity for anger was in the first of these meetings at the end of the year. He shook from the effort to control his emotions. "How," he asked, "can you talk about more months of coursework when instructors are not coming to teach the courses we are supposed to be taking now? The teaching in some of our clinical courses is so sloppy it is degrading to be associated with it."

No one wanted to hear Will make that statement. The Assistant Dean, who walked by our classroom in total detachment every day, feigned shock that he had not been notified about instructors failing to appear. What an actor! Students shouted Will down. Quality of instruction was not a problem to them. The only issue was course titles, semesters and hours: What minimum would it take to be eligible for licensure in the United States? "All that matters is how the transcript looks," was the final word of our representative. How sad!

Street Fighting in the Classroom

In a way, there were the "good guys" who came to Mexico to study medicine, and there were the "bad guys" who only wanted a medical diploma. The bad guys were consistently bad. But the good guys were not consistently good.

When we joined together to form that class of twenty-four aspirants to the practice medicine and surgery we left worlds in which each of us had a recognized place. We entered a sociological limbo of status ambiguity. We had to adjust to ill-fitting roles as doctoral level scientists or practitioners who had become students again. We also had to adjust to a cultural limbo. We joined together in a liminal state in which it was difficult to feel secure about personal values, rules of proper behavior, a sense of self. Only a few, like Will, lived by a code of personal morality that was not challenged by strange ambiguities and uncertainties. Of the eighteen "good guys," eight more or less met the high standards set by Will. Ten reverted at times to the "law of the jungle" as they struggled to survive in an informal system that was a labyrinth of cultural complexity.

What I refer to colloquially as the law of the jungle is a way of settling disputes that many of us encountered as adolescents on school playgrounds, where for some, at least, "might makes right." Some of us encountered it in the armed forces, where each member of a military unit must establish his or her place among fellow soldiers (in my case, fellow sailors) in an unofficial pecking order of fitness for brutality. It was especially apparent on the streets of any inner-city slum and was apparently also learned in Africa and India, because nearly everyone in our class seemed familiar with this jugular approach to conflict resolution.

During the first month of classes we held together much as I remembered from chiropractic college. Apparently, that was the feeling Hugh Thompson had from his background in veterinarian school. We had our first big examination at the end of June in anatomy. We were invited after class to meet at Hugh's house where he and his wife threw a party to celebrate our first academic hurdle. We had already endured some rather poor teaching to make us aware that this was not an outstanding program, but we felt like proper medical students all the same.

Three days later the first brawl took place. Simon, a powerful former weightlifter from Nigeria, became very bossy. He got into the habit of telling people to be quiet or of ordering them to go to the front of the room to teach their assigned topic. He seemed to feel entitled to shout down anybody who made a comment he didn't like. Being big almost made it seem right.

Rajendra, a tall biochemist trained in India was the most outspoken in resisting Simon. Raj began the confrontation a day earlier when he shouted across the classroom that Simon had let us all down by not being present to give his scheduled lecture on the physiology of muscle tissue. On this day, while I was at the front of the room translating a discussion between the instructor and another student, the room suddenly filled with a loud scrapping of chairs and angry shouting. Simon was pushing his way to the rear with his massive fist cocked to smash Rajendra, who for his part stood up to strike a blow of his own. They were pulled apart. We shrugged it off, and hoped we hadn't looked like fools to our instructor.

As the summer dragged on bickering became endemic. Those who attended class were resentful of those who didn't. Those who prepared careful lectures resented those who failed to perform. In our dissection lab, a few of the good guys were always left with the thankless chore of closing up the body and cleaning up the mess while others slipped out the door without offering to help.

As early as July, class solidarity was in tatters. Simon was not the only one to get bossy. Morarji became equally dictatorial. We felt we had elected him as our representative. He interpreted the election as making him our leader. He began to speak for the class entirely on his own authority, conferring with his clique but not with the group as a whole. He became furious with me because I took action on an issue that affected the class as a result of events in our course on genetics. The incident is instructive of what was happening to class interaction.

Our genetics instructor had not been around for days as we met to teach ourselves. Suddenly on a Friday he appeared to set up our final examination. We were told to work together as a class to write a paper that would be turned over to him so that he could use it as the basis for a written examination he would administer in exactly one week. We were stunned. Only seven were present at the time. We were too fragmented to coordinate a research and writing project. It was time for altruism. Gordon Graham and I volunteered to do it together over the weekend on behalf of the entire class. Everyone present loved the idea. They willingly let us do the work. So we did.

Monday arrived, and so did we, with an enormous document we had managed to type. (No computers and no Google search engine in those days.) Morarji and his clique, absent when the assignment was given on Friday, appeared on that day. They knew nothing of what had taken place.

I explained to Morarji what had happened, and that I needed to brief the class on the contents of the paper as soon as the dermatologist finished his morning lecture. Inexplicably, Morarji said that Gordon and I should hand our paper over to him to take directly to the instructor in his office. He also informed us that we could not brief the class. Where did he get the idea that he had that kind of authority?

Muttering "screw you," Gordon stomped off. Neither he nor I was keen to have Morarji turn in our typed paper as though it was his work. I still wanted to review the material with the class, and finally Morarji reluctantly agreed to let me quiet down the class during an idle period and begin my task.

Within minutes, however, Morarji returned to the front of the room to announce that instead of proceeding with my review copies of the paper would be distributed to everyone for their own study use. "That's fine by me," I responded, "but in the future it would be better if you would be attend class, since you would be able to represent us more effectively if you were here to take part in discussions with instructors. We can't easily say that they must talk only with you when you are so seldom present."

I spoke with what I felt was a non-hostile, matter-of-fact way. Absent is absent. His absenteeism was known to all of us. Yet he erupted in a rage. "You are making judgments of me," he sputtered. "I am entitled to be absent a couple of times a week." (Actually, he was usually absent.)

"You are taking advantage of me by telling instructors I am absent and getting me into trouble"

That last charge hurt. In spite of feeling that the few of us who attended and gave lectures were being used by the others, we never passed on a word of criticism to an instructor. Personally, I went out of my way at times to makes excuses for them. "Morarji had to go to the office but he should be back soon." How many times had I exaggerated a class involvement that scarcely existed?

Time to reflect further on my hurt feelings evaporated instantly. "Simon is absent even more!" Morarji screamed, in total irrelevance. That got Simon to his feet as two-hundred pounds of black fury. "You are never here; you don't know who's here or not here." The two large men in their thirties lunged at each other like angry bears. We broke up the fight, but tension grew worse as one month slowly gave place to the next.

By October we had descended into a rougher sort of barracks brawling. The day before the big fight, Morarji approached me between classes to accuse me of nefarious undertakings. "You talked the instructor into changing the biochemistry exam," he charged. I hadn't, and said so, even though the issues seemed trivial. "Others are doing it too," he added, not much mollified. "People change things by talking with the instructor," implying that only he was entitled to negotiate class assignments. "You ought to attend class yourself if you want to have a say in class discussions with teachers," I said, repeating my assertion of some months earlier.

Wow! That wasn't what he wanted to hear. He escalated to screaming again. "It's nobody's business whether I come or not." I left the room. There was no reasoning with him.

The next day, after missing the first several hours, Morarji suddenly walked into the classroom between periods. He came straight to me and repeated his charges that I was working behind the scenes to change things in the program. In my best Sunday School turn-the-other-cheek manner, I quietly repeated that I had never been involved in anything not evident to anyone in the room, and succeeded enough so that he abandoned me for the hallway.

Silently, I sighed in relief. He seemed ready to hit me, and he was both tall and heavy.

In the hall he turned on Jim Bateson, the D.O. Jim is easily aroused, and he didn't care a fig about class spirit. If Morarji wanted to fight, he would give it to him. Not without help, however. He called some of the other good guys to join him. Remember, these men were good in the sense of being good students. They were definitely not good peacemakers. In fact, those nearby seemed to relish the chance to take on a bad guy.

The shouting ended any possibility of study. I closed my book and looked up as Morarji pushed Gordon Graham backwards into the classroom. It was a very uneven match. Graham stood only 5 feet 9 or so, appeared to weigh no more than 135 pounds, and wore glasses like a bookworm. Morarji was a giant. But what Morarji didn't know was that Graham was a captain on leave from a Ranger Battalion in the American Army Reserve. He was fully trained and experienced as a special forces fighter. For my part, I was less the goody two-shoes than I had been in the summer. If they wanted to fight, I wasn't going to interfere. No one else was, either. These two had been stewing for this fight for months. And I confess that I took secret pleasure in knowing what Morarji had gotten into. He was no match at all for the little man, one of us good guys. He was in for a shock

Backing into the room, Graham calmly removed his glasses, folded them, and placed them to the side on a table. Turning, he assumed the stance of a karate expert. I was tempted to laugh, it looked so much like a cheap movie. The slightly built protagonist crouched to face an enraged elephant of a man. I figured no one would get hurt, and I was essentially right.

Morarji charged swinging wildly at air. Gordon gave him a swift kick to the groin. He followed that with swift hard blows to the side of the face, backing away after drawing blood. Astonished and furious, Morarji raised a big, heavy opaque projector high above his head to crash down on Graham's head. Someone got that away from him. Then he raised a chair high in the air, but by that time he was pulled away. Morarji never touched Graham, who deliberately and calmly retrieved his glasses and returned to his seat to wait for the next class, or the next attack. What a guy!

Nothing was settled. Morarji continued to accuse others of secret backstairs negotiations with instructors and administrators. Most of us felt that he feared others were doing what he probably did. Eventually, I realized that nearly everybody in the class at one time or another talked privately with school faculty and staff to advocate some personal plan for modifying our program. Those actions were, I supposed, almost inevitable in a school that failed totally to facilitate communication. It reflected our total failure ever to get the class to discuss issues without shouting and anger.

From that brewing discontent, a more serious issue emerged. The bad six decided that one member of the class constituted a danger to the integrity of our whole program because he had a job. The rules of our program were clear on that point. Working for pay was strictly forbidden, although we knew that some students in previous years had gotten away with it. (I was in the clear on that rule, since I had taken a two-year leave of absence without pay, leaving Edna to support the family in California while I pursued my fantasies.) The evil six feared that medical boards in the United States would disqualify all of us for licensure if it became known that a member of our class held down a job during his student years.

The fear was irrational. The student in question, a pharmacologist, was not that much out of line. He had managed to continue a research project testing two forms of cancer chemotherapy by supervising a post-doctoral fellow in the United States who carried out daily tasks in his laboratory. It did not seem unreasonable to me that a laboratory scientist coming to medical school might feel able to fulfill administrative responsibilities in ongoing research. To the six, however, that employment became a cancer in itself, and they insisted that it had to be eradicated.

For the rest of the year they tried to get him, first, to give up his salary, and, as that failed, to be expelled. You can imagine what that did for class unity, especially when a couple of the good guys began to share the paranoia. But there was more.

A published brochure stated that dentists and veterinarians as well as Ph.D.'s were eligible for advanced standing, but certain other practitioners were explicitly excluded. As mentioned earlier, chiropractors were emphatically not eligible. One brochure and an advertisement, but no other document that I ever saw, specifically stated that osteopaths and podiatrists were also not eligible, and we had one of each. The bad six somehow got hold of that brochure.

That, too, was an empty issue. I cannot believe that our status as graduates of this medical school would ever be affected by the fact that a classmate (who had a Ph.D. in anatomy) was a graduate of the American School of Osteopathic Medicine or that another was qualified by an American school of podiatric medicine.

Yet, paranoia struck again. For months the rumor mill flourished with reports of efforts to get the Dean to expel those three classmates. The victims received anonymous threats by telephone. They learned of calls to the Dean. We were told of phone calls to the American university in which the pharmacologist had his lab. Calls reputedly also went to his funding agency, hoping to get him into trouble for having become a student. Other calls went to the state boards with which the osteopath and the podiatrist were registered. A lot of mischief was done.

I continued to pooh-pooh the fears of Jim Bateson and Frank Smith in early spring, when they decided that Al was one of the conspirators. Al was a good friend to me. He was from Turkey, but lived in the States. Although he was married to an American and had American children, he spoke very cryptic English. It took concentration to understand him. He was a good student, who learned Spanish very fast, speaking it the same way he spoke English, with short-changed grammar and idiosyncratic vocabulary. Still, if you focused on what he said you could usually figure out what he was getting at.

So that morning outside the classroom I understood because I was standing directly next to him. He and Bateson were talking so quietly that I didn't realize at first how angry they both were. Bateson usually escalated faster to shouting. Anyway, as I arrived, he was accusing Al and a student from Hong Kong (by way of Canada) of trying to get him and Frank expelled. "You were talking with the Assistant Dean about getting us out," he sneered. "No, I wasn't," Al replied. "I had to talk to him about insurance papers for my car." Jim refused to believe that, although I did. "You interfer in my life and I'll lay you flat!" Jim uttered through clenched teeth. "Geez," I thought, "a practicing physician and a commander in the Navy Reserve, and you cope with interpersonal problems in that way?"

Still, it just seemed like a shouting match in whispery voices. I could just barely hear Al answer. "You better not try me. I haven't fought since Turkey, when I killed a man. I'll see you dead if you attack me." I could barely hear him, but Jim didn't miss a word of it. "Threaten to kill me, will you," he stammered, lifting his knee toward Al's groin and aiming a fist at his face." Quickly, I pulled him off and others stepped between the two of them. I walked Jim away. He cooled off by fanaticizing how he would have smashed Al's head to a pulp against the marble wall if I hadn't pulled him away. "Thanks, Bob. You did the right thing." I sure did.

Later in the spring, events forced me to reassess the paranoia of Jim and Frank. The physiologist with the Doctor of Science degree from the University of Calcutta did a very foolish thing. He entered his fears for the integrity of the program into a letter directed to the Dean, whose designing of the PhD-to-MD program he characterized as "a stroke of genius." "It requires imagination and a lion's heart to do this; it reflects superb talent to organize this." The poor DSc, though skilled enough to have published on certain enzymes, was foolish enough not only to write that letter, but to let it fall into the hands of other students. "The program has run smoothly so long under your able stewardship, and with such deft management by . . . our venerated Administrator and Assistant Dean, and by the all-out devotion and back-breaking day-and-night hard work of so many students during the preceding 12 years." I nearly retched as this Uriah Heap went on.

"I am proud that to my class belong so many outstanding scientists and veterinarians." He continued, still not getting to the point. "If I may speak for myself . . . I have spent about 18 years in research and teaching. I have been chairman of physiology at a big college in India, a Fellow in Biochemistry, Neurology and Cardiology at Harvard Medical School and an Assistant Professor in Medicine at Duke Medical Center. . . . I have had the distinction of being elected a Fellow of the New York Academy of Sciences, which is a high mark of recognition amongst the American scientists." Hard to believe, Uriah, but get to the point.

On the fourth page of his letter he finally did. "If personal opinions have a place, Sir, it is my opinion that persons holding a diploma in osteopathy, podiatry or chiropractics *(sic)* should never be admitted to this special program. If indeed they have realized their initial mistake now belatedly, I would join my other friends in the class in bidding them a hearty farewell as they proceed to the 5-year program, but, sorry, I would not share the boat with them."

I still don't know why he mentioned chiropractic. It was never mentioned again either in that long letter or in anything that came up in subsequent months. I don't think he or any of the others realized that I was a chiropractor, and I never gave it another thought.

He also went after the dismissal of the pharmacologist who continued to manage his research project at a distance. The letter continued. "the scandal about Santo Domingo schools was not about the length of their academic curricula. I was then a student in Santo Domingo, in one of the school which was not involved in scandals. But I remember the agonizing concern amongst the students there at the time when The Miami Herald published the breakthrough story. A medical graduate from the CETEC medical school . . . held a job elsewhere while he was as a student of medicine at CETEC." The California State Medical Board, he added, "raised a legitimate question: what kind of a medical school is it that allows a student to hold a job simultaneously; how can a medical student divide his/her attention between studies and another profession?" He then concluded that this led to the investigations which "finally resulted in closure of several medical schools . . . and many former graduates . . . who were already practicing in the states found themselves stranded, with their licenses withdrawn." Uriah Heap neglected to add, that the Dominican schools were also proven to have sold diplomas to individuals who were never in attendance, a rather more serious failing that to permit part-time employment by a student.

The classroom was bedlam the morning the pharmacologist grabbed a copy of Heap's letter out of the hands of a careless conspirator. He showed it immediately to Jim and Frank. They converged on Heap, who exited to the hallway to mollify his victims. So committed was he to his assessment of the danger to his M.D. degree that he grew angry too. He entered our program, we then realized, because the Caribbean school he was attending collapsed. He felt desperate. His Gandhian principles smothered in an outrage as he grabbed the pharmacologist by the throat to choke him against the wall. The victim, also a Ghandian and as small and inexperienced in street fighting as his attacker, reached around Heap's arms to land a lucky punch. The fight ended almost before it began with Uriah bleeding profusely from his nose, which was broken.

For weeks after, Heap came to class disfigured by the injury and the time it took for plastic surgery to heal. Two months passed and then, unexpectedly, two plainclothesmen arrested the pharmacologist for assault and battery. He was carted off to jail.

The details of what followed need not concern us here. Heap must have bribed the police to carry out the arrest on a university campus, which is a federal offense in Mexico. The two officers ended up spending three days in jail themselves and forfeited half a month's salary for that illegality. The pharmacologist spent the night in jail without food, water, or a bed until a couple of his classmate-countrymen finally discovered which jail held him and paid his bail. Before a judge, neither the accuser nor the accused would agree to a settlement, so it became a criminal court case. We had the distinction, as the last class to complete the PhD-to-MD degree in twenty-four months, to also be the first ever to have students spend time in prison. The worst until then had occurred three years earlier when an enraged student shot three bullets in the classroom before his pistol was taken from him. That time, no one called the police.

Will and most of the rest of us finished our first year totally committed to high ethical standards and to mastery of the science and skills of medicine. It was hard, however, to emerge from our experiences without cynicism. A few of our classmates exited weak in knowledge and compromised in ethics. It is frightening to contemplate the practice of medicine by a doctor who is not totally committed to the first rule of practice, *primum non nocere*, "above all, do no harm," wrongly attributed to Hippocrates but rightly sworn to by every physician licensed to practice in the United States.

Chapter Thirteen

Clinical Rotations in Mexico

The End of Summer

Four months of crash courses in the basic medical sciences passed with passing of the hundred-degree temperatures of summer. With that also passed our cultural naïveté. We now understood well that the pace of study, the rigor of it, was different from medical schools in the States. We had acclimated to endless hours of hanging around. We expected to wait for instructors who might never arrive on any one day, or who might arrive late and keep us into the following hour. Nothing would surprise us very much.

I received an official letter warning me of dismissal if I did not immediately pay my fees. Was my medical training going to abort on a technicality? Was this another extortion? Worried, I presented myself to the Assistant Dean's office. Of course my fees were paid, his secretaries told me. "Don't worry." The letter became another souvenir of how we endlessly had to fear stumbling into a pit of uncertainties. Weeks later another letter warned that I was in trouble because the documentation of my pre-medical studies was incomplete. That time I had gotten a form letter intended for someone else. My papers were completely in order. In emotional and psychological terms, perhaps the hardest thing about studying in Mexico was to cope with the helplessness of knowing that we could at any moment be dismissed individually or have our program lengthened, changed, abandoned, or made prohibitively expensive without warning and without recourse. The authorities could do absolutely anything as far as we could tell, and we might not even find out about it until later. In actuality, they treated us fairly, but in a completely arbitrary fashion. So, nothing could surprise us very much. We simply had to live with our anxieties.

Joining Fourth Year Students

Summer passed. October arrived and it was time to join main campus fourth year students (equivalent to third year in the States) for our hospital-based training.

We had been warned by last year's students to be very circumspect in following instructions. There were no instructions. So we went by what Mexican students told us. First in priorities was the dress code. We were to become *perros blancos*, "white dogs." In a desperate scramble we shopped around for the white clinic jackets familiar to American medical students (and to chiropractic students, for that matter). In addition, we were to wear white shirts, white pants, white socks and white shoes. We had to be totally white except for neckties, which permitted touches of color. We learned from the lone woman in our MD-to-PhD class that she was permitted to show color in her blouses.

We were also very green. We had to be prepared for times when we might be allowed to assist in surgery. We had to get hold of green hats, masks, shirts, pants and shoe covers, all to be kept on the ready for instantaneous changes. We would also need them later in the dog laboratory when we would be given our introductory training in surgical techniques, beginning with incisions and culminating in suturing uncomprehending canines.

One of the blessings of doing hospital rotations in our school was that we were not asked to show up before 9 a.m. Later, when I did a year of rotations in the United States, the starting time was usually 6:30 a.m. or earlier. For the first week in *Hospital General*, however we arrived only to stand around in white uniforms, because someone who mattered had not been notified that we were scheduled to appear. In chiropractic college I felt like a doctor the first time I walked into the clinic, a passing moment that was to become a growing sense of professional identity. In medical school we looked like milkmen or hospital orderlies. Doctors may have worked in white jackets or lab coats, but only students dressed in white from head to toe. A new sense of professional identity had to emerge much more slowly out of an amorphous white blur of low self-esteem.

My self-esteem got a nudge in an upward direction by the group to which I was assigned. Through student politicking that took place in my absence, I found I was in the only group that already had a lot of experience and training in medicine and surgery. Only Graham, with his research on insects, had no preparation for clinical rounds. Otherwise, our team included Jim Bateson, who had himself supervised American medical students in an American teaching hospital as well as in naval hospitals, Hugh Thompson, who practiced medicine and surgery for animals, and Mike McBride, who prescribed medications and performed surgeries for diseases of the foot.

It was good we had so much capacity to learn from each other, but we learned vastly less than I had hoped. I had eagerly looked forward to bedside training in which every second patient would not be my own superbly healthy mother ready for lunch. What a privilege it would be to access patients without the need to build a private student practice through personal solicitations. What a thrill to encounter seriously sick, truly challenging medical cases rather than my own teenage sons and daughters or other chiropractic students. Well, that expectation turned into another disappointment. We gained good experience in comparison to the chiropractic internship, but it was nonetheless severely limited.

Rotation on the Medical Ward

We spent six weeks in medicine, five of which were with a doctor who rarely stayed with us for more than an hour a day. I came to understand why my first impression of the hospital was of a milling throng of patients mingling with a milling throng of students in white. Both categories of individuals learned to spend hour after hour waiting for something to happen.

On the wards, we found surprisingly few patients. On some days our service would not have a single new patient for us to work up. Usually we would attend to one or two. We never had a day of going from one patient to the next for hours on end, but at least we were not worn down by overwork.

For the first few weeks we were confined to doing case histories of the patients assigned to us. For each, we filled out an identification page entering answers to a sequence of questions we were supposed to memorize: name, age, sex, marital status, occupation, race, place of birth, residence, religion, and so on. Often that was all that got done all morning. We spent afternoons in classes taking courses in the clinical sciences. By the next morning we could expect to start all over again with a different patient. Or, we might go on to the family history. Again, we were supposed to have memorized a sequence of questions. It was weirdly reminiscent of my training in kinship analysis as an anthropologist. For all relatives on a family tree we had to determine if they were living or dead, and if alive, how old they were. What were their past and present illnesses? If dead, what did they die of? It was tiresome but necessary for a patient's immediate family, but we were required to follow it out to all uncles, aunts, cousins, nephews and nieces. Remember, most of our patients were Catholic with little or no education. Family limitation was not in their game book. The number of relatives to trace back could mount by the score. We were there to learn medicine. We seemed to be getting a lot of experience in genealogy. We all ended up resenting those assignments, as did the Mexican medical students with whom we mingled.

The hardest questionnaire to memorize explored personal non-biological antecedents to the chief complaint. Ethnologically, that fascinated me. Cultural factors that make the Third World different from my world in California could be strikingly important: type of work (mostly manual) and level of education (minimal to non-existent). I documented how prone they were to accident and disease, often through ignorance and illiteracy. Dying of lung disease from having smoked before they were ten years old. Women who wore themselves out with endless childbearing and childcare. Poor beyond belief, we learned not to be surprised when a person of thirty looked fifty as a consequence of poor diet, bad housing, inadequate clothing, and overwork. Families of small children were left fatherless by men in their thirties who drank themselves to death.

We were taught to explore those sociocultural dimensions systematically. Our numerous questions on housing included asking: More than one room? Electricity? Running water? Access to a toilet? Garbage disposal? Leaky roof? Solid walls? Vermin?

The answers we elicited were probably not of much use. When we quizzed on personal hygiene, we often got descriptions of baths, clean clothes, and clean bed sheets every week when we knew such cleanliness was inaccessible.

Ours was a charity hospital, so many of our patients were among the worst off in a nation desperately unable to raise its masses out of poverty. Residing in shantytowns lacking electricity and paved streets, with water spigots at a distance, we treaded on their dignity if we explored too callously the circumstances in which those proud people were forced to live. And what did we expect them to say when we followed orders and asked about their diversions and vacations? Vacations, indeed! Their whole lives were vacations from the forty-hour work week and well-lit, well-heated or air-conditioned workplaces for decent pay and retirement benefits. Such lovely human beings. I shed tears for them.

As important as those social and cultural factors were for understanding health and sickness, they were seldom explicit in our work as medical students. It was explained to us that how they disposed of garbage and human excretions affected their health, but we were not tasked with disease prevention (applied anthropology). Preventive medicine is the single most important medical activity needed in a developing nation (and, indeed, in our own world of relative wealth), but it was never expected that we should try to change their life circumstances. We were there to acquire knowledge and skills in curative medicine. A few questions would suffice to identify a probable victim of amoebic dysentery from polluted drinking water, tuberculosis from crowded living quarters, or hepatitis from contaminated kitchens, but we had to move rapidly on to evaluation of the chief complaint, present illness, and then on to the physical examination.

As in my chiropractic internship, I grew impatient with the slow pace. We were still questioning patients. I wanted hands-on experience. After our supervisors left, no one objected when I returned to patients for further work. I made it a practice to slip back onto their wards to examine eyes and ears with my ophthalmoscope and otoscope. With my stethoscope I explored bowel sounds, respiratory noises, and heartbeats. I checked reflexes and palpated abdomens. But it came to an end. Our supervisor got upset if he arrived to find we were not waiting in readiness. Several times I disappeared into a ward where fellow students failed to find me and I missed rounds as a result. Dispirited, I returned to waiting, and waiting, and waiting. After a time, I found I couldn't even use the time profitably to study. I just waited, wondering if someone might be breaking into my car parked on the street around the corner.

We wasted more than half of our six weeks of medicine just loitering in the reception area. At that slow pace we did learn to diagnose and write orders for certain of the illnesses that commonly show up in a charity hospital. Hardening of the liver from chronic alcoholism was frequent. I recall one man, about sixty years old with a swollen belly, yellow skin, and eyes rolled up under his eyelids, as he struggled to emerge from the stupor that brought him to our emergency room. He was thoroughly frightened of dying, as was his predecessor on that ward, a man who also fit that description and who died. But this patient gradually improved as fluid was drained from his abdomen, yet remained very sick. Then he, too, slipped into a coma and passed away. They had cause to be frightened.

Against that backdrop we entered the men's ward one morning to examine a much younger individual with a barrel-shaped stomach. Only thirty-eight years old and the father of five small children, he supported his family as a street vendor. Vendors are lucky if they make enough to live on. Guided by ignorance and the limitations of a hard, drab existence, he had been a heavy drinker from late childhood. Every weekend he consumed raw grain alcohol, thinned somewhat with water, until he collapsed into his unconscious dreams. His liver was nearly destroyed. Yet he was not greatly disturbed. He felt well, and came to the hospital only because his family thought a doctor ought to examine his enormous belly. Over a couple of days, diuretic treatment saw the volume of fluid begin to diminish. Then suddenly he was flat on his back, his face obscured by a naso-gastric tube. During the night he began to vomit blood. A not infrequent complication of alcoholism is bleeding from the esophagus, where they acquire varicose veins secondary to the cirrhosis. He was much sicker than he realized. Still, we saw him gradually return to health.

I grieved for that relatively young man with so dismal a future. I grieved for his eventual widow and children who were surely destined to end up on the streets with other women and children reduced to begging for a living. As little as a vendor made, it provided minimal shelter, clothing and food for seven people. Our supervisor guessed that he would be dead within the year.

Often we examined patients whose infections or degenerative diseases had not brought them to the hospital until they were in an advanced state. Because I had a special interest in the diagnosis and treatment of joint pain, I spent more time than usual with a gout patient who turned up on our ward in intense pain and barely able to walk. Over the preceding thirteen years he had been seen a couple of times by doctors, but for the most part he simply got worse without medical attention. He lost partial function in both hands, and his feet were almost useless. The right foot looked scarcely human, forced out of shape by golf-ball sized swellings and ulcerating lesions. Each morning I assisted the intern as his ulcers were painfully drained and bandaged. He seemed better after a few weeks and then, one morning, I arrived to find him gone. By coincidence I subsequently encountered him on a sidewalk in town. Hobbling painfully, he inched along in agony toward an uncertain destination. I felt so helpless. As a doctor, I wanted to perform a miracle.

Degenerative diseases are discouraging. I also spent weeks seeing a middle-aged man imprisoned in endless pain and nearly complete immobility from severe rheumatoid arthritis. He tried to keep his crooked fingers busy with embroidery, and while we could do very little for him medically or surgically, I repaid his willingness to let me familiarize myself with his hot, painful joints by translating embroidery instructions from English to Spanish.

Infectious diseases could also present frightening experiences when they were far advanced. One young man with a history of drug abuse and alcoholism provided an opportunity to examine multiple system degeneration in a severe septicemia that spread deadly gram-negative bacteria to every part of his body. To a student able to ignore the horrible odor, it was a chance to examine a chest so badly infected on one side that only the other side moved on breathing. Involuntary splinting minimized movement on the worse side. Day after day I returned to monitor his gradual decline, and each day I tried to encourage him in what was a completely hopeless deterioration. Once I arrived to find an open Bible on his side table. He was seeking the miracle we could not provide, but life gave up on him before he could test his new-found faith. He was twenty-three years old.

We were assistants in successes as well as failures. Routinely, our experienced preceptors identified infections that responded well to antibiotics and other treatments. We learned to differentiate pneumonia from tuberculosis and how each should be handled. We learned to tell the difference between one kind of infectious diarrhea and another, and to know how to prescribe for each one effectively.

We took part in the diagnosis of a fifteen year-old boy who had never attended school. I used to bring comic books to read to him. He came from a nice family, but very poor, so he contributed to the family income as a window washer. His diagnosis was straight-forward, but it was my first experience with this not uncommon disease. A couple of weeks earlier he had a sore throat. It was probably Streptococcus, because he arrived with a globular, fluid-filled abdomen that looked much like those from alcoholic cirrhosis of the liver. He was too young for alcoholism, however, showed no signs of jaundice, and displayed generalized edema. His was a not uncommon complication of strep infections, a kidney disorder (post-streptococcal glomerulonephritis). As is common with teenagers, he was a mélange of child and adult who seemed even younger than his years. Still a boy, he had gonorrhea. Both conditions responded well to treatment by doctors wise enough to know that a patient may well suffer more than one disease process at a time. It was a reminder.

The Surgical Rotation

We moved on to six weeks of surgery without surgery. For half of that time we rounded almost without a preceptor. The surgeon only showed up three or four times. His successor, in contrast, was very conscientious. Yet, at best it was surgery without surgery.

Although we had been trained in our surgery technique course to suture wounds, it was only on dogs. When we donned our greens to enter the surgical theater, it was only to watch. We never helped in anyway with procedures. As medical students, we were too low on the totem pole, lined up behind first year interns who were privileged sometimes to suture lacerations in the emergency room or on a ward. They, in turn, lined up behind residents, who alone might hold a forceps while the surgeon cut, clamped, or cauterized. What, then, could we do besides just watch and listen?

Rounds began with a visit each morning to the wards to carry out pre-operative and post-operative examinations of our preceptor's patients. That provided some hands-on experience and orientation to diagnosis. We learned to distinguish an acute appendicitis, with intense lower right quadrant pain, vomiting and constipation, from a possible parasitic infection, with intense lower abdominal pain vomiting, and diarrhea. The one would go to surgery. The other to the medical ward.

A case history and physical exploration allowed us to distinguish a probable acute gall bladder that needed surgery from a duodenal ulcer that probably did not. We examined hernias and more complex abdomens, gaining experience with x-ray interpretation and laboratory studies.

Often we first encountered a patient only after surgery. Especially on a Monday morning when, for example, an emergency surgery had closed the penetrating knife wounds of a drunken weekend brawl. As in all post-operative cases, we gained a feel for how normal tissue should respond, and how to palpate for incipient infection. Not infrequently as we carried out those inspections we confronted veritable works of art in the form of knife wounds and drainage outlets cut through and around tattoos that ranged in interest from crudely rudimentary to exquisitely detailed.

One twenty-two year old lad remains indelibly in mind. On taking his history he seemed a sweet, soft-spoken child-man, small and delicate. Over his head his mother had suspended a rosary, the crucifix dangling just above his nose. He was in for multiple stab wounds. On pulling back the sheets his sutures were seen to cut through an enormous tattoo of a spider web, part of a bipedal art gallery that included a knife dripping blood in one direction and a syringe dripping heroin in the other. He was, in fact, a tough street kid, who, with three younger friends, persistently terrorized the children of a local middle school where our preceptor's wife was a teacher. He had been stabbed by another local hoodlum. We learned that within two days his three friends took revenge. His attacker was cut down in a back alley with eighteen knife wounds, a case of cold-blooded murder by teenagers. So much for a medical student's first impressions of a patient.

From the wards we moved downstairs to the clinic, where our preceptor picked up the folders of outpatients waiting to be seen. While he sat across his desk from a patient, five of us towered over the proceedings, ready to take part in the interrogation, to measure blood pressure, or be sent on an errand. It was good experience. We began to get the hang of practicing medicine. Beginning with the patient's stated reason for why he or she had come we learned to narrow the interview down to diagnostic possibilities.

On our first day, an Indian woman sat down who seemed to be paralyzed on one side of her face. The doctor happened to ask me for a clinical impression. I responded by demonstrating what is known as idiopathic facial hemiplegia with a quick test of cranial nerves, eliminating the likelihood of an intracranial mass or hemorrhage by noting characteristics of frontal muscle function. I enjoyed a big success that morning, thanks to familiarity with the ethnographic study of a Cherokee shaman well-known to the Cherokee Nation and to anthropologists for her treatment of Bell's Palsy, which she knew as "crooked face." I was rarely that lucky, and usually followed up each hour in the consulting room with several hours of detective work rifling through medical textbooks.

At the rear of the consulting room we herded in with patients who warranted physical exploration. Each of us in turn gently pressed into the abdomen, listened to chest sounds or put a joint through its range of motion as we began to get a feel for the physical examination. It was never complete, however, and was always rushed, since we more or less stood in line for the experience. Only rarely was a pelvic or rectal examination undertaken, and in those cases were just watched. It all happened at a rapid pace and soon we were on to the next patient and more likely than not, a very different health problem. We were acquiring experience in diagnostic procedures, but it was limited and we needed much more, and not the least, to actually have a hand in surgical procedures.

Obstetrics and Gynecology

The third of our four hospital rotations brought us to the women's ward for five weeks. If there is one experience in the study of clinical medicine that makes you feel you are a physician it occurs when you first exercise that incredible freedom granted a doctor to expose and explore the body of a stranger. I will never forget the first morning our small entourage was led onto the small obstetrics and gynecology ward by our new preceptor. By medical convention, a woman's modesty is preserved by covering one part of the body while examining the other. Taking care not to uncover her breasts, a woman with a possible abnormal pregnancy suddenly lay before us naked from her waist to her knees.

We had already taken her case history. A thirty-five year old mother of five, she told of missing her last period and of the recent onset of colicky abdominal pain with vaginal bleeding. She was probably pregnant, but in danger of dying from implantation of the embryo in a fallopian tube rather than in the uterus where it belonged. We began the physical examination.

The first act of the physical examination was a visual inspection. So there we stood, six men, staring intently at the exposed abdomen of a woman obviously suffering pain and intense worry. She seemed little mindful of what under other circumstances would have constituted a humiliating exposure. Our white jackets, stethoscopes, and professional mannerisms helped her, I imagine, and helped us to respond appropriately as professionals. She needed help, and the surgeon with his "assistants" could provide it. As it turned out, the surgeon would save her life. Presumably, we students learned how, at sometime in the future, we would also save lives. For a minute or two we stood, stared, and listened as the doctor explained what he was doing and why.

My eye was caught immediately by something totally irrelevant. Descending straight down from her naval was a dark line. I had never seen such a thing before those weeks, but it turned up on a number of women on this ward. I morphed silently from physician to anthropologist as I pondered a racial trait that puzzled me. Why had I never read that Native Mexican physical characteristics included that brown line? Was it in the literature but not noticed by me? Did it correlate with hair form? Short stature? Did it occur outside of Mexico? Did it have a biologic function? Each woman who demonstrated that trait distracted me for a second, after which I returned to my emerging medical persona.

Visual inspection in that case revealed nothing other than an anxious woman. Listening to the abdomen with a stethoscope revealed normal bowel sounds and no more. Palpation, however, elicited exquisite pain in the right lower quadrant and a pelvic examination allowed the doctor to make sense of those findings.

Half an hour later we met the patient in a closed off examination room. For younger women, a nurse, woman doctor, or woman student was usually asked to stand by. This patient, however, was seen without such niceties. Doctors in Mexico didn't seem to worry the way American doctors do about possible lawsuits.

The procedure was very convenient for the doctor. he sat comfortably on a stool with eye-level access to the shaved vulva. it must be extremely disagreeable for a woman to be positioned in that so-called lithotomy position, her legs held up and apart by metal stirrups. The examination itself can be painful, and although our instructor was gentle, he was forced to probe highly sensitive areas.

The pelvic examination is necessary and important. It offers a basic way to get vitally important information. Practice is required to learn to insert two fingers of the right hand into the vagina while palpating overlying parts of the lower abdomen with the left. With those probing fingers one can localize adhesions, growths, or painful areas. In this case an ectopic pregnancy was suggested when the doctor felt an adnexal mass and elicited intense pain. Even in normal pregnancies one looks for changes in and around the cervix, which were absent in this case. Those examination skills should be acquired by every doctor, but we learned only as much as we could by watching. The instructor described what he was doing and answered questions. With a speculum inserted he leaned to the side so each in turn we could catch a glimpse of what was revealed. But we never carried out the procedure ourselves as students.

Backed up with blood chemistry studies and a plain x-ray film of the abdomen, this patient went to surgery. She did indeed have a tubal pregnancy which could have cost her life without its removal. As a fringe benefit, the remaining fallopian tube was ligated. Five children was enough. For several days after we observed as the surgeon inspected the wound. We probed gently around it with our fingers to test for signs of firmness that might indicate infection. Her recovery was uneventful and she rewarded us with a big smile when she learned she would be released to return to her children.

It was common in a gynecology patient to learn enough to arrive at a tentative diagnosis just from the case history and physical examination, even without doing a pelvic. The other woman on the ward had a cyst big enough to be felt by pressing into the abdomen. Again, we only watched as the surgeon performed the pelvic exam and we followed the patient's post-operative recovery. It was not very exciting, but we were growing in experience all the same.

The most dramatic patients in Ob-Gyn were a few pregnant women in toxemic shock (eclampsia). Delivered immediately of their babies their lives seemed to hang by a thread as they lay silently in the intensive care unit. We never lost an eclamptic patient while I was on the service even though they were in great danger. We did come from those experiences with a deep sense of responsibility for knowing instantly how to medicate and supervise a patient who might die if we failed to perform perfectly. It was a frightening responsibility that we experienced, although only vicariously.

Not a lot of babies were delivered in that department. In the social security hospital a mile away, dozens children were born every week. The university hospital where we trained only accepted difficult cases, usually scheduling only one or two deliveries a day. Not once did I actually deliver a baby during that rotation. As students the closest we got was in the give and take of question and answer sessions with our preceptor. For that we read furiously, studied charts, examined mothers ready to give birth, and timed the frequency and intensity of contractions. That was as close as we got. An intern, resident, or doctor actually got to catch the baby. Unless you do it yourself, you don't really know how. Of course, Bateson had delivered many babies and, surprisingly, Graham had been allowed to catch his own first born. They were the experts on our student team.

Pediatrics

The best rotation of all was pediatrics. The doctor in charge of us, graduate of a premier medical school in Mexico, did his residency in pediatric surgery in Boston. He loved tutorial teaching and we loved him.

Working with children is so special that it is somewhat like learning a different kind of medicine. Indeed, for infants and small children, pediatrics resembles veterinarian medicine in that you have to do your case history and physical examination with a patient who can't talk. Children can become quite frightened and uncomprehending. But mainly they are rewarding patients, and I loved working with them.

So pediatrics was a love affair. Our preceptor took time with us as case by case we grew in our capacity to carry out a differential diagnosis. The "differential" is absolutely basic to the practice of medicine. Given the history and findings relating to a patient's complaint you must decide what the most likely cause might be, as differentiated from the second most likely, the third, and so on. Once you know what the problem is, treatment usually follows standardized protocols. Case by case we enlarged our experience and expanded our skills.

Gordon, the devoted father of two small children who had "caught" one of them at birth, hoped to specialize in pediatrics, so he spent all of his uncommitted time on that service. Often he carried a tiny little girl in his arms whose diagnosis was failure to thrive. After a couple of weeks on the ward she was doing well enough to go home, even though she was still very small. A month later Gordon was still holding her when he had time. Her mother had not returned to fetch her. What would her future be?

We saw a lot of brave little kids. An eight-year-old boy whose leg had been amputated above the knee. An eleven-year-old boy who lost his right arm just below the shoulder. A twelve-year-old trying stay calm despite a naso-gastric tube and the anticipation of surgery as horrors he could scarcely have imagine as recently as the morning before when he left home to walk to school and was run over by a car. And there was a sweet ten-year-old who was paralyzed from the waist down after her little brother impetuously stabbed her in the back with an ice pick. How did a little boy get his hands on an ice pick?

Perhaps the bravest baby was our first experience with Down

Syndrome. Even a beginning medical student could make that diagnosis: slanting eyes, a large tongue and a small little finger all pointed to that chromosomal defect. His mother also fit the picture. She was over forty when she got pregnant. The boy's chest x-ray showed the outline of an enlarged heart, a not uncommon complication. Consistent with those signs he came to us with symptoms of extreme respiratory distress, suffering from acute pneumonia. Jim, who had seen many sick children in his practice in Oklahoma, gave the child only hours to live. We believed we were learning what a baby's dying could be like, but the little guy hung on until we left for the day. To our amazement, breathing oxygen from a face mask he was still fighting for breath the next morning. We learned to recognize paradoxical breathing as his broad caved-in chest heaved up while his abdomen sucked down. Each breath was strenuous work requiring the exertion of his whole little body. His doctor flooded him with antibiotics and intravenous nourishment. Nurses monitored him faithfully. Each breath looked as though it would be his last, yet he was still alive the second morning, and breathing easier. Amazed and delighted, we cheered him on, and darned if that little guy didn't recover. His little brain will never function well and he will suffer other medical problems before he fills out his life expectancy of a couple of decades, but he was an inspiration to us, and he brought joy to his aging mother.

Of course we saw a lot of routine childhood diseases. Inflamed tonsils, pneumonias, diarrheas, rashes, coughs. We saw battered children and starving children. We also saw a few over-indulged children who ate too much rather than too little. Our instructor took responsibility for the entire range of cases, including those who would have been referred to subspecialties in the States. Our doctor took them all on, including some remarkable reconstructive surgery on children with congenital defects

He was understandably proud of two boys we observed who had been born without connections between the bladder and the penis. They urinated through openings in the lower abdomen and would have led very abnormal lives had they not benefited from our preceptor. One reconstruction was still incomplete, with more surgery still to be done. The other could pee like any boy after more than a dozen surgical procedures. His missing urethra had been replaced with a graft. Few other surgeons in Mexico could do that kind of complex and frustrating surgery. An earlier surgeon had wanted to amputate the penis and scrotum in order to construct a vagina in their place, a not uncommon practice throughout the world. We know from the medical literature that such a child is almost certainly destined to face psychological problems from being changed to a girl at four years of age.

Most cases, of course, were far more prosaic, the kind that show up in any doctor's office. If we could have stayed on that service for months instead of only weeks we would have learned much. We were even supervised in carrying out simple procedures. As prosaic and unremarkable as it was, with this doctor supervising we carried out our first rectal exams. No big deal, but we never got to do one on an adult. After each of us had done one the preceptor asked, "how many have you done before?" He knew the answer before he asked. It was a well-known failing of the system that could have been easily rectified (no pun intended). "You owe me a Coke," he responded with a smile. By the time the three weeks had passed we owed him quite a few Cokes for providing experiences of various kinds. And, of course, he was fluent in conversational English.

On a Friday afternoon as May Day edged up on the calendar to mark the last five weeks before we were to return to the United States, a scrawled handwritten note appeared on our bulletin board. "No more clinical rotations. New schedule: 8:00 to 10:00, nephrology and 10:00 to 12:00, gastroenterology." We had been attending clinical courses from 12:00 to 6:00 every afternoon. This would commit us to ten straight hours in the classroom, without even a scheduled lunch break. That was depressing enough. But much worse, without prior warning it cheated us of our last five weeks of hospital experience. The sudden upset cost us three weeks of Ob-Gyn and two weeks of surgery. Sick patients who were our best teachers were replaced by dispirited lecturers who often abandoned us to an empty classroom. We were very unhappy with that fiat which, not surprisingly, was handed down without prior discussion, notice, or explanation.

Comparing Chiropractic and Mexican Training

With the end of my pediatric rotation I had completed two

apprenticeships in the care of patients, one in a chiropractic clinic and the other in a general hospital. In some ways the two complemented each other.

In both institutions we were challenged by the heavy demands of paperwork. In the chiropractic clinic we spent hours filling out forms and getting them approved. The file on each patient grew thick from our input, even if very little eventual treatment was administered. It would have been better had our time gone more into working with patients and less into matrix-oriented bureaucratic formalities.

In the hospital it started out in much the same way. For several weeks we struggled with collecting and recording dreary details about family members, life styles, and personal hygiene. Then, however, it did stop, and for the rest of the year we read charts but never filled them out. It was the totem pole again. Interns did the charting under directions from the doctors. We only had to familiarize ourselves with what was written. It made better use of our time since it allowed us to focus on diagnostic workups and treatment plans.

In the chiropractic clinic weeks slipped before we began to work with a first patient. The school wanted to be sure we were thoroughly briefed on every phase of patient care before we took on even supervised responsibilities. We eased into working with patients by first working with fellow students. We never saw a patient without hunting down a supervisor to oversee what we did. Meticulous supervision ensured that no patient would suffer from our inexperience and no patient would be tempted to charge one of us and the college with malpractice (a potential reality given the American legal system). And we did provide diagnostic maneuvers and spinal adjustments (treatments).

Medical school was very different. We were never briefed. We found out what we were supposed to know and do by being told to perform (under threat of embarrassment if we failed). Yet, patients didn't suffer because we never provided treatment. In the hospital we only watched what supervisors, residents and interns did. As training it fell short of what William Osler recommended.

But although we got hands on experience (no pun intended) in chiropractic college and none whatsoever in medical school, we got equal experience in diagnosis in the two institutions, with this caveat. In chiropractic training it was almost completely limited to musculoskeletal complaints.

As a medical student it struck me that I never saw the kind of patients I was familiar with in my chiropractic training. The patient with a wry neck, a stiff shoulder, or a painful low back might present to a private physician, I had no way of knowing, but I did not encounter them in the General Hospital and I did not see them as a medical student. My fellow medical students had no way whatsoever of learning to diagnose and treat those kinds of conditions. They never encountered them.

However, I slipped away some afternoons to observe musculoskeletal patients in the office of a chiropractor located elsewhere in the city. I also spent time with that kind of patient on many occasions when I spent time in the busy practice of a traditional healer, a bonesetter (who referred to himself as a *sobador* or a *huesero*). I even documented his work sufficiently to publish "The Treatment of Musculoskeletal Disorders by a Mexican Bonesetter," (1987) and, with Brad Huber, "Bonesetters and Curers in a Mexican Community," (1996), both in refereed journals.

The richness of the hospital experience was in the patients we did see. As in my chiropractic internship, I spent more time just hanging around than I did with people needing care. But over the course of that first year I benefited from first hand experiences in the signs and symptoms of diseases, the interpretation of simple laboratory reports, and the reading of x-ray films beyond those for bone and joint problems.

In many ways my clinical training in the two professions was frustrating and wasteful. Much more could have been accomplished. But on a positive note, by the end of that year in Mexico we students had been sufficiently exposed to patients to have surmounted a high personal barrier. We were sensitized to the need to explore patients with all of our senses as extended by instrumentation. We learned to feel at ease in doctor-patient relationships, and we learned how to practice a number of elementary physician skills. Let it not be forgotten that in both institutions we students were highly motivated, and the pain of our patients served as a prod to our determination to become good doctors.

From Mexico to the United States

At *La Universidad Autónoma de Ciudad Juárez* our hospital training ended on April 26 and our last day of classes ended in final examinations on May 25. The year ended like any other day in class. The Dean or

Assistant Dean did not visit our classroom to say good by, wish us well, or even provide instructions. We hadn't seen either of them for a long time, so it ended without ceremony. We just grabbed our books and split.

That afternoon I packed the car. In the evening Gordon Graham and I went out for dinner – our meager celebration. The next morning I drove off to California, happy. Within days Edna and I found ourselves in Washington, D.C. where Edna was committed to work in a congressional office and I prepared to apply at local teaching hospitals for clerkships.

Chapter Fourteen

Day One in an American Hospital

My First Clerkship

Washington Hospital Center, Washington, D.C., a teaching hospital for Georgetown University School of Medicine: I was privileged to be accepted there, thanks to Edna, who had gone to the nation's capital on a congressional fellowship four years earlier. She decided to spend that fellowship year in the office of Tom Lantos, a newly elected congressman who until then had been a professor of economics at San Francisco State University. When they first met in his office it was still unfurnished. She joined his staff almost from day one. After returning to Mills in 1982 she continued for the next couple of decades to devote Fridays to work in his San Mateo Office, which turned out to be very important for my career. When I arrived from Mexico, Congressman Lantos saw to it that I was accepted at Washington Hospital Center so that Edna could work on special assignments in his Washington office for the summer and, not incidentally, share an apartment with me after our year of separation.

The First Morning

I was awake from three a.m., worried I would oversleep. My first clinical clerkship was scheduled as a two week rotation through urology. The Chief of Urology was also Medical Director of Education for the huge, 922 bed hospital. In agreeing to take me on he assigned me to his own department. If I met standards for a fourth year student where he could keep an eye on me I would be allowed to go on to other clerkships. If I didn't, I would politely be told that all of their other openings were filled and I would be set adrift, perhaps unable to find any other hospital within commuting distance of Edna that would give me a chance. So I tossed and turned, determined to report for rounds on time at 6:30 a.m.

Suppose I got lost in the dark of early morning? They would think me unreliable. I made a trial run over the weekend, but had not realized I was to report directly to the ward. When Monday came I made my way to the department office in an isolated part of the hospital complex. No one was there that early. Terror struck. Where was I supposed to be? How could I be so dumb? Somebody in a white coat said try the fifth floor and ask for Dr. Nicrovan, the chief resident for urology. I set out to find Dr. Nicrovan.

My God, elevators take forever. Down a long dim corridor, footsteps echoing its emptiness. Sharp right into the light, through double doors and down the hallway to a nurses station in the middle of Ward 5A. "Was Dr Naproxin . . . I mean, Dr. Nicroxin on the ward? "I don't know Dr. Nicroxin," turning to other nurses busy with patient records, "anybody know a Dr. Nicroxin?" Urology, I added. "He must mean Dr. Nicrovan. I saw him heading into 5C" Yes, my mistake, I meant Nicrovan. 5D! "No, 5C" Yes, 5C, and I headed off reeling like an intellectual dinosaur. It wasn't even 6:30 on my first Monday, and I had already made a fool of myself.

After ten minutes that seemed an hour I finally found Dr Nicrovan on 5F. He was alone. Nearly all of the other residents were out of town at a meeting. It was hard for one man to do rounds alone, so he was glad to have a medical student to help. As we walked from the room where I found him he switched immediately to a quick summary of the patient we were about to see. I tried to pay attention, but we were moving fast and I found it hard to concentrate and at the same time keep pace at his elbow as we dodged in and out among other busy people on the ward.

We turned abruptly through a door and woke up my first American patient.

Dr. Nicrovan seemed supportive of me. Later I learned that he was a foreign medical graduate himself, so no doubt he knew how I felt. Just before reaching the patient he asked in a quiet voice, "We need to check the surgical wound, can you do it?" "Yes, of course," I replied. What luck. I had done that many times under supervision at *Hospital General* in Mexico. I began to feel I might survive the morning. "Good morning, Mr. Arnold. This is Dr. Anderson. He's going to check your wound." Gently, facing each other across the bed, Dr. Nicrovan and I peeled back the bandage, and under his watchful eye I felt for tenderness or edema and noted with authority that there were no signs of inflammatory erythema. "It's fine," Dr. Nicrovan reported to the patient. "We can remove the drain. This may hurt a little." I held sterile four-by-four squares of gauze while he deftly pulled out the surgical drain. "Now we can bandage you up," he went on as he placed four-by-fours over the wound. "Do you have any tape?" he asked, glancing briefly at me. "No, I'll get some," and off I went.

I didn't want to keep him waiting, but I wasn't really sure how I was going to find tape. At the nurses station they directed me to the supply room. There, alone, I looked helplessly at shelves of small packages, all unfamiliar and not a single one looking like tape. A nurse came in. "Thank God," I said to myself, but she wasn't a nurse, just a housekeeper. She knew no more than I. Suddenly, Dr. Nicrovan was there. "Here it is," he said, and together we returned to our patient. The bandage finished, he handed me the tape and scissors. "On a surgical rotation you should always carry tape and a pair of scissors with you," but he didn't seem annoyed. I wasn't the first medical student he had broken in.

The next patient had been draining urine through a foley catheter that ran to a plastic bag hanging from the side of the bed where the amount of urine could be measured. Dr. Nicrovan took me to a small bulletin board nearby where nurses posted the patient's fluid consumption through intravenous and oral intake along side of the output of urine. "On post-surgical patients, always keep a close eye on fluid intake and output. They should roughly balance," and with that we jointly made a rapid calculation and turned to the patient. "How would you like to get rid of the catheter?" Of course, the patient was eager for that. Dr. N. then told me to hold a basin and explained that he cut rather than unplugged the part of the catheter that held injected water so the water bulb inside the bladder would drain and permit the catheter to be pulled out of the penis. He explained each step as he performed that simple maneuver. Before the patient was aware that it hurt, it was done, and we left the room.

Two patients later we encountered a similar situation. No blood was apparent in the urine bag and the intake-output balance had been holding steady. "How would you like to get rid of that catheter," Dr. N. intoned in what I recognized as a little bedside ritual. The patient, of course, was very agreeable to that. "Fine. Dr. Anderson will take care of it for you," and with that he was out the door. "Oh, no! Not yet! I'm not ready for this" I thought, as I heard myself say, "Just lie back and relax."

I pulled the blanket aside as though I had done it a thousand time, while my head was spinning in utter dismay. It was such a simple, safe procedure, but suddenly I blanked out on how Dr. N. told me to hold the tubing so it wouldn't spray the patient and me with urine. How fast should I pull? Putting myself in the place of the patient, I was sure it would be painful no matter how I did it. What did he do with the urine bag when he finished? I couldn't remember a thing, but I did it. Actually, it was quite simple, and from then on I did the job routinely. However, the stress would be similar every time I made that critical shift from watching and listening to instructions to carrying out a new procedure myself.

I was only one hour into my next twelve months of training and had already learned a lot. Back at the nursing station we sat down at a shelf-like table to enter our findings and record what had been done in each patient's chart. We were running late, since we were understaffed. Dr. N. hastily wrote his notes while I leaned over his shoulder to see how it was done. This was to be another task I would have to learn on the pedagogical principle frequently repeated in medical school, "see one, do one, teach one." But he wrote very fast and I got lost in the complexity of it, even though written in English rather than Spanish.

And, to be sure, the next day he let me do some of the charting. On the ones I wrote I signed as Robert Anderson, MSIV (medical student fourth year), but my entries had to be countersigned, and he inevitably found I had neglected to enter some pertinent data. It didn't upset him, I knew that he would expect rapid improvement during those first days. The time did come when supervising residents trusted me enough to merely skim my entries and countersign, but let me get back to my first day.

Rounds were finished at a time on the clock when at General Hospital we would just be arriving to begin our tedious waiting around. No waiting here. Rushing down the corridor, his unbuttoned clinic coat swirling behind him, Dr. N. sipped from a paper cup of coffee as we rushed towards surgery. I passed on the coffee. My stomach was as tight as a walnut. How long could I keep going at this pace before I would smash into that solid wall of my own ignorance? How long before I would display a stupidity that would entitle them to reject me as "Made in Mexico?" Surgery. Oh My God!

While these thoughts tangled my brain my voice provided camouflage. "What kind of surgery will we be doing?" "A TURP," he muttered as we rounded a corner to a door that seemed to jump aside as we passed a sign marked, surgery entrance - for physicians only. "A TURP. What's a TURP?" I mused, afraid to ask. "I'll meet you in the cysto suite down the hall to the right. Get your scrubs over there," he pointed.

In Mexico we had to provide our own "greens," so it was nice to find it all there, fresh and clean. I found a locker, changed, and headed for the cysto suite of surgery rooms equipped for operations carried out by inserting what looked to me like a narrow stainless steel bicycle pump. Properly called a cystoscope, it was designed for insertion through the penis into the bladder. I waited until Dr. N. appeared in his scrubs and introduced me to the attending physician. The etiquette is that the operation is technically done by the attending, a private doctor, but since Dr. N. was then finishing six years of residency (two in general surgery and four in urology), the attending just supervised while Nick did the work. The chart listed me as the second assisting surgeon. My technical status in the hospital as such was actually that of clinical extern.

Later, when I did my rotation in general surgery, and later still in obstetrics and orthopedics, I would have things to do after I scrubbed in. All of the skilled work was done by residents and attending physicians, but I would be expected to hold the wound open with retractors, to keep the area clean with a suction tube or gauze pad, to cut sutures after they had been tied, to hold tissues with forceps, to place called for instruments in the surgeon's hand, all things I had done toward the end of World War II forty years earlier as a Navy corpsman assigned to the Eye, Ear, Nose, and Throat (EENT) Department at Long Beach Naval Hospital.

The high point in terms of being given more responsibility than in Mexico was to take place later in the year, but I will recount now how it happened. I was assisting a dermatologist. He took cancer prone patients to surgery to remove as many as fifteen to thirty small growths (nevi) from skin on the front part of a patient's body, and then turn the patient over to do as many again on the back. With so many small sites to excise, everybody kept busy. Residents found it boring because it was so repetitive, which created a learning opportunity for a fourth year extern.

The first time with that dermatologist was my chance to suture a human being instead of a dog. I made mistakes. With patience, the doctor demonstrated how he wanted them done and asked me to undo my errors. I had to resist the temptation to laugh out loud – or cry out in anguish – or both. The patients were wide-awake, anesthetized with local injections that only numbed the areas of incision. The attending did not want anything to be said that might frighten the patient, so he had us work in near total silence. He instructed with hand signals, a nodding forehead, and an occasional whisper. He definitely would not countenance a laugh or jest. I felt a perspiration of anxiety break out on my forehead. The surgeon did all of the excisions, but he gladly turned suturing over to others. My hands trembled the first couple of times as I had to stab three or four times before I hit the right spot and could push through to tie off the wound. Quietly, the surgeon showed me how to hold the needle holder to reduce shaking. I felt strengthened by knowing that I knew what to do, if only I could get it right.

My nervousness was the same the first time I scrubbed my hands with soap and brush for a full ten minutes and was assisted by a nurse into a sterile gown and gloves. I had been thoroughly drilled in our surgery courses in Mexico, and that good training provided a sense of confidence that gave me hope. After the first two or three nevi removals

I calmed down and from then on I sutured without difficulty. It began to get tedious.

The next time I was assigned to the dermatologist every one of the surgical residents had been called elsewhere. He only had me for assistance, poor man. The operative record listed me as first assistant surgeon. We scrubbed side by side in silence and entered the operating room to be gowned. A friendly first-year had told me by then how to observe operating room etiquette, so I always scrubbed another minute or two after the surgeon finished in order to be the last to enter the surgical theater and to be gowned and gloved. On that day, I assisted in draping the patient and faced the attending over the body of the patient. He turned to the instrument nurse and quietly said, "a scalpel for Dr. Anderson."

Mercifully, he then looked away at his own work to give me privacy as I cut into a living human being for the first time in my life. The panic of my first suture reappeared, but was easier to control this time. I converted instantly into a wonderful actor, a veritable television star. "Suture, please," I intoned as I held a gauze pad over the open cut to stench the flow of blood and then, glancing over the top of my face mask, I held the knot so the nurse cut the suture threads, muttering quietly, "thank you." I was the surgeon and a nurse was assisting me! I left the hospital that night in ecstasy, even though I had not cut through deeper layers of skin, touched an organ, or confronted pathology more complex than a mole. I was very easy to please.

But, to return to that first day when I scrubbed and gowned for a TURP (transurethral resection of the prostate). As men get older it is not uncommon for the prostate gland that is wrapped around the urethra to grow large and strangle urine flow. It is a benign kind of hypertrophy, except that men die from it if the backed up urine causes infection or kidney disease. Men often fail to have the problem attended to until they show up at the emergency room in fear and agony because they can't urinate and the full bladder is causing extreme pain. It is a simple matter to thread a catheter into the penis to drain off the blocked fluid, but the underlying condition requires surgical repair.

Historically, the resection of an enlarged prostate involved pelvic surgery that had a high risk for complications. By 1985 it was done with a cystoscope, which meant that there was nothing for me to do, since excision of the prostate tissue was carried out at the far end of the scope. I was told to don operating attire so I could assist in minor ways. The payoff was that the surgeon from time to time moved his head aside to let me have a look to the far end of the tube while he explained what I was looking at.

The scope focused on one small area at a time, but more vividly than if it were in the open for bare eyes to see. So, on that day I could see how he was cutting away obstructive tissue. I expected to see a bloody mess, but to my amazement, since it was done by nipping out small pieces at a time, it produced a very clean, beautifully trimmed opening. It was exquisite. Moreover, patients recovered quickly and with little apparent discomfort, as I learned on subsequent days when we saw those patients on urology rounds.

Another time, when conducting a diagnostic examination inside a bladder, I marveled to see urine dripping in from a kidney. It was beautiful. The resident doing the surgery taught me how to identify trabeculations, waves of overdeveloped muscle in the wall of the bladder, telltale signs that a man had been straining those muscles to pass urine through his strangled urethra. On yet another day, the surgeon entered a kidney to remove stones that evolve from excess minerals in the urine, and with that my views of the urine trail reached as far up as where urine is produced.

That first TURP took less than an hour, after which I helped move the patient onto a gurney and into the recovery room. There, while skilled nurses in the surgical intensive care unit took charge, the surgical resident wrote up his post-op orders.

I had to pay attention, because I would soon be expected to relieve him of that chore. It required another bit of memorization, with adjustments for specific circumstances. "VS Q 15 min until stable & Q 4 hrs" was usually the first line. It meant that the nurse was to take vital signs (temperature, pulse, blood pressure) every fifteen minutes until those measures no longer fluctuated, and then to continue to check every four hours. The next line just read "I & O," meaning record fluid intake and output. Orders continued with instructions for diet, bed rest and ambulation, medications, breathing care, intravenous fluids, and wound care. Normally, while the medical student wrote those orders the resident got busy dictating his post-operative report describing the complete procedure. Working together, we might have time for a cup of coffee or a hasty lunch before starting all over again on the next operation.

Meanwhile, other staff cleaned up the cysto suite and brought in the next patient. I scrubbed again, got into a fresh sterile gown, and stood to one side waiting to begin. I didn't know where the resident was at that moment, so I introduced myself to the attending, whom I had not met before. I was quite relaxed, since I had no responsibilities more complicated than to hand over an instrument or hold something, with good opportunities to observe. The attending asked where I went to school. "Mexico," I said, unsure of how he would react. He merely nodded, but I felt on trial from that moment on. He probably treated me exactly as he would any other student. "Where's your home?" "California." "What happens to water in the bladder when you are doing a cystoscopy?" he asked, as though that followed naturally in polite conversation. I shivered as though hit by a blast of cold air.

It was still the morning of my first day on an American clerkship, and I was hit with something I had already learned to fear in Mexico. Later, other medical students told me it is called "pimping." It was hard enough on medical rounds to discuss a patient in the hallway, but it was unnerving when I was assisting in surgery, trying to cut a suture while being tested on my knowledge of anatomy, physiology and pathology. "I beg your pardon?" I said, stalling for another three seconds in the vain hope that an answer would come to mind. "What happens to water in the bladder," he repeated with no sign of emotion in his voice

Why does my mind go blank at times like that? "Does it go to the veins?" he said, giving me a small mental shove. Well, that seemed logical, so I said, "yes, it would do that." "How much is absorbed that way?" He gave me plenty of time to think, but it was hopeless. I had only just learned that in conducting a cystoscopy a stream of water is jetted into the bladder and that we actually are looking through water when we visualize the prostate and bladder wall. I had no idea at all of how much water was involved, and had never thought about water absorption. "I really don't know," I responded. In the whole year, I rarely heard another student or resident admit that kind of total ignorance. They might not know, but they could be clever at stalling, or they would introduce some physiologic kinds of speculation that kept them afloat.

I started off really badly with that surgeon who had determined that I was from a Mexican medical school. How did he respond to my abject confession? Only his eyes were visible between his mask and his cap. He said nothing. Was he disgusted? Did I confirm a low opinion of foreign medical students? "About a liter an hour, usually," he finally said, giving me a little help. Great. At least I will know the next time I am asked, and I turned my head, thinking the quiz was over, but it wasn't.

"What happens if that much water is absorbed?" "Oh, shit," I thought. I'm still in trouble. But I began to cope. I could visualize my instructor asking that same question in the course on renal physiology at the chiropractic college. If only that had been yesterday instead of four or five years earlier. But I came up with an acceptable answer. "It would just be filtered out by the kidneys," I murmured weakly. "And what if the patient has poor renal function?" the doctor continued, like a long distance runner. "It would cause hypervolemia," I responded, hoping that would be the end of it. "And what harm would that do?" he shot back. Still able to think physiologically, I responded adroitly that it could result in pulmonary edema, cardiac insufficiency, and congestion of the liver." That seemed close enough to what he wanted, but then came the next question, which I later learned was always the pattern. No matter how well you answer, they always to come up with more questions until either you stumble into your blind alley on that subject or the time comes to start working with the patient. "How would that effect electrolytes?" On my second stab I hit upon sodium balance. A better student would have known that instantly.

On the questions to that point I rated myself an F, a second F, three B's in a row, and a C. I ended with a final F for the total. "What is the normal amount of sodium in the blood?" I looked at my feet, and then at him. "I don't know." "You should know that," he said harshly, turned away, and that was it. l had memorized that value at least a couple of times for exams both in chiropractic college and at the *Instituto de Ciencias Biomédicas*, but it wasn't there for me when I really needed it. The previous year when doing rounds in Mexico, laboratory values were always printed out together with the normal values, and the same had been true when I was a chiropractic intern, so I had not been under pressure to retain them. That night I memorized them.

For the rest of the year I always tried to find out what surgical or medical cases I would work with the next day, or at least later in the day. Given a bit of time to review, pimping wasn't so devastating, especially since the information was usually in our pockets in the paperbound *Washington Manual of Medical Therapeutics* that every medical student carried in the big pocket of her white jacket.

Even so, questions were often shot at us without warning, especially in radiology, where we moved rapidly from one case to the next, each different. Ultimately, the only way to answer well when pimped is to know medicine and surgery very thoroughly. Two years on rotation can move you in that direction. I was going to have to work very, very hard to make up for the slow start we got in our first year in Ciudad Juarez, but I wasn't afraid of work, and to judge from that first morning in an American teaching hospital, each day would build up my qualifications over the coming twelve months.

The First Afternoon

It was one-thirty when we got out of surgery. I wasn't sure where we were going. I just pulled my short white jacket on over the pajama-like scrubs and followed Dr. N. as he headed toward another part of the hospital. We were nowhere near the cafeteria or near food. During that first day I left the apartment without breakfast and I worked through the day without lunch or dinner, but that was unusual.

Eating breaks were normal respites that buoyed my spirits and provided relaxation and a bit of earthly pleasure. Drawing on my years at the chiropractic college, I suppose, I wondered why hospital food was so unhealthy? In every hospital I worked in (which eventually included three in San Francisco and nearby Daly City), cafeterias offered cheap food for students, residents, and, inexplicably, doctors. It was always heavy, heavy, heavy; and we all loved it. Quite aside from how it was clogging my arteries, I began to worry about gaining weight. Since I was getting little sleep and no exercise I began to wonder how I would stay healthy. But those were not my thoughts on that first day. I was too hyped up and tense to care much about that missed lunch. I simply rushed along as we headed to the outpatient clinic.

In the clinic I met Justo Gonzales, M.D., chief resident designate and the only other urology resident in town that day. He was swamped with patients, which is why Dr. N. and I rushed from surgery to help out. Introductions were brief. Later I learned that Justo had his M.D. from the Dominican Republic, where he was a born citizen, the country with the worst possible reputation at that time for medicine. Although a foreign medical graduate, he qualified over American-trained physicians, as had Nick, and for that matter, the chief resident in surgery whom I was to work under later in the summer. It heartened me to realize that graduates of foreign schools could become highly competent and respected in medical and surgical specialties. Justo certainly seemed to be doing well with the waiting crowd of outpatients. A couple of extra hands would speed things up, though, so we all set to work, except that I was nearly useless that first day.

I accompanied Justo as he tended to the next few patients. With so much going on, it was hard to focus on his procedures, but I tried to take note of the basic clinic routine. After briefly greeting the patient, I stood over Justo's shoulder as he glanced over the chart and then turned to the patient to ask what had brought him in. "Did you leave your urine specimen with the nurse?" "Yes," so off we went to the microscope alcove to examine it. "Take a look and tell me what you see," I was told. I couldn't get the thing to focus. It had been several years since I last examined urine slides in the clinical chemistry course at chiropractic college. A nurse showed me how. "Any blood cells?" Justo called out as he left to start the next patient, while the first waited for us to return. I squinted down the scope and identified a couple of crystals and promised myself to review *The Washington Manual* on urine analysis at night when I got home. I also made out a few cells that looked like tiny fried eggs. "Probably epithelial cells," I mused, knowing they couldn't be red cells, which ought to look more like little doughnuts. "None," I said, when Justo came back. He double checked, and there were none. Later, as days passed with lots of practice on urine slides, I learned that blood cells were smaller and harder to find than I had thought, so I was lucky that first time. I probably would have missed them if they had been there.

Returning together to the small examination room, Justo asked if I had done rectal exams before. "Only on plastic models," I answered, figuring that small kids didn't count. "OK, today you had better just watch." While he did the examination, he described how to position the patient and oneself and what to feel for with one's fingers. The next day in surgery I did my first adult rectal exam – on an anesthetized patient. EUA, examination under anesthesia, is a superb way to learn. Later, when I clerked in gynecology, I learned to do a pelvic exam the same way. But on that day in the cysto suite, while we were draping the patient for his TURP, one of the residents did a rectal exam on the unconscious man and then had me repeat the exam, explaining what I should be feeling as I repeated the procedure under his guidance. Several experiences like that got me moving in the right direction, and later in the clinic I was given opportunities to examine fully conscious patients who might or might not have rectal or prostatic pathology, always double-checked by a resident or attending.

On day two I took patients as did the residents. With the patient seated on the examination table, I sat at a small desk to check his records and ask why he had made the appointment. I then took a brief history, asking questions relating mainly to the chief complaint, with only a cursory question or two about general health. I then asked him to lie down on the table, recorded vital signs, and did an equally hasty but focused physical examination. When the resident joined me to review my findings he re-did all crucial parts of the exam and added a few questions of his own.

We might carry out some sort of simple procedure. The first time I catheterized a patient was on a man who squirmed in discomfort as I struggled to hold his slippery, limp penis with one hand while observing good sterile technique with the other that pushed a wiggling rubber tube through the tiny opening, up the shaft, and into the bladder. We were both perspiring that first time, but eventually I learned to do it better so the patient was less uncomfortable and I wasn't uncomfortable at all.

As four o'clock drew near, the last patient was seen and nurses began to lock down the clinic. We headed out. I was exhausted and began to realize that I was also hungry. Nick took off. Nobody tells students when their supervising residents leave, perhaps because it is obvious.

Justo and I continued on. "You can go home, if you want to," he told me kindly. I would have loved to take off immediately but my fellow students and I had agreed before we left Mexico that we would always volunteer for extra duty because it was one way to make ourselves more welcome. So, I said I would like to do evening rounds with him.

Evening of the First Day

Evening rounds were harder than those in the morning. First, we repeated the morning routine of checking each patient, preparing them for the night. "Be sure to order a sleeping medication," Justo advised, "if there is any possibility it will be needed, or you will be awakened at 2 a.m. on your call night to scrounge meds for a manic patient."

With ward patients settled down for the night we moved on to new patients admitted for surgery or treatment the next morning. We had four that evening, and so, while others were eating dinner we got to work. "You take Mr. Smith. He's scheduled for a TURP, Justo said, "and remember to concentrate on the GU [genito-urinary] system. Just hit the main things in your general history and physical.

I felt like I was walking on my knees. I was very tired. I was burned out from the stress of learning so many new routines and procedures. I was exhausted from working with patients on the thin edges of my limited knowledge and skill. And now I was assigned to carry out a general medical examination. I walked into the room and it did not go well.

The elderly man I encountered was hostile and agitated. He demanded to know why his personal doctor wasn't there. Softly, I explained that his doctor was completely in charge of his care, but that other hospital personnel always took care of the routine admission formalities. Responding to my own stress, I added that it was dinner time and the doctor needed to give attention to his family. Years of ethnographic field encounters helped me get moving. I began with the key question, "What brought you to the hospital this evening?" "It's all in my chart," he grumbled, turning to look at the bed he aimed to sit on. "I gather you have a problem with your prostate," I countered, hoping to get him interested in talking about himself. Hostile people usually will end up talking if it is about something that interests them, like their own health. But it didn't work with that man. "I already went over all of that with Dr. Jones. Just ask him. He already knows it all."

He was the toughest informant I had ever encountered, ethnographically or medically. He was damned if anybody other than his doctor would do. I tried again, and a third time, but I got nowhere. I decided to shift to the physical examination.

I listened to his heart and lungs, palpated his abdomen, and reached for rubber gloves and lubricant the nurse had left for me. "Lie on your side, please, Mr. Smith. I need to examine your prostate" I decided I had to do the exam, the first in my life on a real person, because it was routine and no decisions would be made based only on what I might think I had found. Also, I wanted Justo to realize that I did know how to do a history and physical, even though I freely admitted that my experience was very limited.

So I reached for the gloves just as the patient jumped off the bed, turned to the table next to it, grabbed the phone, and started to dial, casting dagger-like words in my direction. "I'm calling Dr. Jones. He knows all about my case. You can just ask him yourself."

I froze. With irrational despair I feared I would be kicked out of the program if the attending thought I was a stupid medical student agitating his patient and interrupting his dinner, quite unappreciative of the doctor's ability to gauge what was going on. "Please don't," I shot back. "I have all the information I need, and you can talk with Dr. Jones later when he comes to see you." With that, I beat a hasty retreat into the hallway. Now what was I to do? I had botched my first H & P. Manfully, I paged Justo and dragged myself off to face him.

To my relief, he explained that no one is expected to do much with an uncooperative patient. I had gotten enough of his history for a barely adequate entry on his chart, and at least I could make a note of his vital signs. We would simply add that the patient had refused a rectal exam, and let it go at that.

The next day, on a gurney outside the operating room, Mr. Smith called me by name as I walked by. He apologized, explaining that he realized later I was only doing my job. He was very upset at the time, he added, and "my daughter said I should apologize." I reassured him that I understood, that anyone might get tense under those circumstances.

It was time to do the last two patients, but one had not shown up yet, and Justo could do the other. He urged me to go home. It was 8 p.m. I thanked him for taking so much trouble with me and headed for my locker and my clothes. It was a big relief to be spared another patient intake.

The next day I was able to talk with two medical students about that H & P. They told me what I needed to worry about and what I did not need to bother with. More importantly, they made a list of abbreviations for me so I could interpret what others entered on charts and so I could add my own entries. You start off, for example, with a general impression of the patient. It usually reads somewhat as follows, A & O x 3 (alert and oriented to time, place and person), WD (well developed), WN (well nourished), NAD (in no apparent distress), and then on to vital signs and the various body systems (skin, head, thorax, and so on).

I made a neat list of all of that on a card and referred to that and others cards frequently those first months until they became routine. When I made mistakes, I was corrected. A medical student is entitled to make mistakes, although some were gentler than others in their corrections. At times I was embarrassed when I missed something simple and obvious, but no one dwelt on those failings, and there were always new patients to see and more medicine and surgery to experience.

Chapter Fifteen

The American Year

Teaching Hospitals in San Francisco

I departed Mexico with recorded credit for the completion of twenty-two weeks in four clerkships. Clerkships the following year in American hospitals were recorded as hours completed rather than as weeks.

- General Medicine (6 weeks)
- General Surgery (6 weeks)
- Obstetrics and Gynecology (5 weeks)
- Pediatrics (5 weeks)

In San Francisco as in Washington, D.C., Edna was the key to arranging my first clerkship in that city. In those years she was Head of the Department of Education. One of her many innovations was to pioneer a program to train teachers for work with hospitalized children. To develop that program she appointed a renowned specialist to the faculty, Evelyn Oremland. As it happened, Professor Oremland provided a second key by putting me in the hands of her influential husband, Jeremy Oremland, M.D., who was Head of the Department of Psychiatry at Children's Hospital of San Francisco. Through Dr.

Oremland I met with, and was approved by, his colleague, Stanley Steinberg, M.D., who was in a position to admit me because he served as Director of Training at the hospital. It is unlikely I would have been accepted into the Children's Hospital teaching program were it not for highly placed professionals who were willing to give me a chance.

At Children's Hospital I earned credit for:

- Psychiatry (96 hrs)
- Inpatient Psychiatric Consultation (96 hrs)
- Child Psychiatry (120 hrs)

Those assignments kept me busy from September 2 to October 18. I am happy to report that my sponsors' trust in me was justified. The record read, "Dr. Anderson's work during the 7-week period of his clerkships was of highest quality."

At that point in my career as a medical student a colleague became my benefactor, Arthur H. White, M.D., an orthopedic surgeon at St. Mary's Hospital and Medical Center, San Francisco. Just three years earlier, in 1982, Dr. White became founding director of the St. Mary's Spine Center. Similar centers could be found in other major cities, but St. Mary's was the first that was explicitly and aggressively multidisciplinary. His program included physical therapists and other non-surgical medical specialties as well as a range of alternative health care providers, including chiropractors. Because I was a board-certified and licensed chiropractor, a medical anthropologist and an academician, he decided I was well positioned to contribute to his state-of-the-art program and he integrated me with gusto. He had me design and administer clinical trials under the Center's auspices and make presentations at annual national clinical conferences of an organization known as *The Challenge of the Lumbar Spine.* Not the least, he arranged for me to complete all of my remaining clerkship requirements at St. Mary's.

In the summer of 1986 I wrote a long letter to Dr. White to bring him up to date on one of the research projects on back pain sponsored jointly by Mills College and the Spine Center (Anderson, 1992). I used that letter to thank him for his support, and I reprint the closing paragraph below, because it allows me to acknowledge my debt to a terrific human being. Sponsored by Dr. White, between October 19, 1985, and May 25, 1986, I completed the remaining required clerkships at St. Mary's:

- General Surgery (168 hrs)
- Ophthalmology (56 hrs)
- Orthopedics and Traumatology (168 hrs)
- Otorrhinolaringology (56 hrs)
- Electives in Surgery [all spinal] (120)
- Free Electives [non-surgical spinal] (96)
- Cardiology (160 hrs)
- Endocrinology (40)
- Gastroenterology (160 hrs)
- Hematology and Oncology (32 hrs)
- Nephrology (96 hrs)
- Respiratory Diseases (160 hrs)
- Gynecology (152 hrs)
- Obstetrics (160 hrs)
- Pediatrics (168 hrs)
- Neurology (96 hrs)

The following paragraph (shortened and redacted) concluded my letter to Dr. White on July 31, 1986, a few weeks after I completed two years and twenty-three clerkships:

> I am so happy to be back into my regular life again, Art. I anticipate being more effective as a medical anthropologist now that I have medical qualifications. That would not have happened last year had I not been invited into hospital training by highly respected department heads in several American medical centers. You, especially, made extremely valuable opportunities available to me. Because of my prior commitment to research on back pain, the chance to be based for seven months in the St. Mary's Hospital Spine Center provided the richest possible training. Not the least, your unfaltering support made it possible to live in my

own home with my wonderful companion, Edna, rather than in a motel in some remote area doing clerkships in a less stimulating hospital. I am deeply grateful.

Clinic Highlights from American Clerkships

During that year in the United States clinics surpassed wards and operating rooms for hands-on experience. Clinics were busy places with streams of patients moving in and out as long as the doors were open. They provided endless opportunities to take responsibility for appropriate aspects of patient care. Urology clinics twice a week got me started, but none was more rewarding than obstetrics and gynecology, partly because my training in Mexico made me useful to house staff. Many of our patients were Latina and it proved helpful that I could handle medical Spanish. On the rotation in Mexico I was assigned to elicit medical histories and perform preliminary physical examinations, but never to undertake more aggressive maneuvers such as pelvic examinations or to deliver babies.

In my American rotation willing residents initiated me rapidly into taking complete initial responsibility for clinic patients, my work carefully checked at each step. Moving beyond the general history and physical, they taught me how to manipulate a speculum to examine the cervix and scrape off tissue for pap smear analysis. I acquired basic skills such as how to identify pathology digitally by performing a bi-manual vaginal examination.

To help in processing the flow of waiting patients I was assigned to perform prenatal examinations, learning how to feel for the position of the fetus, to listen to and interpret the fetal heart-beat and to measure the growing abdomen as those findings were correlated with the normal expectations of fetal growth. I soon learned how to order a sonogram or lab work, practiced how to enquire for symptoms of trouble, such as headaches with edema that might forewarn of a life-threatening toxemia of pregnancy. In all, I was coached and double-checked on skills that any fully qualified doctor would consider very basic, but which excited me as I moved beyond observing to hands-on participation (participant observation as we would say in anthropology).

It was scary at times to take on those simple responsibilities, especially when two lives at once were at stake. In the labor and delivery rooms I was taught to implant small wires in an unborn baby's head in what I was told was not a cruel, unnatural procedure so much as a wonderful instrument to alert the obstetrician to fetal distress, with its possibilities for hideous consequences that could transform a healthy fetus into an impaired, perhaps palsied baby. And, like other medical students, I learned to interpret the wavy lines that flowed across an oscilloscope as a monitor of the baby's response to increasingly frequent and heavy contractions.

No moment in my entire professional career ever matched the thrill of delivering a baby for the first time. I was backed up by two nervous Ob-Gyn residents who were understandably uneasy about my skill-level, but acknowledged that I had assisted in enough births and studied enough assigned readings to be ready for my initiation. I arrived one morning to be told that the next delivery would be mine.

My patient was an immigrant from El Salvador who arrived to deliver her first child. Her husband was at work, not because he was unaware that he could be present at the birth if he chose, but because he needed his daily wage and besides, in his home village men stayed away when their wives delivered. I spent much of the day in a labor room with that young, frightened and hurting mother-to-be. Although I spoke colloquial Spanish imperfectly, probably on a level with her immigrant husband's English, we had time to talk, and it meant a lot that she could share her experience with me. I explained what was taking place as the hours passed. I reassured her when she thought the monitor meant that her baby was in trouble. I jollied her along by reminding her that her child would be an American citizen. I held her hand as contractions squeezed into excruciating pain and she groaned, " I can't take it anymore." What could I say to help? Perhaps it helped just to have me say, "Yes, I know," or, following an even deeper groan, "I'm sorry, but you have to get through it." Once, in her agony, she laughed when I said, "OK, we'll take five minutes for a Coke break, but then we have to get on with it again."

The resident palpated with her rubber glove to ascertain the position of the baby and how far down its head had descended. With permission of the patient, I checked too. There is no other way to learn how the cervix feels as it widens and thins and how the fontanel's of a baby's head can be differentiated so you know which way the baby has turned.

Finally we rushed to the labor room, and while the residents and I scrubbed and gowned the delivery room anesthesiologist and nurses prepared the parturient. Seated on a stool to "catch" the baby, and with a resident at each elbow (because they really were uneasy about my level of readiness), I talked my patient through the process. The head was crowning. "She needs an episiotomy," one of the residents muttered, handing me a pair of scissors. A quick snip widened the birth canal. Abruptly, the head began to emerge. I was supposed to place my hand against it and instruct the mother to stop pushing so the vaginal tissues could have a few seconds to stretch, but it happened far faster than I expected, and suddenly I had the head in my hands. From then on I performed adequately. Automatically, from many rehearsals, I turned the head and lowered it to ease out the first shoulder, then raised it up for the second, and WOW, I had the whole baby in my hands, held low to permit blood to drain into it before we cut the umbilical cord.

The cord cut, I handed the infant to a neonatologist who did an evaluation, found it healthy, put on its identification bracelet, and had it "sign" the birth record with imprints of its feet. I occupied myself with extrusion of the afterbirth while telling the mother, "it's a girl, and she's perfect." Soon she was holding the baby and cooing to it, all smiles and indifferent to our labor as we sutured the episiotomy.

She suffered a fourth degree tear. One of the residents told me as we departed the delivery room that she was bound to tear, based on evaluation of the birth canal. But the other gave it to me straight. She probably would not have torn so badly if I had stopped the delivery for a few seconds as I had been taught. I felt terrible, and was only slightly consoled to be reminded that she would heal completely, which she did, and, also, that even the world's most experienced obstetrician had to deliver a first baby. Fortunately, I did have two skilled doctors backing me up.

It is an anomaly of teaching hospitals that medical centers headed by the most skilled clinical professors are also those that may assign part of one's care to new residents or even to an occasional medical student capable of making mistakes.

When I saw the new mother the next morning she introduced me to her husband and to her beautiful baby, who now had a name. Her husband, whose broken English was much more fluent than my stilted Spanish, thanked me for all I had done in staying with her through labor as well as for doing the delivery, and she did too. But something was gone from our relationship. It had become formal again. The previous day, as I held her hand, wiped her brow, and provided what solace I could, we achieved a heart-warming intimacy. I shall never forget her despairing face just inches from my own as she pleaded, "I can't take it anymore." She clung to me as we moved rapidly down the corridor that separated the labor room from the delivery room. She trusted me as she struggled under surgical lamps, unaware that I felt nervous and uncertain. We exulted together as we shared that darling little baby whom she drew gently to her heart. Each of us in our own way will never forget that moment of shared fear and ecstasy. What an unparalleled experience for every new mother, and for every new doctor. Can any other profession match it?

The Emergency Room

I got far less emergency room experience than I would have liked during my two years of hospital training. When a rapidly evolving emergency occurs, even a medical student can get heavily involved and learn a lot. In Mexico I mostly watched while others got hands-on experience. My ER experience in the United States wasn't much better, since I never did a formal rotation in emergency medicine. From time to time, however, I hurried along with a resident or attending when we were called in for a specialty consultation.

The first experience occurred during my first week in the United States, when I went with Justo to attend to a patient who had been in the ER all day with nobody able to figure out what was causing his problem. He had come in complaining of back pain and of passing blood in his urine. Justo was called in to check him out, since it sounded like a genitourinary problem. As we pushed open the door to the examination room, Justo told me that the ER doctors were stumped. They checked out the usual causes of hematuria and nothing positive showed up. Checking for bladder infection or a lesion in the urethra came up negative. An x-ray pyelogram ruled out kidney stones. He did not present a history of trauma to the kidneys. The rectal exam eliminated prostate hypertrophy. What could it be?

As we approached the patient Justo pimped me. "What test would you order now?" With that I made one of the best diagnostic guesses of my student career. Of course it is very un-chic to guess, and on the whole I did restrain myself, since you are never rewarded merely for a lucky guess. The practice of medicine is not a lottery. If you win it is because you demonstrated well thought out reasoning. If your suggestion turned out to be wrong but you had reasoned well, you still looked pretty good. But I hadn't learned that yet, so I responded with a guess. "I would order a test for sickle cell disease."

Justo responded in the predictable pimping way by asking, "Why?" Still one more time, being an anthropologist helped. The patient was black. I knew that almost ten percent of African Americans carry the sickle cell gene. In chiropractic training I was taught that the disease can manifest in multiple organ systems. Without crediting chiropractic college, and benefiting from knowing that all of the most likely causes had been ruled out, I explained that the underlying problem in all manifestations of the sickle cell disease involved clogging of capillary blood vessels by deformed red blood cells. My guess was that it could occur in a kidney.

Happily, Justo found my justification adequate, and let me enjoy a triumph that was otherwise his alone. He had already decided, without telling me, that the man was probably experiencing a sickling crisis. And the truth is, I had no idea why sickled blood cells would turn one's urine red. I hunted that night for the answer, and read that obstructed capillaries deprive affected parts of the kidney of oxygen. That caused blood cells to breakdown. I am still unclear about the underlying chemistry. You can spend a lifetime mastering medicine, which is why it can seem quite overwhelming to a student. Anyway, I did well enough on that, and soon after was informed that my next rotation at Washington Hospital Center had been approved. I would be allowed to finish out the summer there.

But on to San Francisco in the fall, where I got some additional ER experience by responding whenever I could if the loudspeaker announced a "Code Blue." It meant that somebody was in cardiac arrest, and people rushed in from all over the hospital, since speed was essential. I rarely did more than watch, run off to carry a tissue specimen to the laboratory for analysis, or hold something for a doctor. In principle, I learned the basics of what one should do, but I would have panicked if ever had to do more than hold the fort by administering cardiopulmonary resuscitation (CPR). If I was nervous the first time I had to remove a foley catheter, went into a spasm the first time I sutured a simple skin incision, reacted too slowly to ease the delivery of a baby, you can imagine that my first time as the responsible physician in an arrest would be scary – for all concerned – but it never happened.

My biggest personal responsibility for providing emergency care as a medical student fell reasonably well within my capabilities. It began when I was assisting Dr. Zuckerman in the cast room at St. Mary's. "We" had just pulled a fingernail out of the crushed finger of a patient who nearly went through the ceiling from pain and fright. My contribution was to spray the finger with a freezing solution while Dr. Z. tugged at the nail with his forceps.

We got it done and were preparing to leave when the head nurse poked her head in the door. "Dr. Zuckerman, come quickly, Mr. Mario is having a seizure." We dashed down the corridor and pushed through a small knot of people surrounding the patient. In addition to nurses and doctors the cluster included the man's wife, mother, father, and brother, each expressing anguish as the patient contorted in massive waves that climaxed in a full body spasm known as opisthotonos. All of the muscles of the back, legs and neck contracted to raise his body into a cantilevered arch supported only at the heels and head. It was very dramatic. (In a microsecond of recall I flashed back to a chiropractic classroom and a moment when the medical doctor teaching our class laughed at me for incorrectly pronouncing opisthotonos.)

Dr. Z. pushed directly through to the head of the table, boldly pulled back the eyelids to fix his gaze on the patient's gyrating pupils. I looked too. "He's not having a seizure. He'll be OK in a minute," and out he went to examine a possible ankle fracture in another room.

I followed, bewildered. "That's not a seizure. The guy's a jerk," Dr. Z. told me. "In a true seizure the eyes are fixed, not moving around. Also, this guy was answering questions, even though his neck and face were so contracted that he could only gasp his words. People in seizure are non-responsive when you talk with them. You're interested in psychiatry, Bob. He's your patient."

Fresh out of my psychiatry clerkships, that suited me fine, so back I went. The father caught up with me in the corridor. The family originated from a part of the Mediterranean where men like to talk face-to-face at a distance of about six inches. It makes most Americans feel uncomfortable, but I knew about that cultural trait from an anthropologist colleague, Edward Hall, so that didn't bother me in itself, although his sour breath was rather off-putting.

The father was outraged. "What kind of a doctor is that," he gesticulated, "taking ten seconds to look at him and make a diagnosis. How can he know anything without looking at his records. Somebody has to take care of my son. It will kill his mother," at which point we both turned to look into the room where the mother was screaming in an hysterical fit.

Mario was twenty-five years old and had been married for only a year. He earned a meager living as an artist and lived with his attractive young wife in a small apartment built on to his parent's home. His three brothers also still lived at home. It was a great case for an ethnographically informed psychiatrist, I mused, as I learned that Mario had been rear-ended in a minor automobile accident that caused a painful whiplash injury to his neck. He suffered a lot of pain but no pseudoseizures, as his episodes are called, until he submitted to a cervical myelogram in our hospital.

Before the radiologist did the myelogram he warned that the procedure might cause a severe headache, and - on quite rare occasions - a seizure, but side-effects would subside - usually in a day. Mario evidently responded, at least subconsciously, to the possibility of seizure, but not to the time limitation. He had suffered pseudoseizures ever since.

I saw the patient as a candidate for psychotherapy, but what could I do in an emergency room? Whiplash was a neck-related problem. Cervical pathology undoubtedly fed into his seizures. Even Dr. Zuckerman agreed on that. So I decided to examine his neck. At the least, from what I had been taught in chiropractic college, he might benefit from a bit of gentle hands-on stroking.

Back with the rest of the family and Mario, who had quieted down,

I moved to where Dr. Z. had stood. Gently, I stroked my fingers down the back of his neck, feeling for nodules or restrictions of movement that might suggest benefit from a gentle massage.

Immediately, Mario's eyes fluttered. "He's seizing again," the father groaned. "He can't take nothing on his neck." The whole family started to tense up along with the patient. What could I do? Instead of making him feel better I had triggered a recurrence of opisthotonos (pronounced with emphasis on the middle syllable).

I stepped outside to consult with Dr. Z. He ordered a quick acting intravenous tranquilizer, an offshoot of valium. With that, Mario eventually calmed down. When I checked in on him later he was laughing and chatting with his brother. He always felt fine after an attack, as though nothing had happened, except for a couple of days of soreness from the muscle cramps. His appetite was fine, and even though his life was a mess, he manifested what is known in the psychiatric literature as *la bell indifférance*.

Eventually a psychiatrist dropped in and concluded he would be willing to see Mario on a once-a-month basis, but only if he could see the family as a whole in at least some of those sessions. Then the psychiatrist slipped away to see another patient. It was left to me to ease Mario and the family out of the emergency room. I spent six hours with them that day.

Clerkship Related Programs

Although the emphasis was on clerkships, students spent hours each week away from wards and clinics to attend conferences of various kinds. Professional meetings, such as the annual *Challenge of the Lumbar Spine*, were rare. A student might attend the annual meeting of a medical specialty, with several days of sessions that report updates on current topics or new research findings. When I began urology, for example, several of the residents were out of town to attend their annual convention. While I was a medical student I attended an annual meeting of the Society for Medical Anthropology, but I did not make it that year to a strictly medical convention, which was probably typical for medical students, if only because they are often located in distant places.

A student was more likely to attend a regional medical meeting. I attended one while doing my rotation in psychiatry. For two days during a sunny fall weekend I rubbed shoulders with psychiatrists, psychologists and other health care professionals sitting in on a series of lectures that assembled clinician-scientists from all over the country to address the issue of doing intensive psychotherapy with disturbed individuals. That type of meeting was also rare in a student's experience.

Grand rounds, in contrast, were frequent and valuable. Throughout the second half of my American year I attended at least two a week, one every Monday in general surgery and another every Tuesday in general medicine. In addition, when I could be released from clinical duties, I occasionally sat in on grand rounds in cardiology, psychiatry, rheumatology, and other specialty fields. The typical format was that of a lecture. The speaker might come from some distant medical school, or she might be one of our own attending staff, and frequently it was a resident who undertook a thorough review of the current literature to provide an overview lecture.

A common format was to focus grand rounds on a complex problem in diagnosis and treatment. In one of our medical grand rounds, for example, a resident started the meeting by presenting the case of a moderately ill forty-seven year old white female, previously in excellent health, with complaints of diarrhea, joint pain and a nodular rash on her arms and legs. After that summary introduction she summarized the patient's past medical history as well as findings in her review of systems, none of which was very relevant. Laboratory findings and other test results were summarized and management of the case was described.

After that detailed overview, the senior attending physician discussed the case and the kinds of problems it presented. Finally, an open discussion among physicians in the audience took place. That patient was of particular interest to me, since she was diagnosed with joint disease secondary to ulcerative colitis, and I was eager to learn all I could about normal and abnormal joint function.

Each subfield of medicine and each teaching hospital scheduled its own version of departmental conferences that met for an hour to explore a topic in basic science or some clinical topic that was relevant to the specialty field. On the whole, they were run in a manner similar to those of grand rounds, except that they covered topics sequentially throughout the year, much as is done in a course taught at the university.

Departmental conferences provided the didactic component of post-graduate residency training. Medical students were expected to attend the lectures while they were clerking in the department. It could add up to only a couple of weeks. The longest I got was six weeks on Ob-Gyn. However, because I was especially interested in certain fields, I managed to attend some conferences independently of my clerkships.

I began each day with an hour-and-a-half in radiology. During the first half-hour I usually did one of two things. Often I sat with a radiologist as she read urgent films taken during the night or in time for morning rounds. Alternatively, I joined radiology residents, each of whom in turn was assigned to present some particularly interesting or complex case, which might be based on standard plain or contrast radiography, CAT scans, sonograms, magnetic nuclear resonance films, or xerograms (radiographic images on paper). Case presentations always began with identifying normal anatomy and whatever pathology could be detected. The focus was on the differential diagnosis and whatever additional studies were needed as appropriate treatment came under review. I found that radiology provided an intense ongoing involvement in every field of medicine and surgery, with each patient, although not present in the flesh, a basis for reviewing or learning a lot of medicine in a matter of minutes.

After that half-hour warm-up, an instructor from the nearby University of California School of Medicine took over. Usually each teacher showed up once every two weeks (and unlike medical school in the State of Chihuahua, they never stood us up). In that way, we were systematically guided through major subspecialties such as neuroradiology, which included reviews of brain anatomy focused on the structures we needed to be able to identify on CAT scans. Nuclear magnetic imaging and other imaging techniques were also taught. Other sessions covered the chest or the abdomen and pelvis, also with constant visualization of the involved anatomy from various perspectives, always with identification of pathology, the differential diagnosis, review of treatment options, and expectable outcomes. Pediatric radiology had its own hour

Because I especially wanted to learn as much as I could about musculoskeletal disorders, radiology related to the skeleton especially captured my attention. I joined the program at St. Mary's thinking that X-ray and CAT scan examination of the bony anatomy would be fields in which I would excel. As a chiropractor, I had a California State License to Supervise and Operate X-Ray Equipment. However, I soon realized that my personal experience was very limited compared to what those residents and instructors knew, and I had to work hard those months to keep from looking ignorant.

I was there as a medical student for an unusually long time. Every three weeks, two or three new interns and an occasional medical student joined us for a shorter rotation. American medical students seemed rather lost in all fields of film interpretation, but interns were quite sharp. With good training, they were learning a lot in their first post-graduate year.

Before and after those morning sessions in radiology I was off doing clerkship duties on the wards, in treatment rooms, or in surgery. Usually I managed to get free for lunch hour presentations with residents in internal medicine.

Internal medicine offered a session each week on topics such as gastroenterology, nephrology, neurology or general internal medicine. I missed their Thursday sessions in order to continue the conferences in psychiatry. The most relevant to my focus on back pain were the neurology sessions in which several different neurologists covered major disease categories. AIDS that year was a new and growing concern in every field of medicine, and not the least in neurology, where understandings of the enormous neurological and psychiatric complications of that devastating disease were increasing at a mind-boggling pace. I also learned some neurology from the gerontologist who lectured to us regularly. Those noon sessions, along with radiology, provided a richly rewarding coverage of general medicine with a focus on diagnosis and patient care. It was gratifying to round out and deepen what I had learned in chiropractic college and during my first year in the PhD-to-MD program in medical school.

Not the least, from four to seven on Monday evenings and from four to five on Tuesdays, I sat in a windowless classroom in the basement of the hospital where residents in orthopedics convened their classes on bone and joint diseases. With that I got a review of slightly over half of the major skeletal systems, and was particularly fortunate that they included the spine, hip, knee and foot. As a major plus, a series on pediatric orthopedics introduced me to a field in which I especially needed training.

The pediatric lectures differed from those in psychiatry, radiology and internal medicine that were presented by qualified experts. In the pediatric meetings residents taught each other, much as my cohort had done in Mexico, but with an important difference. First, the teaching standards were very high. A resident normally devoted several days to careful preparation. Second, attending physicians always joined us to evaluate and discuss each lecture. Third, it was always considered important to include the most current information in the literature. Fourth, once a week the head of the residency program discussed relevant x-rays with us. Fifth and extremely important, it was usually possible sooner or later to examine a patient who manifested the disorder under discussion. Always, teaching in the hospital moved easily and consistently from the classroom to the bedside and back to the classroom.

Since the arrival of patients was unpredictable, it was impossible to put specific diseases on the teaching calendar. We had to be ready to cope with problems of all kinds at any time. Reminiscent of pop quizzes in a liberal arts college that might harshly challenge an undergraduate who had partied all night, on rounds a medical student might get exhaustingly pimped on a new case after being up all night on call.

Once a month on rare occasions when I was able, I attended morbidity and mortality conferences, known as M & M's. In those, staff physicians and house officers reviewed all deaths that had taken place, along with all cases in which questions of poor or improper treatment might come into in question. As a variant of those, in one hospital I attended a couple of meetings of the tumor board in which clinicians from different fields focused on problems in the treatment of cancer.

The surgery residency program included a meeting every week of what they referred to as a text club. Reading a major textbook on general surgery together, each resident in turn presented a chapter review. As often as not, a resident might just write lecture notes directly from the text and read from them in a flat and uninspiring way. Those meetings were a good time to sit in the back of the room and catch up on sleep.

Even if I tried hard to get something out of one of those presentations, I just couldn't stay awake. We were all sleep deprived.

Journal clubs were common in all of the hospitals in which I trained in the states. They usually met once a month, when a resident was supposed to summarize and evaluate current publications. Usually those topics were highly technical and remote from the basic medicine and surgery I was learning, so more often than not I did not find them useful. I startled the chief resident in urology once when he said, "Bob, I'll run off some copies of the articles we'll be discussing tomorrow so you can read them in advance and have them for your files." He was such a nice guy, but I had just looked over the articles and concluded that only a fully trained urologist would find them interesting or useful, so, thinking of his time and the cost of photocopying, I thoughtlessly said, "Oh, don't bother." He was so shaken he had to laugh. Apparently no medical student had ever said no to that offer before. I boxed myself in a corner with that foolishness, and had to struggle from then on to demonstrate in every way I could that I really was a serious student.

I have saved one kind of instruction for the last. From time to time, more frequently on some services than on others, the representative of a pharmaceutical company got involved in the conference program. A rep usually got our attention by providing food. If we were lucky it would be a buffet lunch of delicatessen foods, or an afternoon snack. But we were also pleased to accept gifts of pens, flashlights, and other goodies. For a while I kept a shirt that read, "one night only" to advertise Clotrimazole in tablet form as an overnight cure for vaginal itching. I was never able to decide where I might wear it. Whatever the gift might be, a Big Pharma Rep typically asked for fifteen minutes to explain a product and how it could be prescribed, leaving free samples for doctors to pass on to patients. Similar presentations were also made at the medical school in Mexico and in chiropractic college, where sales people demonstrated treatment aids for chiropractors to sell to patients.

All in all, then, I had a busy classroom schedule during my training year up north. During the first five months I averaged a dozen meetings every week, which increased to an astonishing twenty a week for the final seven months. Those sessions added up to more classroom time than is usual for a full load of courses in an undergraduate university program. It was also much more than the average medical student attended.

In addition, we were expected to do outside reading and to pass examinations at the end of each clerkship. The exams were not as difficult as you might imagine. They were generally informal and quite non-threatening. A couple of times my exam was to present a topic to residents in their weekly conference. Most of my exams were to examine a patient, discuss the differential diagnosis, and explain my treatment plan. The focus in hospital teaching was on helping students grow. I thrived in that atmosphere.

My Last Two Days at St. Mary's Hospital

It was 7:00 a.m. on Thursday, May 15, 1986 when I entered the doctors' dining room at St. Mary's Hospital and Medical Center. It was comforting to realize I had completed my last clinical rotation and had attended my last conference as a medical student. My plan was to walk across Golden Gate Park later in the morning to UCSF where Vert Mooney, M.D., a distinguished spine surgeon from the University of Texas Southwestern Medical School, was scheduled to give a talk. I knew Vert well from *The Challenge of the Lumbar Spine* and once even shared the speaker's stand with him. But I had arrived early enough to relax over a morning snack first.

With time to spare and a cup of coffee in hand I noticed that Jim Metcalf, the President and CEO of St. Mary's, had also dropped in for a cup of coffee. Mr. Metcalf, whom I had not met before, invited me to sit at his table and the timing couldn't have been better. I would need to have Dr. White's signature notarized on official papers that would also need to be embossed in the president's office with the corporate seal. I was worried about the corporate seal, because my status at the hospital was irregular. Mexican medical students were not eligible for clerkships at that time.

Mr. Metcalf was very supportive. I told him exactly how I had arrived at St. Mary's. It didn't bother him at all since I was officially sponsored by Dr. White as Medical Director of the Spine Center, and that was all that mattered. Metcalf commented that schools attach more importance to the corporate seal than they should, and that was all there was to it.

The next day, I arrived at the president's office at 9:45 only to learn that the secretary who had the seal and the notary public authority was in a meeting until 10:30. However, it worked out fine. When she returned she paged Dr. White out of surgery and got all of my papers signed, notarized, and embossed with the corporate seal of the hospital. That did it! I had finished my formal training.

Ten days later Edna and I packed the car and set out for Texas. We were in the audience at the University of Texas Southwestern Medical School on May 31 in time to celebrate my son Scott's graduation with his new M.D. degree. Scott eventually went on from there to the University of California at San Francisco and Berkeley to earn a Ph.D. in medical anthropology – all through the front door. Our daughter Kris - also through the front door - was a medical student that year at George Washington University. The next year she completed a clinical clerkship at Washington Hospital Center where I had clerked.

After Scott's graduation Edna flew off to work for a month in the Washington office of Congressman Lantos and I continued driving to the twin cities of El Paso and Ciudad Juarez, where I spent the last fourteen days of a journey that started eight years earlier when, for the first time, I opened the door and walked into the president's office at Pacific States Chiropractic College.

The Exit Examination in Mexico

I found myself back in Ciudad Juarez on Monday, June 2, and spent the day paper chasing. It was tedious, with moments of uncertainty, but by the end of the day the Assistant Dean signed off on my two years of clerkships. I paid a $6,000 tuition fee for that year in the states, and was pronounced qualified for the last hurdle, the exit examination, which was to be my last formal examination.

I had passed Day One of the FMGEMS (qualifying examinations for foreign medical graduates), covering basic medical sciences, in El Paso a year and a half earlier. I found the basic science exam to be very difficult, but quite fair. We sat for two 2-hour exams in the morning and a third 2½ hour exam in the afternoon. I knew from what others had told me that to pass you had to move rapidly from one question to the next without slowing down to ponder any one question. I had attended medical school classes faithfully and studied to do well in those courses, resisting the temptation to practice more than minimally for the exams, but nonetheless I passed Day One on the first try. I passed Day Two of the FMGEMS a year later in San Francisco. In addition to a test on English, that exam also came in three parts, two hours each, all three on clinical sciences. Again, I passed on the first try.

At the end of the two years, with both parts of the FMGEMS out of the way, all that remained for certification as a medical doctor by the Educational Commission for Foreign Medical Graduates (ECFMG) was to meet what they refer to as medical credential requirements. The final requirement for that was to return to Juarez to take an exit examination at the *Instituto de Ciencias Biomédicas*.

In Juarez to get over that last hurdle, the secretary who processed our official transcripts that Monday told us the exam would probably be given four days hence on Friday and Saturday, and it would be probably take three weeks after that before we would be issued our diplomas. But although that guess about diplomas was framed in the usual uncertainties, her speculation that the exit exam would be administered on Friday and Saturday made sense.

On Thursday, the day before we expected to be examined, the Assistant Dean announced a different date for the exit exam. Now we were told it would probably be the following Monday, eight days after we were first informed about dates by the secretary. But what kind of a test should we be preparing for? Multiple choice? Practical? Other? Should we appear in white medical student attire? We could only wonder and guess. And although we were within days of becoming qualified M.D.'s, we were experienced enough to worry that something might come up to postpone or even terminate our medical careers.

The Monday of the big test came and went with no examination and no explanation. Following instructions we gathered at 9:00 a.m. in our old classroom. After hanging around for over an hour a secretary told us we should come back after lunch. After lunch she explained that the Assistant Dean was on the phone and wanted her to tell us that they were still processing our papers, so the exam would be delayed until

Wednesday and would continue on through Friday. However, we should return the next day for confirmation.

The next day, Tuesday, we showed up to be told that it could not be Wednesday as hoped. Given so much uncertainty we all showed up on Wednesday in the classroom anyway.

That was when one of our fellow students said he was told by the Assistant Dean that we would have to stay in Ciudad Juarez all summer to take the exam unless we were willing to pay. If we handed over a payment we would be able to get it done the following two days (Thursday and Friday), after which all of the paperwork would be taken care of for us and we could return to our homes that coming weekend. Was his statement fact or rumor? Was there any truth behind it? We talked it over and decided to refuse to negotiate. Later, two students, Fred and Wally, did offer to pay $250 each, but they were turned down, presumably because it was not enough. Or were they turned down because a bribe was considered inappropriate? After hanging round for another couple of hours, thoroughly confused, we all gave up and returned to our lodgings.

The rumor was that if we paid a bribe we could take the exam beginning on Thursday, so that Thursday morning we gathered in our classroom to consider our options. We finally agreed we would march to the Assistant Dean's office to protest that we wanted to take the exit examination now without making an under-the-table payment, but as we deliberated one of our classmates suddenly burst through the door breathless to gasp that we had to get to the hospital across town immediately. Several school doctors were already waiting to examine us. The time had come, eleven days after we first presented ourselves in the PhD-to-MD office and a full week after the first anticipated date.

I drove to the hospital, parked, and walked in carrying my whites on my arm. An instructor I remembered from the end of the first summer, when we sat for the comprehensive examination on basic sciences, attempted to stop me because I was not dressed in white. I quickly slipped past him.

Gordon Graham and I were assigned to a patient. Our test began with doing a history and physical (H & P). Before we could get started we were joined by a third assigned student, Seti, one of the bad guys. He was useless. He didn't speak Spanish at all. He had managed to get credit for two years of clerkships in Mexico without ever having done an H & P.

We got started. The man had no front teeth. He had worked in Texas for 18 years, but didn't speak a word of English. Although I could handle formal medical Spanish adequately, I faltered perilously on colloquial Spanish and was truly challenged by the edentulous patient with slurred speech. Fortunately, he was very cooperative and understood the virtue of speaking as slowly and distinctly as he could.

On examination of our 67-year-old patient, we identified a traumatic injury to his ankle that was complicated by poor circulation. It was a pretty simple case with no hidden surprises; not a difficult exam at all. No laboratory values were made available, so we had to depend entirely on what we could elicit in conversation (the history) and what we could see and feel (the physical examination.)

With those findings in hand we drove to my quarters to work them up. Gordon and I collaborated easily, but Seti was useless. He couldn't even type or write. (His English speech never included definite or indefinite articles.) We agreed on a differential diagnosis, moved on to indicate what laboratory and x-ray work we would order to confirm and refine a diagnosis, and proposed possible treatment plans. By the time Gordon and I had typed our report it was 9:00 p.m., so I took him out for dinner to celebrate and learn more about his North American year.

The next morning, June 13, I showed up for the oral examination at 8:30 a.m. The faculty arrived at ten, and I survived the orals. However, diplomas would be delayed until all formal paperwork for the full two years had been approved; maybe by sometime next week. I argued to no avail. Some of my fellow students felt I was too confrontational.

I was so discouraged. I decided to see if a gift (bribe) would hasten the process. The following day I arrived at our classroom before anyone else, and fortunately the Assistant Dean was nearby in his office. I was permitted in to talk with him right away. I figured from his rejection of Fred and Wally, that he would accept $500 or maybe $1000. I began by explaining that I had to leave. He asked if I needed my papers before August. I said no, I didn't, because I was returning to teaching. "OK," he replied, "I'll take care of your papers as long as you don't need them before August." I politely asked how much he would need to take care of it. To my astonishment he said, "nothing."

I will never understand the bribery system down there. However, I thought it would be prudent to sign over a travelers check for $100 as a gift (to ensure his good will), but I clearly did not need to. I also gave $20 bills to each of the secretaries.

He agreed as part of our conversation that he would sign two letters, one to the Dean of the Faculty at Mills College to certify that I had completed the full five-year medical school curriculum in two years. The other to the Commission for Foreign Medical Graduates to verify that I had completed all requirements, but that my graduation papers were still being processed and would be delayed. I mailed that one by registered mail from the Juarez post office.

Medically Qualified at Last

It seemed too good to be true. I was ecstatic when I left his office, and soon found myself on the bridge driving over the Rio Grande for the last half-hour bumper-to-bumper crossing I would need to make. Quickly packing up my temporary apartment I paused for a short refreshing swim after which I headed my car onto Highway I-10 to drive home to Oakland

It was eventually certified officially (signed and embossed) that I had survived the last comprehensive examination. My diploma, signed by the Rector of the University and the Governor of the State of Chihuahua, qualified me for the title of physician and surgeon (*el Titulo de Médico Cirujano*), which meant that I was fully qualified to apply for a license to practice in Mexico. The *Titulo* was a more advanced degree than the certificate (*la Acta de Examen Profesional*) normally awarded to graduates at the end of their fifth year, which I also received.

Back in the United States, as a new M.D. with ECFMG certification awarded exactly 30 years after I was granted a Ph.D. by the University of California at Berkeley, I had at last qualified to enter an American residency program as an intern, Post Graduate Year One (PGY-1), should I chose to pursue a license to practice. Of course, I was committed to return to my career as an anthropologist, which had been my intent from the start. An unforgettable ethnographic adventure had ended successfully. Not without mishap, but with success.

Chapter Sixteen

Was it Worth While?

Ethnography as Cultural Description

An anthropologist typically does research by immersing oneself in a society, learning the language if need be, spending a year or two observing, asking questions, getting involved, photographing, videotaping, and writing copious notes on how people live their lives; in other words, on how they experience and manifest their culture. Anthropologists call that method "participant observation," and the goal is to produce a cultural description that can be shared with any and all who might be interested.

To that end I set out to learn about and eventually write about chiropractic as a prominent and important field of alternative medicine. As is common in anthropology, that seemingly straight- forward objective detoured in unanticipated directions. It became a voyage of discovery that brought me to the shores of medicine as well as of chiropractic. I had not anticipated that I would document two similar cultures rather than one. And I had not anticipated that the shores on my voyage of discovery would be a chiropractic college and a foreign medical school.

As an additional unintended consequence of setting out to learn what I could about the culture of chiropractic, I ended up matriculating in the two schools I studied. What began as an ethnography of "the other" became an autoethnography of how I joined fellow students to become a chiropractor in one school and a medical doctor in the other.

As an autoethnography targeted at cultural description it is not meant to serve as a biography. It is only incidentally about me. It is not offered as a window into my soul, although it inevitably does serve as a window. It is offered, rather, as a mirror of my fellow students, their instructors, and their professional communities, of the culture of chiropractic and the culture of medicine. Its purpose and justification was to produce ethnographic descriptions.

As I wrote the cultural descriptions printed here, however, I became aware of still one more unintended consequence. This autoethnography also constitutes a cultural description of the profession of anthropology itself, as a case study of how one ethnographer identified a need for research, oriented potential research to what was already described in the writings of others, identified a community to approach and eventually to live with in order to learn about it by employing the method of participant observation. Other ethnographers might well have exemplified fieldwork differently, just as Norman Kline and I worked differently in Bali. We are all different, but underlying those differences, we are all more or less alike as professional students of humankind.

Description as Autoethnography

The first phase of this long-term ethnography lasted from 1978 to 1983 as I documented student and faculty culture during the start-up years of a new college of chiropractic. It revealed not only how students were trained to become practicing chiropractors, but surprisingly, how they also studied medicine.

In the chiropractic college I attended the intent was not that graduates would ever practice medicine and surgery in any form. However, in the larger national perspective it should be noted that, as a rarely pursued option, chiropractic students in the State of Oregon could, and still can, elect to complete 36 hours of additional course work for certification to practice minor surgery and proctology. It should also be noted that osteopathy was also originally limited to spinal and joint manipulation in ways analogous to the practice of chiropractic, but unlike chiropractors, osteopaths were very aggressive in integrating the study of medicine and surgery. The result was that osteopaths were admitted to full membership in the American Medical Association in 1969.

The second phase of my research, from 1984 to 1986, documented student and faculty culture in the PhD-to-MD program I completed at a medical school in Mexico. It began with a summer of intense course work in the basic sciences designed specifically for us as advanced placement students. The rest of that first academic year placed us in courses on medicine and surgery that were also established specifically to meet our needs. But in addition, it simultaneously placed us in clinical clerkships alongside of regular fourth and fifth-year students.

The second year required us to complete 19 clinical clerkships in American teaching hospitals. I recorded my experiences from Washington Hospital Center, The Children's Hospital of San Francisco, and St. Mary's Hospital and Medical Center in San Francisco.

Ultimately, our most valuable achievement as cultural anthropologists is that we document how people lived their lives while we were with them. In that way we create contemporary descriptions that eventually become historical treasures, irreplaceable archives of the past. To that end I described the chiropractic college I attended as it was thirty years ago during its first four years of solving start-up problems. (My observations should not be taken to represent the college as it is now.) Similarly, I describe the university medical school in Mexico that I attended as it was twenty-five years ago. (Again, my observations should not be taken as descriptive of the school today.) Finally, as an autoethnography, those descriptions also constitute a case study of how one cultural anthropologist conducted a ten-year fieldwork project. Now located in the past, I offer these cultural descriptions as historical documents still alive with contemporary relevance, which is what all professional historians hope for.

Comparative Analysis

Although ethnographic documentation constitutes the pivotal practice for every cultural anthropologist, there is, in fact, a second methodology that is equally important (and I refer here only to cultural anthropology, setting aside biological, archaeological and linguistic subfields). The second method is comparative analysis. It is the method that shapes how we look for ways in which a culture documented by participant observation or autoethnography is both similar to and different from a different culture equally well described. To that end I have described what it was like to study medicine in two contrasting institutions that were similar in that neither was a part of an accredited school of medicine and surgery in the United States. It should be stressed that both were fully accredited in appropriate ways. The chiropractic college was accredited by the Council on Chiropractic Education (CCE) as authorized by the United States Secretary of Education, and the Mexican medical school was regulated by the State Government of Chihuahua. The three hospital teaching programs in the United States in which I did all but four of my twenty-three clinical clerkships were also fully accredited to American medical schools.

Chiropractic Medical Course Work

As demonstrated from my experience as a student, it was possible to learn basic medicine in the chiropractic college I attended, but with four serious limitations.

First, medical subjects were poorly taught. Even several courses taught by a retired medical doctor on the faculty were pedagogically impaired. His instructional technique was to read aloud from the textbook in a monotone as our eyes trailed along with him, page by page and line by line. Only occasionally did he lift his head to insert an illustrative comment from years of general practice.

Second, students had to be self-motivated to work hard on mastering medical subjects. They enrolled in chiropractic college to learn spinal manipulation, not how to prescribe medicine or practice surgery for which they would never be licensed. Also, the courses were difficult for most of my fellow students who enrolled only minimally prepared by undergraduate premedical science courses. On the whole, the class seemed to view medical subjects as unwelcome detours from the chiropractic program that truly inspired them.

Third, surgery and pharmacology as central therapeutic subjects in a medical school curriculum were not taught. Because the college was committed to a "straight" as opposed to a "mixer" philosophy, the use of medicine and surgery for most kinds of illness, and especially for almost all musculoskeletal disorders, was disparaged and discouraged. The school was required to teach medicine by the Council on Chiropractic Education (CCE), so understandably the subject was of interest only as a way to learn as much as possible about harmful side effects and unintended consequences. Surgery was outlawed for chiropractors in California and instead of pharmacology a course on toxicology was taught.

Fourth, and perhaps most significant, medicine was taught almost entirely in the absence of opportunities for students in the teaching clinic to examine patients for medical problems. Medical cases would have been most welcome. They would have been appreciated as teaching cases for how chiropractic spinal adjusting or other non-pharmaceutical remedies might offer potential alternatives to medical treatment. However, patients seeking care in the clinic were self-selected for musculoskeletal health problems.

Although the program in medicine was weak, I would stress that our training for the chiropractic evaluation and management of spinal and peripheral joint pain and dysfunction (subluxations) was intense and thorough. Our classes included upper cervical specific adjusting (the "hole-in-one" approach developed by B. J. Palmer), which we studied in one of two popular versions competing as the Gonstead technique or as the National Upper Cervical Chiropractic Association (NUCCA) method. They seemed to offer no more than placebos. However, we graduated well trained and rehearsed in an extensive armamentarium of full-spine adjusting techniques, many of which have been demonstrated in randomized controlled trials to be effective for the relief of pain and immobility (Bronfort, 1992: 415-441).

Students were thoroughly dedicated to the principles and practice of chiropractic, and more broadly to natural healing methods. Classroom teaching and informal student-initiated experimentation inspired mutually reinforcing interests in natural foods and healthy life styles. The result was communitas. Students respected one another, helped one another, taught one another, and contributed labor and money to making the school better to the extent they could. It was inspiring in that way.

Medical School Abroad

My training in Mexico was very different. I have no doubt that the five-year medical school program produced physicians and surgeons well qualified to serve the Mexican people. Keep in mind that I can only report on a set-aside program intended for foreign students qualified for advanced placement.

In our program, as unthinkable as it would seem, instructors frequently failed to convene classes and teach, and some were not qualified for the subjects they taught. Fortunately, our class included well-trained scientists as well as experienced practitioners of medicine and surgery in the persons of four veterinarians, a podiatrist, and even a fully qualified American physician and surgeon. During our intensive summer devoted to basic medical sciences, and continuing throughout the first academic year of additional courses, we lectured and tutored one another on a high scientific and skill level that largely made up for failures in the formal program designed for us. That said, our experiences demonstrated two serious failings.

First, much of our time doing clerkships, which were the same as those set up for regular five-year students, was spent just standing around waiting for assignments and supervision. A lot of valuable time was wasted. A year of clinical clerkships in that program offered only half as much as in North American hospitals.

Second, as a particular shortcoming of our two-year set-aside program, half a dozen of our fellow students abused the system. By the end of a year with them it seemed undeniable that they were failing to study and learn medicine and surgery. It seemed clear that they were motivated to earn an M.D. degree as a way to achieve high status and eventually to be well paid. They demonstrated no commitment to the humane purposes of medical practice. Certainly, this much can be said: they did not study, they did not learn much medicine, and they created a bad environment for the rest of us. Whereas we students in the chiropractic college luxuriated in communitas (the benefits of mutual support and encouragement), in medical school we endured scheming, cheating, and even physical violence.

But that was only during the first year. For the second year we all went our separate ways. I didn't see any of my fellow students or even stay in touch with them. We were all far too busy and rushed for that. Although I have no idea how their clerkships progressed, I can testify that mine offered outstanding opportunities to work with doctors, nurses, technicians, patients and administrators in state-of-the-art facilities and under completely supportive conditions. I was privileged, and all the more so because I benefited from special opportunities in the Spine Center to expand what I had learned about back and neck pain in chiropractic college and during my few short months in part-time practice as a licensed chiropractor.

Finally, I must add that I have no information at all about what ultimately happened to the scheming six who cheated. It is possible, even likely, they were awarded the *Acta* or the *Titulo* or both. One or another may also have obtained a license to practice in his home country. However, it would seem unlikely that they would ever advance to licensing in the United States.

First, they would likely have been blocked by the FMGEMS. Those exams required a broad and detailed knowledge of medical and clinical sciences that they did not possess. Even well-qualified applicants were frequently unable to pass on a first or second try. When we returned to Juarez for the last two weeks I was astonished to learn that Gordon Graham had flunked both days of the FMGEMS. Gordon was the assistant professor of entomology who taught human dissection courses at his university and who was assigned to partner with Seti and me for the exit exam. He was clearly was on his way to becoming a skilled and caring doctor. (Remember, he was the one who carried an abandoned baby in his arms for weeks when we clerked in pediatrics.) He and his wife, who was expecting baby number three at any time, were planning to move back to their former apartment in El Paso so he could do one more year in Ciudad Juarez while he crammed to retake the qualifying exams for foreign medical graduates. I am happy to report that he passed during that following year. The last I heard he had completed a residency in the states and was doing well in Texas as a new specialist in family practice.

I did not see that potential in the six bad guys. The FMGEMS, for which bribery and cheating would not work, could only open the door to residency training. If somehow one or another of them managed to gain certification by the Educational Commission for Foreign Medical Graduates, he would still have to find a residency program that would accept him in spite of obvious weaknesses in clinical skills. If, wonder of wonders, admittance was gained, it would require a remarkable turnabout in ethical and professional commitment for him to succeed well enough to finish an internship year and qualify for licensure. I think it most likely that all of them eventually were diverted into other careers.

On to an Ethnography of Practice

Many anthropologists dedicate themselves to using what they have learned about the myriad of different ways people cope with problems of living to recommend and help implement solutions to practical problems, to practice applied anthropology or public interest anthropology. My training prepared me for involvement in recent and evolving changes in the design, implementation and evaluation of public policy relating to the provision of health care.

Within the medical establishment, nurse practitioners, clinical nurse specialists, certified nurse midwives, certified nurse anesthetists, and physician assistants, as well as podiatrists and dentists, optometrists and others pursue professional careers that coordinate with those of medical doctors in ways that have evolved greatly in recent years.

Career lines in complementary and alternative medicine are also part of the mix. Either in combination with conventional medical practitioners (complementary medicine) or as competing forms of practice (alternative medicine) they include a mind-boggling diversity that ranges from truly bizarre to well supported by clinical research.

Medically qualified practitioners – not all by any means, but an increasing number each year – now collaborate with, coordinate with, or at least acknowledge as sincere some kinds of practitioners they would have shunned half a century ago. They include traditional practitioners from non-Western societies, such as providers of Traditional Chinese Medicine (TCM), including herbalists and acupuncturists, as well as practitioners of Qi Gong and Tai Chi. Ayurvedic Medicine from India, except for yoga, is much less known than TCM in the United States, but it too has become increasingly available. Unani (with ancient Graeco-Arabic roots) is available in places. Native American Healing, including sweat lodges and herbal remedies, and survivals of other folk medicine traditions have also grown in popularity.

The origins of many kinds of alternative medicine are much more recent. For back pain, as an example, sufferers can now access practitioners of specialties named after innovators who were still alive when I was a medical student. Most prominent among those are the Feldenkrais Procedure, the Alexander Technique, or Rolfing as well as programs such as the McKenzie Method, the Trager Approach, and Aston Patterning. Other conservative options include naturopathy, homeopathy, a range of meditation techniques, biofeedback, and hypnosis.

Dr. Arthur White was my mentor for the implementation of those policy changes. He got it right early on. His subspecialty as an orthopedic surgeon focused on back and neck pain. When he convened annual meetings of *The Challenge of the Lumbar Spine* his welcoming address always emphasized a very important reality. Low back pain impairs at least 80 percent of all of us at some time in our lives. At any one time, around 20 to 30 percent of us will be afflicted. Many people suffering pain and dysfunction would certainly benefit from professional care.

Early on, however, Dr. White realized that very few of his back and neck pain patients were candidates for surgery. He became an expert on non-surgical approaches, on *The Conservative Care of Low Back Pain*, as he titled the book that he and I edited (1991).

To minister to all Spine Center patients he put together a team of medical practitioners who, in addition to three spine surgeons, were skilled in non-surgical approaches: specialists in internal medicine, physical medicine, psychiatry, nutrition and clinical psychology. Skilled occupational therapists and physical therapists for their part evolved beyond ameliorative hands-on therapies to teach a back school program so that patients could learn to heal themselves and prevent recurrences.

With success, Dr. White became a renegade in his time. He added alternative and complementary medical practitioners to the Spine Center staff. I remember as though it were yesterday, although I do not recall his exact words, that he opened lumbar spine conferences by stating categorically, "None of us can offer cures for all people suffering with back pain. Each of us can help some and not others. We need to stop thinking about competition and develop our capacity for collaboration."

In his introduction to the book he and I edited for practitioners in the field, he described his program this way. "Conservative care commends itself as the first resort for all but the very rare patient who comes to you as a surgical emergency. Conservative care commends itself, when properly carried out, as the only kind of treatment that will be needed for ninety-nine percent of your back pain patients." To that he added, "You may be a physician, a physical therapist, a chiropractor, an osteopathic physician or specialist in some other field of health care. Whatever your field, if it includes the conservative care of low back plain disorders, your primary interest and concern is the well-being of your patient" (1991: 3)

He went on to ask, "Who are we, the specialists in spine care, to whom patients turn?" And in answer to his own question, he said, "We are skilled. We are confident. But we are unorganized, with inadequate means of inter-professional communication. We know too little about the expertise of those outside our own practice. We tend to feel competitive, even jealous, of one another. Patients do not benefit from these attitudes. Society does not benefit. It is clear that we as practitioners also do not benefit" (1991: 5).

In my guise as a practicing anthropologist, I would suggest that Dr. White's philosophy should inform the whole of the heath care community. It is not yet a reality and it will be difficult to implement. Yet it is time to move aggressively in that direction, motivated and supported by the National Center for Complementary and Alternative Medicine (NCCAM), a branch of the United States National Institutes of Health that got its start in 1992. The promise of complementary and alternative medicine reaches far beyond back and neck pain to inspire new ways of thinking about health and health care universally and holistically. But complementary and alternative approaches must be implemented following scientific guidelines based on an ancient ethical principle, *primum non nocere*, "First, do no harm," and well designed clinical trials of efficacy will be required as basic to the practice of evidence based medicine, including complementary and alternative medicine.

Applied Anthropology from Iceland

Not just for back pain, but in the practice of medicine in all of its dimensions, the medical doctor, although captain of the ship, is not the only sailor needed to reach port safely. To allow the crew to function effectively, and most importantly, for practitioners to find pleasure in their work and to be accorded respect in their communities, the big unsolved problem is not only what works in healing. It is about the self-identity of health care providers.

A very big issue for my fellow students in chiropractic college and for chiropractors in their lives, was that it was important for them to be respected as doctors. It was a need in two dimensions. One was that potential patients would be more willing to seek services from a provider qualified as a "doctor." No surprise there. However, the other dimension was usually not discussed or much thought of. It was the need for respect and a social status worthy of respect.

I experienced that in my autoethnography when I was a mere boy and wanted to grow up to be a doctor like Dr. Newton, or like my Uncle Harry, the evangelist. I know it was important to my uncle to be respected as "Dr. Anderson."

I was heavily exposed to it in the chiropractic community, where "doctor" both as a term of address and as a term of identification was constantly articulated and demanded.

Although less a reality in medical school in Ciudad Juarez, it was present in subtle ways. Identification as an M.D. not only promised work that was more challenging and remunerative, it also promised higher status and role benefits.

Meanwhile, in the medical and dental communities of the United States, the high status of the doctor is granted at the expense of those whose work and responsibilities are less central, but nonetheless demanding, important and professional. Those professionals are not addressed as "doctor." I have in mind the nurse specialist, for example, or the dental hygienist. I would argue that we would all benefit from leaving titles aside as invidious and counter-productive symbols of personal worth.

The public school teacher is as important in our communities as the medical doctor. Terms of address should not rank them. And that brings me to Iceland.

It was my privilege in 1998 to teach at the University of Iceland as a Fulbright visiting professor. I learned so much from those remarkable people, and even completed a study of the diagnosis and treatment of low back pain (2000) and of religious beliefs and practices (2005). But most importantly, I learned to appreciate living in a thoroughly egalitarian society. Every Icelander is respected for achieving potential as an individual. Of course, some achieve more than others, and in their occupations some are wealthy and others just get by, but in social life they encounter one another as human beings all equally entitled to respect and appreciation.

Consistent with that egalitarian ethic, titles are used to describe jobs – she is a doctor, he a priest, whatever. But they do not serve as titles of address. Individuals are addressed by first names – not last names and not last names preceded by titles – just by first names. A highly placed physician, the Surgeon General of Iceland (*Landlæknir*) wanted to talk with me once about my ongoing research on alternative medicine, so I biked to the edge of Rekjavik to talk with him in his office. His name was Ólafur Ólafsson, but we chatted together as Ólafur and Bob. Not as Surgeon General. Not as Doctor. Not as Professor. Just as Ólafur and Bob. It would have been the same had he been the President of Iceland and I, the janitor in his building.

I sense that we are shifting that way in subtle ways in the United States today. We are less formal than we were a generation ago. Unfortunately, in hospitals and medical or dental offices, custom still almost always demands that practitioners be addressed as "Dr." The best a patient or nurse can hope for is Mr. or Ms., because not uncommonly they are addressed by their first names. It is time we moved on. If the surgeon general can be just plain Ólafur in Iceland, and if every Icelander is on a first name basis with every other Icelander, then let us learn from them. That is how applied anthropology works. We learn from other cultures how our own culture can be improved, just as we help people in developing nations adapt their cultures for greater economic, community, and political success. Students at Mills now address me as Bob. I wouldn't have it any other way. Think about it.

The Interdisciplinary Potential

Interdisciplinarity permeates academe these days and I'm all for it. Usually interdisciplinary research or teaching requires the collaboration of two or more professionally trained specialists. However, I came to realize that to some extent I could benefit from an interdisciplinary approach to research without the struggle of organizing a research team. Trained and experienced as an anthropologist in the subfield of medical anthropology, but also possessing qualifications in chiropractic and medicine, I undertook a kind of research that drew on the intersection of those fields.

The challenge of the spine and neck was especially compelling because the incidence of spinal disorders is very high in all kinds of societies, from simple hunters and gathers to rural villagers to factory workers to desk-bound intellectuals (Anderson, 1999: 333).

In order to undertake cross-cultural research on health and healing that would take advantage of my hard-earned new knowledge and skills as a chiropractor, I devoted much of my field research in medical anthropology to one major category of disease (spinal misalignments) and to world-wide forms of healing known as bonesetting in non-literate folk societies and as spinal manipulative therapy (or chiropractic) in urban literate traditions. My basic question was, How were these healing cultures alike and different? Two chiropractic skills allowed me to do a kind of research that intrigues me still and that only one other anthropologist chiropractor, Norman Kline, is also qualified to do. (I'll tell you about my friend Norman later.)

One of those skills is that a chiropractor is trained and experienced in diagnosing back pain and immobility that is biomechanical in origin (the chiropractic method of motion palpation). That skill served me early on for documenting the prevalence of back pain among farmers in the hills of Nepal and urban bus drivers in California. For an ethnographer working with indigenous healers in different parts of the world, including alternative practitioners in the United States, it makes a big difference to be able to authenticate or reject a healer's diagnosis in terms of anatomic, neurologic, and physiologic pathology. They often miss the diagnosis. An ethnographic documentation is far more valuable if it is informed by that fact (see Anderson, 1991).

A second useful skill if the problem is diagnosed as biomechanical is to use a chiropractor's clinical experience to evaluate the effectiveness of whatever treatment is provided. Perhaps the most important result of that kind of research is to document whether or not bonesetters provide curative or ameliorative treatment with their biomechanical manipulations. It makes all the difference in the world when doing ethnographic reporting on traditional healers to know whether or not their treatments actually elicit more than placebo benefits, as I will illustrate below. That has been a missing component of almost all ethnographic work on healing.

To take advantage of chiropractic skills in these two ways it must be stressed that scientific research has confirmed the efficacy of chiropractic methods. Some years ago I was privileged to collaborate with five outstanding chiropractic researchers to carry out an early review of 23 randomized controlled clinical trials of spinal manipulative therapy (SMT) that we published as "A Meta-Analysis of Clinical Trials of Spinal Manipulation." Two of those scientists have since made it big time in the profession: William Meeker is now President of Palmer Chiropractic College West (California) and Robert Mootz is Associate Medical Director for Chiropractic in the Washington State Department of Labor and Industries. At that time, our analysis demonstrated that "SMT proved to be consistently more effective than were any of an array of comparison treatments" (Anderson, et al, 1992: 181).

Since then additional clinical trials have clinched the case we were able to make, indicating that SMT is superior to comparison treatments for the management of acute low back pain (Redwood, 2008; Meeker & Haldeman, 2002). Recently, SMT has also been found in clinical trials to be superior for the treatment of chronic low back pain (Wilkey et al, 2008).

My work as a chiropractor ethnographer provided a lot of rich personal and professional experiences – often rewarding to share with students by means of short video clips that illustrate varieties of healing cultures and stimulate discussions. Most of that research could not be based on in-depth ethnographic fieldwork requiring long residency and language fluency, as was possible in my most recent five-year project (Anderson, 2008). Instead, I did blitzkrieg ethnographies that could be completed in a couple of weeks because they were narrowly focused on the diagnosis and treatment of back pain.

That worked really well with being married to Edna, whose commitments as a professor of education and an institute director took her all over the world. Wherever she went I tagged along to follow my passion while Edna took care of her responsibilities. I will now offer you the longest run-on sentence I have ever composed.

Over the years our parallel careers allowed us to document at least one *kloge mand* in Denmark, *sobador (huesero)* in Mexico, *curendero espiritista naturista* in Peru, *lomilomi kupuna* in Hawaii, master of *tuina* from China, *nganga* among the Shona of Zimbabwe, *andalæknir* in Iceland, *shekesta band* in Afghanistan, *nau vaidya* in Nepal, and, not the least, *balian uat* in Bali (Appendix B), which brings me to the related research of Norman Kline, Professor of Anthropology and Head of the Department of Anthropology at California State University, Los Angeles, but just a young assistant professor when he and I learned to enjoy each other's company at anthropology meetings a long time ago. I want to briefly describe our later collaboration in order to illustrate what might be called "chiropractic ethnography," including resort to autoethnography.

Norman and Bob: An Unexpected Collaboration

Although we had been friends for years, it was a totally unanticipated coincidence that Norman decided to enroll in a chiropractic college in Los Angeles just after I enrolled in San Lorenzo. He outdid me by far in developing chiropractic skills, however. Norman established and maintained a part-time private practice for more than a decade after he survived his versions of the three parts of red tape.

In 1996, Norman used a sabbatical leave to produce a video documentary of a bonesetter in Bali titled *The Balian of Klungkung*. Two years later Edna had reason to be in Bali for a couple of weeks, so of course I was determined to go with her. Norman and I agreed that I could use my time there to re-visit the balian who practices in Klungkung.

The research design had good potential for two reasons. It expanded our understanding of Balinese culture insofar as I was able to expand on Norman's work by adding two other practitioners as a basis for identifying intracultural variability. The three balians were found to be alike in some ways but also significantly different in others. That's what anthropologists have learned to expect in non-institutionalized healing traditions. No surprise there, but it does mean that we cannot extrapolate from our small sample of three to the dozen or so others who practice on the island.

All three displayed some traits in common, however, as I learned by carrying out fieldwork as an autoethnography whereby for some purposes I could report on personal experience as cultural evidence. That succeeded when I presented myself as the patient-subject for a Chinese master of *tuina* at the American College of Traditional Medicine in San Francisco, for a deceased doctor (*andalæknir*) in Iceland, and for a *shekesta band* in Afghanistan. I was eager to do so again for the three balians in Bali.

I presented myself to each *balian uat* in the same way. Explaining that I was experiencing low back pain I pointed to my right sacroiliac joint, adding that just days earlier I had spent 30 hours on airplanes and in airports between San Francisco and Denpasar. My purpose was to document (experience) how they would manage an uncomplicated, self-diagnosed biomechanical lesion (but self-diagnosed by a doctor of chiropractic).

I found that in each case the balian proceeded to treatment without doing a history (inquiring about how I experienced the pain) or a physical examination (to confirm the accuracy of my finger pointing). As for treatment, I could feel (and verify on Edna's video) that each of the three was decidedly off target in attempting to mobilize or manipulate the sacroiliac joint, which expectably would have provided relief.

There was much more to my autoethnographic findings in Bali than that, but my purpose here is merely to provide a sense for how chiropractic ethnography can be carried out in field research. In all, the three balians were quite ineffective in the treatment of joint pain, although I do not doubt that patients profited psychologically. My low back pain did not diminish in response to their treatments. On the contrary, two of the three caused excruciating pain that provided no therapeutic benefit as they massaged heavily and deeply against muscles, ligaments, and tendons along the spine from the neck to the tail bone. One caused intense momentary pain and risked causing ligamental damage by harsh manipulation of a non-symptomatic knee that should have just been left alone. Not the least, another left me with three days of neck pain as a result of heavy routine massage of the cervical spine that provided no benefit that I could detect.

I submit that without the autoethnographic component, my field ethnography might have left me to assume that all three were as effective as chiropractors expectably would be, which is exactly what happened to Norman.

It is very likely that balians are helpful for patients with other painful or psychosomatic conditions, and that their patients benefit from the placebo effect, my field study was not designed to investigate that. However, my simple experiment did demonstrate that the obvious practice-building success of each of the three balians should not be taken as a measure of their skill as bonesetters in the management of low back pain.

An additional reason for feeling that our research design would be provocative was that anthropologists have long been intrigued with the finding that when a second anthropologist independently restudies a community she almost predictably will produce a new ethnography that differs strikingly from the earlier one. Bronislaw Malinowski and Annette Weiner on the Andaman Islanders illustrate that regularity (Weiner, 1976). And it turned out to be true for Norman and me.

Norman's documentary emphasized a supernatural (shamanic) dominance in their repertoires. In contrast, I experienced and described their work as strictly naturalistic. So his documentary of *The Balian of Klungkung* and mine of *Bonesetters in Bali* produced very different ethnographic accounts of balian healing culture.

Later, when we put our heads together over that major discrepancy, we realized that we were both right. We were reporting on contrasting aspects of their healing art, just as Malinowski focused on the culture of Trobriand men with only superficial reference to women, in contrast to Annette Weiner, who years later documented the powerful social, economic, and political roles of women that Malinowski missed. Theirs was a finding of importance for ethnographic fieldworkers and we hope ours will be too (Anderson & Klein, 2004).

Yes, I Feel it was Worth While

Doing research and writing as an anthropologist excites me. My autoethnographic adventures in chiropractic and medical education allowed me to grow intellectually, academically and as a teacher. I fully expected to devote the rest of my life to medical anthropology. Then, quite unexpectedly, that 1998 sabbatical semester in Iceland turned out to be the last time I undertook field research based on training in chiropractic and medicine.

I had no intention of exploring another subspecialty when I returned to Mills that spring. I merely decided I should offer to do community service along with some of my students who were volunteering in a failing inner-city high school nearby in East Oakland. I volunteered to teach an anthropology course to high school kids. That small beginning evolved into ten years of intense commitment to Fremont High School. The need was desperate, not just for the school or for the Oakland Unified School District, but for the very survival of our *Nation at Risk*.

So I shifted my major area of specialization yet one more time. It culminated a decade later when I introduced a new course titled Educational Anthropology (2009) and published two books on school policy, *The Labyrinth of Cultural Complexity* (2008) and *Headbutting in Academe* (2010). In 2009 I deleted medical anthropology courses from the college catalog. Health care is very important, but if American democracy is to survive and flourish nothing is more important than to educate our children properly, because we are *A Nation at Risk*.

Appendix A

Publications as Life-West Research Director

"Introducing Chiropractic to the People's Republic of China." *World-Wide Report*, Vol. XXI (3), March, 1979: 2A-4A.

"Chiropractic Research on a Global Scale." *World-Wide Report*, Vol. XXI (9), September, 1979: 2A-3A.

"Chiropractic: Recognized but Unproved." *The New England Journal of Medicine*, Vol. 302 (6), 1980: 354.

"Anthropometry and Spinal Biomechanics." *The Upper Cervical Monograph*, Vol. 2 (1), July, 1980: 609.

"Bonesetters in England." *World-Wide Report*, Vol. XXII (9), September, 1980: 2a-3a.

"Chiropractic Instrumentation." *World-Wide Report*, Vol. XXII (10), October, 1980: 2a.

"Report from the States." *British Association of manipulative Medicine Newsletter*, October, 1980: 7-9.

"The Importance of Communication." *World-Wide Report*, Vol. XXII (11), November, 1980: 2a-3a.

"Osteological Research." *World-Wide Report*, Vol. XXII (12), December, 1980: 4a.

"Initiating Anatometer Research." *The Upper Cervical Monograph*, Vol. 2 (10), January, 1981: 1, 9.

"The Haldeman Conferences." *World-Wide Report*, Vol. XXIII (1),

January 1981: 4a.

"Chiropractic-Acupuncture in Japan." *ICAC Journal*, International Chiropractors Association of California, March, 1981: 3-4.

Review of Modern Developments in the Principles and Practice of Chiropractic by Scott Haldeman, M.D., Editor. *British Association of Manipulative Medicine*, March, 1981: 3-4.

"On Responding to Research: The Case of Iridology." *The Digest of Chiropractic Economics*, Vol. 23 (6): May/June, 1981: 68-72.

"New Instrumentation for Anthropometry." *The American Chiropractic Association Journal of Chiropractic*, Vol. 18 (6): June, 1981: 43-47.

"We Have Good News and We Have Bad," with Norman Klein. *Archives of the California Chiropractic Association*, Vol. 5 (1), 1981: 9-12.

"Manual Medicine versus Chiropractic: Dimensions of a Confrontation," with Edna Mitchell. *Archives of the California Chiropractic Association*, Vol. 5 (1), 1981: 49-58.

"Report on Research and Training," with Amerigo Biollo. *The Upper Cervical Monograph*, Vol. 3 (1), June, 1981: 39.

"Geriatrics." *World-Wide Report*, Vol. XXIII (8), July/August, 1981: 3.

"Medicine, Chiropractic and Caste." *Anthropological Quarterly*, Vol. 54ll (3), July, 1981: 157-165.

Abstract, "Rotation at the Atlanto-Occipital Joint." *International Review of Chiropractic*, Vol. 35 (2), Summer, 1981: 39.

"Anatometer Research Team." *ICAC Journal*, International Chiropractors Association of California, May/June, 1981: 2, 4.

"A Radiographic Test of Upper Cervical Chiropractic Theory." *Journal of Manipulative and Physiologic Therapeutics*, Vol. 4 (3), September, 1981: 129-133.

"Bonesetting: A Medical Bone of Contention." *The American Chiropractic Association Journal of Chiropractic*, Vol. 15, October, 1981: 89-100.

"The Neglect of Chiropractic in Congressional Research Planning." *The American Chiropractor*, October, 1981: 24-34.

"Medicine, Chiropractic and Caste." *American Chiropractic Association Journal of Chiropractic*, Vol. 18 (12), December, 1981: 24-34.

"Students Involved in Research Department." *Neurologica*, December, 1981: 4.

"Anatomic Rotation at the Atlanto-Occipital Joint." *Proceedings of the Eleventh Annual Biomechanics Conference on the Spine*, December, 1980: 113-140. Boulder, CO: University of Colorado, Biomechanics Laboratory.

"Wharton Hood, M.D., The Rejected Father of Manual Medicine." *Archives of the California Chiropractic Association*, Vol. 5 (2), 1981: 59-63.

"The Position of the Atlas: Rotation and Laterality in Pre-Adjustive patients," with Amerigo Biollo. *The Upper-Cervical Monograph*, Vol. 3 (2), December, 1981: 6-7.

"The Practice of Chiropractic in Japan." *Bulletin of the European Chiropractors Union*, Vol. 29, 1981: 170-172.

"The Concept of Normal in Chiropractic Theory." *Proceedings: Twelfth Annual Biomechanics Conference on the Spine*. December, 1981: 259-272. Boulder, CO: University of Colorado, Biomechanics Laboratory.

Abstract, "The McIntyre Maneuver for Symptomatic Relief of Raynard's Phenomenon." *International Review of Chiropractic*, Vol. 36 (1)l, Spring, 1982: 31.

"Is Chiropractic Marginal or Mainstream?" *World-Wide Report*, Vol. XXIV (7), July, 1982: 4a.

"The Legitimation of Chiropractic: Extra-Legal Mechanisms in Denmark." *The Digest of Chiropractic Economics*, Vol. 24 (4), January/February, 1982: 44-46.

"Chiropractic in the Far East." *World-Wide Report*, Vol. XXIV(4): April, 1982: 4a.

"Hawaiian Therapeutic Massage." *World-Wide Report*, Vol. XXIV (5), May, 1982: 4a.

"Traditional Chinese Medical Theory and Chiropractic." *The American Chiropractor*, May/June, 1982:22-24.

"Should Chairs be Abolished from Classrooms?" *World-Wide Report*, Vol. XXIV (6), June, 1982: 4a.

"The Research Challenge for Chiropractic," *The Journal of Chiropractic Science*, Vol. 1 (1), Spring, 1982: 12-24.

Abstract, "The McIntyre Maneuver for Symptomatic Relief of Raynaud's Phenomenon." (reprinted) *International Review of Chiropractic*, Vol. 36 (2), Autumn/Winter, 1982: 59.

"Sclerosant Injections for Back Pain." *Chiropractic Technology*, Vol. 1 (1), August, 1982: 4a.

"The Myth of Medical Madness." *Chiropractic Technology*, Vol. 1 (2), September, 1982: 4a.

"Doctors as Patients See Them." *Today's Chiropractic*, September/October, 1982: 17.

"The University of California Looks at a Chiropractor." *Chiropractic Technology*, Vol. 1 (3), October, 1982: 4a.

"The University of Zurich Looks at Chiropractors." *The Digest of Chiropractic Economics*, Vol. 25 (3), November/December, 1982: 28.

"The University of Zurich Looks at Chiropractors." (Reprinted) *News in Review*, Vol 1 (7), November, 1982.

"An Historical Perspective on the Founder of Chiropractic." *Archives of the California Chiropractic Association*, Vol. 6 (1), 1982: 61-66.

"Chiropractic in American History: The Ins and Outs of Museums." *Chiropractic History*, Vol.2 (1), 1982: 15-19.

"Annual Biomechanics Conference," *World-Wide Report*, Vol. XXIV (12), December, 1982: 5.

"Spheno-Occipital Relationships: A Contribution to Osteopathic Cranial Theory." *Proceedings of the Thirteenth Annual Biomechanics Conference on the Spine*. November 6-7, 1982: 209-221. Boulder, CO: University of Colorado, Biomechanics Laboratory.

"Bad Times at the Smithsonian," *World-Wide Report*, Vol. XXV (1), January, 1983: 4a.

"Chiropractic in Medical Sociology." *California Chiropractic Association Journal*, Vol. 8 (2), February, 1983: 9.

"The Doctor's Role in Nuclear War." *Chiropractic USA*, February, 1983: 11.

"The Challenge of the Lumbar Spine." *California Chiropractic Association Journal*, Vol. 8 (2), February, 1983: 8.

"Cranial Mechanisms." *Chiropractic USA*, March, 1983: 8

"On Manipulative Medicine in China." *British Association for Manipulative Medicine Newsletter*, March, 1983: 9-10.

"The Hazards of Overtreatment." *California Chiropractic Association Journal*, Vol. 8 (3), March, 1983: 8.

"California Conference on the Lumbar Spine." *British Association for*

Manipulative Medicine Newsletter, February, 1983: 8-9.

"The Smithsonian Looks Better." *Chiropractic USA*, April, 1983: 3.

"Low Back Pain: A Trend in Orthopedics, Chiropractic Care." *The American Chiropractor*, March/April, 1983: l14, 17, 21, 39.

"Arthritis and Body Type." *California Chiropractic Association Journal*, Vol. 8 (4), April, 1983: 226-228.

"Angulation of the Basiocciput in Three Cranial Series." *Current Anthropology*, Vol. 24 (2), April, 1983: 226-228.

"Medical Prejudice: The Case of Bonesetting." *European Journal of Chiropractic*, Vol. 31, 1983: 5-12.

"Beware the Third-rate Clinic!" *International Review of Chiropractic*, Vol. 37 (1), March/April, 1983: 15.

"More on Manipulative Medicine in China." *British Association for Manipulative Medicine Newsletter*, May, 1983: 3-4.

"Successful Spinal Treatment in Ancient Greece and Modern China." *California Chiropractic Association Journal*, Vol.8 (l5), May, 1983: 12.

"A Medical Study of Chiropractic Success." *California Chiropractic Association Journal*, Vol. 8 (6), June, 1983: 13-14, 22.

"Find it, Fix it, Leave it Alone." *British Association for Manipulative Medicine Newsletter*, June, 1983: 6-7.

"The Gravity Stress Analyzer for Measuring Spinal Posture." *Journal of the Canadian Chiropractic Association*, Vol. 27 (2), June, 1983: 55-58.

"A Medical Study of Chiropractic Success." *World-Wide Report*, Vol. XXV (7), July, 1983: 8.

"Biomechanics in the West." *World-Wide Report*, Vol. XXV (7), July, 1983: 11.

"The Validation of Manipulation." *California Chiropractic Association Journal*, Vol. 8 (7), July, 1983: 11.

"Who Makes a Good Doctor?" *World-Wide Report*, Vol. XXV (8), August, 1983: 4.

Abstract, "Deviations from a Sagittal Orientation of the Spine Utilizing the Gravity Stress Analyzer," with M. Winkler & J.-P. Martinet. In Barry P. Davis, Ed., Advances in Conservative Health Science, Vol. 1. *Proceedings of the 1982 Logan/CRC Conference on Manipulation, Diagnosis and Therapy* (pg. 130). St. Louis, MO: Logan College

Academic Press, 1983.

Abstract, "An Orthopedic Ethnography in Village Nepal." In Barry P. Davis, Ed., Advances in Conservative Health Science, Vol. 1. *Proceedings of the 1982 Logan/CRC Conference on Manipulation, Diagnosis and Therapy* (pg. 130). St. Louis, MO: Logan College Academic Press, 1983.

"The Bagelmacher in Israel." *California Chiropractic Association Journal*, Vol. 8 (8), August, 1983: 12.

"An American Contribution to Third World Medicine: Spinal Manipulative Therapy." In John Morgan, Ed., *Third World Medicine and Social Change: A Reader in Social Science and Medicine* (17-27). Lanham, NY: University Press of America, 1983.

"Empirical Approaches to the Validation of Manipulation." *British Association for Manipulative Medicine Newsletter*, September, 1983: 7.

"Fiorinal for Tension Headaches." *World-Wide Report*, Vol. XXV (9), September, 1983: 3.

"X-Ray a Research Tool." *California Chiropractic Association Journal*, Vol. 8 (9), September, 1983: 10.

"Research: A Garden of Roses." *The American Chiropractor*, September/October, 1983: 6-8, 13, 15, 17-18.

"The Biomechanics Conferences of Dr. Suh." *World-Wide Report*, Vol. XXV (10), October, 1983: 7.

"Instrumentation in Research." *California Chiropractic Association Journal*, Vol. 8 (10), October, 1983: 10.

"Sharing in Science." *California Chiropractic Association Journal*, Vol. 8 (11), November, 1983: 10.

"Conservative Health Science Research – 1983." *California Chiropractic Association Journal*, Vol. 8 (12), December, 1983: 10.

"On Doctors and Bonesetters in the 16th and 17th Centuries." *Chiropractic History*, Vol. 3 (1), 1983: 11-15.

"A Research Trial of Cervical Manipulation." *California Chiropractic Association Journal*, Vol. 9 (5), May, 1984: 17-18.

"The Success of Swiss Chiropractors." *Today's Chiropractic*, Vol. 13 (1), January/February, 1984: 38-39.

"Back Pain in Transit Workers," with Laura Nathan. *California Chiropractic Association Journal*, Vol. 9 (2), February, 1984: 12.

"On Practice-Building Seminars." *California Chiropractic Association Journal*, Vol. 9 (1), January, 1984: 10.

Appendix B

Publications as a Chiropractor Anthropologist

"Chiropractic: Recognized but Unproved." *The New England Journal of Medicine*, Vol. 302 (6), 1980: 354.

"Anatomic Rotation at the Atlanto-Occipital Joint." *Proceedings of the Eleventh Annual Biomechanics Conference on the Spine*, December, 1980: 113-140. Boulder, CO: University of Colorado, Biomechanics Laboratory.

"Medicine, Chiropractic and Caste." *Anthropological Quarterly*, Vol. 54 (3), July, 1981: 157-165.

"The Concept of Normal in Chiropractic Theory." *Proceedings of the 12th Annual Biomechanics Conference on the Spine*, 1981: 259-272. Boulder, CO: University of Colorado, Biomechanics Laboratory.

"Spheno-Occipital Relationships: A Contribution to Osteopathic Cranial Theory." *Proceedings of the Thirteenth Annual Biomechanics Conference on the Spine*, 1982: 209-221. Boulder, CO: University of Colorado, Biomechanics Laboratory.

"Angulation of the Basiocciput in Three Cranial Series." *Current Anthropology*, Vol. 24 (2), April, 1983: 226-228.

"Misalignments in the Human Pelvis Measured on Radiographs." *Journal of Human Evolution*, Vol 13, 1984: 593-600.

"An Orthopedic Ethnography in Rural Nepal," *Medical Anthropology*, 8 (1). 1984: 46-59.

"The Treatment of Musculoskeletal Disorders by a Mexican Bonesetter *(sobador)*. *Social Science and Medicine*, Vol. 24 (1), 1987: 43-46.

"Back Pain in Transit Workers," with Laura Nathan. *California Chiropractic Association Journal*, Vol. 9 (2), 1989: 12.

"Chiropractors For and Against Vaccines." *Medical Anthropology*, Vol. 12 (2), 1990: 169-186.

"The Efficacy of Ethnomedicine: Research Methods in Trouble." *Medical Anthropology*, Vol 13, 1991: 1-17.

"An American Clinic for Traditional Chinese Medicine: Comparisons to Family Medicine and Chiropractic." *Journal of Manipulative and Physiological Therapeutics*, Vol. 14 (8), 1991: 462-466.

"An American Clinic for Traditional Chinese Medicine: Comparisons to Family Medicine and Chiropractic." *Journal of Manipulative and Physiological Therapeutics,* Vol. 14 (8), 1991: 462-466.

The Conservative Care of Low Back Pain, with Arthur H. White. Baltimore, MD: Williams and Wilkins, 1991.

"The Diagnosis and Treatment of Low Back Pain since 1850" (8-20). In *The Conservative Care of Low Back Pain.*

"Emic and Etic in a Chinese-American Clinic." *Jahrbuch für Transkulturelle Medizin und Psychotherapie*, 1991: 161-169, 199.

"The Efficacy of Ethnomedicine: Research Methods in Trouble" (1-17). In Mark Nichter, Ed., *Anthropological Approaches to the Study of Ethnomedicine*. Amsterdam, The Netherlands: Gordon and Breach Science Publishers, 1992.

"Standards for Interprofessional Relations" (163-178). In Herbert J. Vear, Ed., *Chiropractic Standards of Practice and Quality of Care*. Gaithersburg, MD: Aspen Publishers: 1992.

"A Meta-Analysis of Clinical Trials of Spinal Manipulation." *Journal of Manipulative and Physiological Therapeutics*, Vol. 15 (3), 1992: 181-194.

"Unintended Psychotherapy in the Practice of Traditional Chinese Medicine in the United States." *Jahrbuch für Transkulturelle Medizin und Psychotherapie*, 1992.

"Physicians and Healers – Unwitting Partners in Health Care." *New England Journal of Medicine*, Vol. 326 (22), 1992: 1503.

"Comfrey in the Chinese Materia Medica." *Asian Medicine Newsletter*, International Association for the Study of Traditional Asian

Medicine, New Series, Nr. 2, July, 1992: 7-11.

"Spinal Manipulation Before Chiropractic" (3-14). In Scott Haldeman, Ed., *Principles and Practice of Chiropractic*, 2ed ed., Norwalk, CT: Appleton & Lange, 1992.

"Spinal Manipulation: The State of the Art." *European Journal of Physical Medicine & Rehabilitatiokn*, Supplement No. 2, 1992: 3.

"Douleur et Anthropologie" (117-134). with Scott T. Anderson. *La Douleur "Au-Dela des Maux*. Editions des Archives Contemporaines. Yverdon,Suisse: Gordon and Breach Science Publishers: 1992.

"The Back Pain of Bus Drivers: Prevalence in an Urban Area of California." *Spine*, Vol 17 (12), 1992: 1481-1488.

"Traditional and Alternative Healing in Mainstream Medicine: Field Notes from the Americas to Zimbabwe." American Back Society Annual Meeting, Syllabus, December 1-4, 1993: 25-26.

Spinal Manipulation: The State of the Art" (260-270). In E. Ernst, M. Jayson, M. Pope and R. Porter, Eds., *Advances in Idiopathic Low Back Pain*. Vienna, Austria: Blackwell-MZV: 1993.

Shamans Possessed by Spirits and Patients Possessed by Witches: Report from Zimbabwe. Video Documentary, American Back Society Annual Meeting, December 1-4, 1993.

"Culture and Pain" (120—138), with Scott T. Anderson. In *The Puzzle of Pain*. (Translated from the French edition.) Basel, Switzerland: Gordon and Breach Arts International: 1994.

"Ethics in Fieldwork: Whose Welfare Must We Promote?" *Anthropology Newsletter*, Vol. 35 (1), January 1994: 43.

Review of The Body of Frankenstein's Monster: Essays in Myth and Medicine by Cecil Helman, 1992. *Medical Anthropology Quarterly*, New Series, Vol. 9 (4), December, 1995: 511-513.

"Ethical Standards for Medical Anthropologists Consulting on Ethnomedicine." *Human Organizon*, Vol. 55 (4). 1996: 484-487.

"Bonesetters and Curers in a Mexican Community: Conceptual Models, Status, and Gender," with Brad R. Huber. *Medical Anthropology*, Vol. 17, 1996: 23-38.

"Is Chiropractic Mainstream or Alternative? A View from Medical Anthropology." *Advances in Chiropractic*, Vol. 4, 1997: 555-578. (Reprinted from the 95th Annual Meeting of the American Anthropological Association, San Francisco, November 20-24,

1996.

Magic, Science, and Health: The Aims and Achievements of Medical Anthropology. Fort Worth, TX: Harcourt Brace College Publishers, 1996.

"Is Chiropractic Mainstream or Alternative? A View from Medical Anthropology" (555-578). In Dana J. Lawrence, Ed., *Advances in Chiropractic*, Volume 4. American Chiropractic Association. St. Louis, MO: Mosby, 1997.

"On Being a Doctor of Asian Medicine." *Journal of the National Academy of Acupuncture and Oriental Medicine*, Vol. 5 (1), 1998: 13-16.

"On Quantitative and Qualitative Research." *Journal of Alternative and Complementary Medicine*, Vol. 4 (2), 1998: 203-204.

"Human Evolution, Low Back Pain, and Dual-Level Control" (333-349). In Wenda Trevathan, E. O. Smith, and James McKenna, Eds., *Evolutionary Medicine.* New York, NY: Oxford University Press: 1999.

"Creating Clinical Efficacy by the Delphi Process." *Clinical Acupuncture and Oriental Medicine*, Vol. 1 (1), 1999: 61-64.

"A Case Study in Integrative Medicine: Alternative Theories and the Language of Biomedicine." *Journal of Alternative and Complementary Medicine*, Vol. 5 (2), 1999: 165-173.

Alternative and Conventional Medicine in Iceland: The Diagnosis and Treatment of Low Back Pain. Monograph. Public Health in Iceland, Supplement 2000, Nr. 1: 2000.

"Forward." In Sidney E. Skinner, *An Introduction to Homeopathic Medicine in Primary Care* (xi-xiii). Gaithersburg, MD: Aspen Publishers, Inc., 2001.

"Indigenous Bonesetters in Contemporary Denmark," (5-22). In Kathryn S. Oths and Servando Z. Hinojosa, Eds., *Healing by Hand: Manual Medicine and Bonesetting in Global Perspective.* Walnut Creek, CA: Altamira Press, 2004.

"Two Ethnographers and One Bonesetter in Bali," with Norman Kline (147-169). In Kathryn S. Oths and Servando Z. Hinojosa, Eds., Healing by Hand: Manual Medicine and Bonesetting in Global Perspective. Walnut Creek, CA: Altamira Press.

"The Ghosts of Humanitarian Doctors, (40-43). In *The Ghosts of*

Iceland. Belmont, CA: Wadsworth, a Division of s Thomson Learning, Inc.: 2005.

References

Anderson, Robert, 1971.
> *Traditional Europe: A Study in Anthropology and History.*
> Belmont, CA: Wadsworth Publishing Co, Inc.

Anderson, Robert, 1981.
> "The Concept of Normal in Chiropractic Theory."
> *Proceedings of the Twelfth Annual Biomechanics Conference on the Spine*, 259-272. Boulder, CO: University of Colorado, Biomechanics Laboratory.

Anderson, Robert, 1982.
> "An Historical Perspective on the Founder of Chiropractic."
> *Archives of the California Chiropractic Association*, 6 (1): 61-66.

Anderson, Robert, 1984.
> "An Orthopedic Ethnography in Rural Nepal," *Medical Anthropology*, 8 (1): 46-59.

Anderson, Robert, 1991.
> "The Efficacy of Ethnomedicine: Research Methods in Trouble,"
> *Medical Anthropology*, 13: 1-17.

Anderson, Robert, 1992.
> "Standards for Interprofessional Relations." In Herbert J. Vear, Ed., *Chiropractic Standards of Practice and Quality of Care*, (163-178). Gaithersburg, MD: Aspen Pubishers, Inc.

Anderson, Robert, 1992.
> "The Back Pain of Bus Drivers: Prevalence in an Urban Area of California." *Spine*, Vol. 17 (12): l1481-1488.

Anderson, Robert, 1999.

 "Human Evolution, Low Back Pain, and Dual-Level Control," (333-349). In Wenda R. Trevathan, E. O. Smith, and James J. McKenna, Eds, *Evolutionary Medicine*. New York, NY: Oxford University Press.

Anderson, Robert, 2008.

 The Labyrinth of Cultural Complexity: Fremont High Teachers, The Small School Policy, and Oakland Inner-City Realities. Lincoln, NE: iUniverse, Inc.

Anderson, Robert and Laura Nathan, 1984.

 "Back Pain in Transit Workers," California *Chiropractic Association Journal*, 9 (2): 12.

Anderson, Robert, William C. Meeker, Brian E. Wirick, Robert D. Mootz, Diana H. Kirk, and Alan Adams, 1992.

 "A Meta-Analysis of Clinical Trials of Spinal Manipulation," *Journal of Manipulative and Physiologicl Therapeutics*, 15 (3): 181-194.

Anderson, Robert & Norman Kline, 2004.

 "Two Ethnographers and One Bonesetter in Bali" (147-169). In Kathryn S. Oths and Servando Z. Hinojosa, Eds., *Healing by Hand: Manual Medicine and Bonesetting in Global Perspective.* Walnut Creek, CA: Altamira Press.

Anonymous, 2008.

 "Chiropractic Treatment Techniques." Google: *Wikipedia*

Bean, William Bennett, Ed., 1950.

 Sir William Osler Aphorisms: From His Bedside Teachings and Writings. New York, NY: Schuman.

Benedict, Ruth, 1934.

 Patterns of Culture. Boston, MA: Houghton Mifflin.

Blair, William G., 1964.

 "A Synopsis of the Blair Upper Cervical Spinographic Research." *Science Review of Chiropractic*, 1 (1): 4.

Bonner, T. N., 1959.

 The Kansas Doctor: A Century of Pioneering. Lawrence, KA: University of Kansas Press.

Bronfort, Gert, 1992.

 "Effectiveness of Spinal Manipulation and Adjustments." In

Scott Haldeman, Ed., *Principles and Practice of Chiropractic*, 2ed edition (415-441). Norwalk, CT: Appleton & Lange.

Coulter, Ian D., and P. G. Shekelle, 2005.
"Chiropractic in North America: A Descriptive Analysis," *Journal of Manipulative and Physiologic Therapeutics*, 28: 83-89.

Davis, Matthew A., Louise McDevitt, Kimona Alin, 2007.
"Establishing a Chiropractic Service in a Rural primary Health Care Facility." *Journal of Alternative and Complementary Medicine*, 13 (7): 697-702.

del Mundo, W. F., W. C. Shepherd, and T. D. Marose, 2002.
"Use of Alternative Medicine by Patients in a Rural Family Practice Clinic," *Family Medicine*, 34: 206-212.

Dunn, William N., 2008.
Public Policy Analysis: An Introduction, 4th ed. Upper Saddle River, NJ: Pearson (Prentice Hall).

Eisenberg, David M., R. B. Davis, et al, 1998.
"Trends in Alternative Medicine Use in the United States, 1990-1997: Results of a Follow-Up National Survey," *Journal of the American Medical Association*, 280: 1569-1575.

Fishbein, Morris, 1932.
Fads and Quackery in Healing: An Analysis of the Foibles of Healing Cults. New York, NY: Blue Ribbon Books.

Flexner, Abram, 1910.
Medical Education in the United States and Canada. New York, NY: Carnegie Foundation.

Flexner, J. T., 1962
Doctors on Horseback. New York, NY: Collier.

Franz, Burkhard, and Colin Anderson, 2007.
"The Potential Role of Joint Injury and Eustachian Tube Dysfunction in the Genesis of Secondary Meniere's Disease," *International Tinnitus Journal*, 13 (2): 132-137.

Freeman, Lyn, 2004.
Mosby's Complementary & Alternative Medicine: A Research-Based Approach, 2ed. ed. St. Louis, MO: Mosby, Inc.

Gatterman, Meridel I., Ed., 1990.

Chiropractic Management of Spine Related Disorders. Baltimore,
MD: Williams & Wilkins.

Gebhard, B., 1976.
"Interrelationships of Scientific and Folk Medicine." *American
Folk Medicine: A Symposium.* U.C.L.A. Conference of American
Folk Medicine. Berkeley, CA:University of California Press.

Gennep, Arnold van, 1909.
The Rites of Passage. London: Routledge and Kegan Paul.

Gevitz, Norman, 1982.
The D.O.'s: Osteopathic Medicine in America. Baltimore, MD:
Johns Hopkins University Press.

Gibbons, Russell W., 1980.
"The Evolution of Chiropractic: Medical and Social Protest
in America: Notes on the Survival Years and After." In Scott
Haldeman, Ed., *Modern Developments in the Principles and
Practice of Chiropractic* (3-24). New York, NY: Appleton-
Century-Crofts.

Gibbons, Russell W., 1981.
"Physician-Chiropractors: Medical Presence in the Evolution
of Chiropractic." *Bulletin of the History of Medicine* 55 (2):
233-245.

Gielow, Vern, 1981.
*Old Dad Chiro: A Biography of D.D. Palmer, Founder of
Chiropractic.* Davenport, IA: Bawden Brothers.

Gorski, Timothy N., 1994.
"Healthy Skepticism: Chiropractic." *The Newsletter of the North
Texas Skeptics,* 8 (4): 1-3.

Greenland, M., L. Reisbord, S. Haldeman, and A. Bluerger, 1980.
"Controlled Clinical Trials of Manipulation: A Review and a
Proposal." *Journal of Occupational Medicine* 22 (10): 670-676.

Hirschfeld, Lawrence A., 2002.
"Why Don't Anthropologists Like Children? *American
Anthropologist,* 104 (2): 611-627.

Ingelfinger, I. J., 1978.
"Medicine: Meritorious or Meretricious." *Science,* Vol. 200
(May 26).

Keating, Joseph C., Jr., A. K. Callender, and C. S. Cleveland, III, 1998.

A History of Chiropractic Education in North America: Report to the Council on Chiropractic Education. Davenport, IA: Association for the History of Chiropractic.

Keating, Joseph C., Jr., 2002.
"Early Chiropractic Education in Oregon," *Journal of the Canadian Chiropractic Association*, 46 (1): 39-60.

Keating, Joseph C., Jr., 2002.
"The Meanings of Innate," *Journal of the Canadian Chiropractic Association*, 46 (1): 4-10.

Kluckhohn, Clyde, and William Kelly, 1945.
"The Concept of Culture," In Ralph Linton, Ed., *The Science of Man in the World Crisis.* New York, NY: Columbia University press.

Koch, David, 2008.
"What a Bunch of Bunk! Debunking Some of the Common "Myths" About Chiropractic," *Today's Chiropractic LifeStyle: Nurturing Spirit, Mind & Body*, June/July: 58-61.

McCorkle, Thomas, 1961.
"Chiropractic: A Deviant Theory of Disease and Treatment in Contemporary Western Culture." *Human Organization* 20 (1): 20-P22.

Meeker, William C., 2000.
"Public Demand and the Integration of Complementary and Alternative Medicine in the US health Care System," *Journal of Manipulative and Physiological Therapeutics*, 23: 123-126.

Meeker, William and Scott Haldeman, 2002.
"Chiropractic: A Profession at the Crossroads of Mainstream and Alternative Medicine," *Annals of Internal Medicine*, 136: 216-227.

Mencken, H. L., 1955.
"Chiropractic" (148-153). In Allistair Cooke, Ed., *The Vintage Mencken.* New York, NY: Vintage Books (Random House).

Miller, Barbara, 2002.
Cultural Anthropology, 2ed. Ed. Boston, MA: Allyn and Bacon.

Murphy, Dan, 2008.
"Research Review," *The Chiropractic Choice*, 7 (2): 10-11.

Northup, George W., 1966.
> *Osteopathic Medicine: An American Reformation*. Chicago, IL: American Osteopathic Association.

North City Chiropractic Health Clinic, 2007.
> "Chiropractic Techniques. "http://www.webstyr.com/Markos/techniques.htm

Peterson, Cynthia, Meridel I. Gatterman, and Tyrone Wei, 1990.
> "Chiropractic Radiography" (90-110). In M. I. Gatterman, Ed., *Chiropractic Management of Spine Related Disorders*, Baltimore, MD: Williams & Wilkins.

Redwood, Daniel, 2008.
> "Chiropractic Management of Chronic Low-Back Pain: Commentary on Wilkey et al," *Journal of Alternative and Complementary Medicine*, 14 (5): 451-452.

Roe, Emery, 1994.
> *Narrative Policy Analysis: Theory and Practice*. Durham, NC: Duke University Press.

Savage, Peter, 2001.
> "Problem Oriented Medical Records," *British Medical Journal*, February 3.

Swidler, Ann, 1986.
> "Culture in Action: Symbols and Strategies." *American Sociological Review*, 51: 273-286.

Turner, Victor, 1969.
> *The Ritual Process: Structure and Anti-Structure*. Ithica, NY: Cornell University Press.

Vallacher, Robin R. and Daniel M. Wegner, 1989.
> "Levels of Personal Agency: Individual Variation in Action Identification." *Journal of Personality and Social Psychology*, Vol. 57 (4): 660-675.

Vear, Herbert J., Ed., 1992.
> *Chiropractic Standards of Practice and Quality of Care*. Gaithersburg, MD: Aspen Publishers.

Weed, Lawrence L., 1969.
> *Medical Records, Medical Education, and Medical Care: The Problem Oriented Record as a Basic Tool*. Cleveland, OH: Case Western Reserve University Press.

Weiner, Annette, 1976.

Women of Value, Men of Renown: New perspective on Trobriand Exchange. Austin, TX: University of Texas Press.

White, Arthur H. and Robert Anderson, Eds., 1991.

The Conservative Care of Low Back Pain. Baltimore, MD: Williams and Wilkins.

Wildavsky, Aaron, 1977.

Speaking Truth to Power: The Art and Craft of Policy Analysis. Boston, MA: Little, Brown and Company.

Wiles, Michael R., 1990.

"Viseral Disorders Related to the Spine," 379-396). In Meridel I. Gatterman, Ed., Chiropractic Management of Spine Related Disorders. Baltimore, MD: Williams & Wilkins.

Wilkey, Adam, Michael Gregory, David Byfield, & Peter McCarthy, 2008.

"A Comparison Between Chiropractic Management and Pain Clinic Management for Chronic Low-Back Pain in a National health Service Outpatient Clinic," Journal of Alternative and Complementary Medicine, 14 (5): 465-473.

Winsor, Henry, 1921.

"The Evidences of the Association, in Dissected Cadavers, of Visceral Diseases with Vertebral Deformities of the Same Sympathetic Segments," Medical Times, November: 1-7.